Fulvio Tomizza
Writing the Trauma of Exile

LEGENDA

LEGENDA is the Modern Humanities Research Association's book imprint for new research in the Humanities. Founded in 1995 by Malcolm Bowie and others within the University of Oxford, Legenda has always been a collaborative publishing enterprise, directly governed by scholars. The Modern Humanities Research Association (MHRA) joined this collaboration in 1998, became half-owner in 2004, in partnership with Maney Publishing and then Routledge, and has since 2016 been sole owner. Titles range from medieval texts to contemporary cinema and form a widely comparative view of the modern humanities, including works on Arabic, Catalan, English, French, German, Greek, Italian, Portuguese, Russian, Spanish, and Yiddish literature. Editorial boards and committees of more than 60 leading academic specialists work in collaboration with bodies such as the Society for French Studies, the British Comparative Literature Association and the Association of Hispanists of Great Britain & Ireland.

The MHRA encourages and promotes advanced study and research in the field of the modern humanities, especially modern European languages and literature, including English, and also cinema. It aims to break down the barriers between scholars working in different disciplines and to maintain the unity of humanistic scholarship. The Association fulfils this purpose through the publication of journals, bibliographies, monographs, critical editions, and the MHRA Style Guide, and by making grants in support of research. Membership is open to all who work in the Humanities, whether independent or in a University post, and the participation of younger colleagues entering the field is especially welcomed.

ALSO PUBLISHED BY THE ASSOCIATION

Critical Texts
Tudor and Stuart Translations • *New Translations* • *European Translations*
MHRA Library of Medieval Welsh Literature

MHRA Bibliographies
Publications of the Modern Humanities Research Association

The Annual Bibliography of English Language & Literature
Austrian Studies
Modern Language Review
Portuguese Studies
The Slavonic and East European Review
Working Papers in the Humanities
The Yearbook of English Studies

www.mhra.org.uk
www.legendabooks.com

ITALIAN PERSPECTIVES

Editorial Committee
Professor Simon Gilson, University of Warwick (General Editor)
Dr Francesca Billiani, University of Manchester
Professor Manuele Gragnolati, Université Paris-Sorbonne
Dr Catherine Keen, University College London
Professor Martin McLaughlin, Magdalen College, Oxford

Founding Editors
Professor Zygmunt Barański and Professor Anna Laura Lepschy

In the light of growing academic interest in Italy and the reorganization of many university courses in Italian along interdisciplinary lines, this book series, founded by Maney Publishing under the imprint of the Northern Universities Press and now continuing under the Legenda imprint, aims to bring together different scholarly perspectives on Italy and its culture. *Italian Perspectives* publishes books and collections of essays on any period of Italian literature, language, history, culture, politics, art, and media, as well as studies which take an interdisciplinary approach and are methodologically innovative.

APPEARING IN THIS SERIES

20. *Ugo Foscolo and English Culture*, by Sandra Parmegiani
21. *The Printed Media in Fin-de-siècle Italy: Publishers, Writers, and Readers*, ed. by Ann Hallamore Caesar, Gabriella Romani, and Jennifer Burns
22. *Giraffes in the Garden of Italian Literature: Modernist Embodiment in Italo Svevo, Federigo Tozzi and Carlo Emilio Gadda*, by Deborah Amberson
23. *Remembering Aldo Moro: The Cultural Legacy of the 1978 Kidnapping and Murder*, ed. by Ruth Glynn and Giancarlo Lombardi
24. *Disrupted Narratives: Illness, Silence and Identity in Svevo, Pressburger and Morandini*, by Emma Bond
25. *Dante and Epicurus: A Dualistic Vision of Secular and Spiritual Fulfilment*, by George Corbett
26. *Edoardo Sanguineti: Literature, Ideology and the Avant-Garde*, ed. by Paolo Chirumbolo and John Picchione
27. *The Tradition of the Actor-Author in Italian Theatre*, ed. by Donatella Fischer
28. *Leopardi's Nymphs: Grace, Melancholy, and the Uncanny*, by Fabio A. Camilletti
29. *Gadda and Beckett: Storytelling, Subjectivity and Fracture*, by Katrin Wehling-Giorgi
30. *Caravaggio in Film and Literature: Popular Culture's Appropriation of a Baroque Genius*, by Laura Rorato
31. *The Italian Academies 1525-1700: Networks of Culture, Innovation and Dissent*, ed. by Jane E. Everson, Denis V. Reidy and Lisa Sampson
32. *Rome Eternal: The City As Fatherland*, by Guy Lanoue
33. *The Somali Within: Language, Race and Belonging in 'Minor' Italian Literature*, by Simone Brioni
34. *Laughter from Realism to Modernism: Misfits and Humorists in Pirandello, Svevo, Palazzeschi, and Gadda*, by Alberto Godioli
35. *Pasolini after Dante: The 'Divine Mimesis' and the Politics of Representation*, by Emanuela Patti

Managing Editor
Dr Graham Nelson, 41 Wellington Square, Oxford OX1 2JF, UK
www.legendabooks.com

Fulvio Tomizza

Writing the Trauma of Exile

MARIANNA DEGANUTTI

Italian Perspectives 38
Modern Humanities Research Association
2018

*Published by Legenda
an imprint of the Modern Humanities Research Association
Salisbury House, Station Road, Cambridge CB1 2LA*

*ISBN 978-1-78188-593-2 (HB)
ISBN 978-1-78188-594-9 (PB)*

First published 2018

All rights reserved. No part of this publication may be reproduced or disseminated or transmitted in any form or by any means, electronic, mechanical, photocopying, recording or otherwise, or stored in any retrieval system, or otherwise used in any manner whatsoever without written permission of the copyright owner, except in accordance with the provisions of the Copyright, Designs and Patents Act 1988, or under the terms of a licence permitting restricted copying issued in the UK by the Copyright Licensing Agency Ltd, Saffron House, 6–10 Kirby Street, London EC1N 8TS, England, or in the USA by the Copyright Clearance Center, 222 Rosewood Drive, Danvers MA 01923. Application for the written permission of the copyright owner to reproduce any part of this publication must be made by email to legenda@mhra.org.uk.

Disclaimer: Statements of fact and opinion contained in this book are those of the author and not of the editors or the Modern Humanities Research Association. The publisher makes no representation, express or implied, in respect of the accuracy of the material in this book and cannot accept any legal responsibility or liability for any errors or omissions that may be made.

Trademark notice: Product or corporate names may be trademarks or registered trademarks, and are used only for identification and explanation without intent to infringe.

© *Modern Humanities Research Association 2018*

Copy-Editor: Charlotte Brown

CONTENTS

	Acknowledgements	ix
	Introduction	1
1	Istria: A Frontier Land	11
2	Borderland, Language, and the Trauma of the Exile: A Theoretical Approach	42
3	Before Exile: Bilingualism and Self-translation in *Materada* and *La miglior vita*	70
4	The Exilic Rift in *La ragazza di Petrovia* and *L'albero dei sogni*	101
5	After Exile: The Writer in Translation from *L'amicizia* to *Franziska*	127
	Conclusion	158
	Bibliography	166
	Index	179

To Gemma and Gaetano

ACKNOWLEDGEMENTS

This book originated from a doctoral thesis which was submitted to the Faculty of Medieval and Modern Languages at the University of Oxford. The thesis was made possible by a Doctoral Award from the Arts and Humanities Research Council, for which I am truly grateful. I would like to express my special appreciation and thanks to everyone who has supported me during my time in Oxford, first to my supervisor, Ela Tandello. I would like also to thank my college, St Hugh's, for its support. A special thanks also go to Laura Levi Tomizza, who has supported my project, and to Diana Rüesch and Karin Stefanski of the Archivio Prezzolini of Lugano, where Fulvio Tomizza's Archive is held, and Tiziano Chiesa from the Fondazione Arnoldo e Alberto Mondadori. I wish to especially thank Safet Zec for the painting appearing on the cover. Words cannot express how grateful I am to my parents, to whom I dedicate this book.

Translations in the text are my own unless otherwise stated.

M.D., London, September 2018

INTRODUCTION

In his *Bosnian Chronicle*, a novel set in the Napoleonic era in the Bosnian town of Travnik, Ivo Andrić presents a crucial chapter in the troubled history of the Balkans, drawing a portrait of the region and the innermost character of its inhabitants. Centring around the French and Austrian consuls and a succession of three viziers, a borderland emerges from the novel's multicultural dynamics and exchanges. Andrić presents a dialogue between the young French consul and an Illyrian doctor, Cologna, in which the latter characterizes vividly the condition of living in a land that straddles two different cultures:

> No one knows what it means to be born and to live on the brink, between two worlds, knowing and understanding both of them, and to be unable to do anything to help explain them to each other and bring them closer. To love and hate both to hesitate and waver all one's life. To have two homelands, and yet have none. To be everywhere at home and to remain forever a stranger. In short, to live torn on a rack, but as both victim and torturer at once.[1]

Doctor Cologna summarizes the challenge of belonging simultaneously to two civilizations, possessing, most probably, two languages, two rules of behaviour, and two sets of feelings. He seeks to describe the situation of hybrid identities, that is, those who lie between two groups without truly fitting into either and who forge their own world.

Here, at the intersection of diverse religions and cultures, people experience a problem concerning identity. As Doctor Cologna points out in the same passage, identity may be replaced by more fluid forms that better define borderland dwellers: he states that he is 'neither Christian, nor Jew, nor Parsee, nor Muslim [...] neither from the East, nor the West, neither from the land, nor the sea'.[2] However, Andrić's contribution would have been less remarkable if he had described the condition of living in a frontier land at a time of peace. In his analysis of the Bosnian region he shows the way in which a region characterized by multiple identities can be shaken by the imposition of new boundaries and changes of administration. He notes:

> They are people from the frontier, spiritual and physical, from the black and bloody line which was drawn, after absurd misunderstanding, between people, God's creatures, between whom there should not and must not be any boundaries. They form the narrow edge between the sea and the land, they are condemned to perpetual movement and unrest. They are the 'third world', where all malediction settled as a result of the division of the earth into two worlds. They are.[3]

This condition is shared by Fulvio Tomizza (1935–99), a writer from Istria — a frontier region that shows great similarities to that of Andrić. Tomizza's literary production cannot be fully understood without considering the special nature of this homeland where Latin and Slav civilizations have created an Italo-Croato-Slovene mixture. This combination of three heritages led to new linguistic and cultural formulations, creating hybrid belongings put under pressure by the large-scale movements of people resulting from the redefinition of borders after the Second World War.

This study focuses on this sudden change of regime that occurs in Istria, the consequent mass movements of exile, and the consequences — the surfacing of all the complexities and contradictions of a frontier land — as explored in Tomizza's works. Exile is experienced as trauma, an event which dramatically splits life into a before and an after. These phases are marked by the linguistic and cultural richness of the Istrian homeland and, in contrast, a monolingual life abroad. The fulcrum of this analysis is therefore language, which gives us a privileged perspective from which to view Tomizza's unique exile.

To be an exilic author means facing the issue of language. As Axel Englund and Anders Olsson suggest, exile always means there is 'a gap in one's language and identity'.[4] The reaction of writers to their voluntary or forced removal varies:

> Some writers continue to work in their native tongue, which is nevertheless altered or influenced by the alien context; others take the leap into another language, in part or completely, and thus bring the experiences of their own language across into a foreign one; others yet mix multiple languages in their work and thus create a literature that resists translation by sprawling across linguistic borders.[5]

Even when authors decide to maintain their native tongue abroad, language is stimulated by a new environment and conditions: 'Continuing to write in one's mother tongue even when one is removed from its native environment does not necessarily lead to linguistic stagnation. Ewa Thompson proposes the possibility of '"linguistic cross-fertilization" and enrichment of the literary koine'.[6] This means that exile always represents a change in the relationship between the self and its environment, and this could also be conceived as 'a rupture in the sense of an unusually sharp break from the old and entry into the new'.[7] But this is also a break that specifically affects language: 'A traumatic experience, not just because of the physical displacement from the native land but because [the exile's] professional tools are inextricably related to the cultural and linguistic realities of his/her country of origin'.[8] Exile will be considered as trauma in this analysis, because, as suggested by Lloyd Kramer, 'The experience of living among alien people, languages, and institutions can alter the individual's sense of self about as significantly as any of the traumas known to psychologists'.[9] Exile for Tomizza is exactly this sort of overwhelming experience. It can be best understood through the evolution of his language, given that in exile 'the self must come into being in the first place in an active relation to language'.[10]

I will associate Tomizza's exile with the notion of trauma to characterize his linguistic transition. While the vast majority of exiles experience a shift from a more homogeneous 'linguascape' (to use Yasemin Yildiz's term) to a more heterogeneous one, in Tomizza's case it is the contrary.[11] By transferring his pronounced Istrian multilingualism into a narrative that becomes ever more Italian he undergoes a drastic linguistic reduction. This linguistic trauma may be part of a wider loss, as suggested by Susan Levy and Alessandra Lemma:

> Trauma always involves loss. The losses may be actual such as the loss of a loved one, of one's home and country, or they may be more symbolic, the loss of identity, meaning or hope. Often, the traumatized individual is faced with both; an experience of exile, for example, which involves the literal loss of country, family and language can precipitate a sense of internal disorientation and loss of identity.[12]

This transition is further complicated by the troubled political situation found in Trieste, Tomizza's new home, where hostility against the Slav population was seen daily.[13] Tomizza's passage from the Istro-Venetian/Čakavian double dialect to Italian 'may be devastating, depriving the subject of access to the living world'.[14] In practical terms this meant having to lose the subtlest meanings and nuances related to his native land and thus the possibility of fully expressing himself: 'Once a writer chooses a language that is not his mother tongue there remains the problem of distance: that is, you are expressing yourself in a language with which you have no emotional tie'.[15] As the Yugoslavian writer Danilo Kiš states, Tomizza would have needed a great variety of languages and dialects at his disposal:

> To be true in the way its author dreams about, [the story] would have to be told in Romanian, Hungarian, Ukrainian, or Yiddish; or, rather, in a mixture of all three languages. Then, by the logic of chance and of murky, deep, unconscious happenings, through the consciousness of the narrator, there would flash also a Russian word or two, now a tender one like *telyatina*, now a hard one like *kinjal*.[16]

The plurilingual text is always 'more than just the addition of another language to provide for local color'.[17] Tomizza's plurilingual texts will be explored in this analysis to show that his progressive Italianization meant the suppression of his dual or plural linguistic background, which was then able to emerge only occasionally. Despite this, though, the employment of a remarkable form of self-translation constitutes a rich creative process, and Tomizza was still able to generate fruitful linguistic ideas.

Tomizza is among the Italian authors who have most extensively explored the experience of exile, and he pushes this theme to the point where new perspectives are gained. Despite this he has been relatively poorly considered within the literary panorama of the novecento. In the Triestine context, he is acknowledged by critics who consider him the successor of Italo Svevo and Scipio Slataper, who as I will explain in Chapter 1, are its most important authors. Tomizza carried forward themes of identity and language that had already been explored by his predecessors. However, outside Trieste, Tomizza is largely neglected and his work still struggles to gain the attention it deserves. Although the Istrian peninsula does not cover a wide area, it offered him the chance to examine in depth the phenomenon of exile. As in the case of Andrić, the hybrid land shaken by exile — which is not a common starting point for a writer — led to new discoveries and to the overturning of parameters derived from the more common experience of exile where multilingualism and multiculturalism are the result rather than what is left behind.

Writers such as Ovid, Dante, and Petrarch, and in recent times James Joyce, Josip Brodsky, and Milan Kundera, have been involved in forced or voluntary removals from their home country. They have often included this experience in their works, looking at the meaning that should be attributed to detachment from one's homeland, how they felt in the new country, their sense of loss and laceration, their experience of writing from a foreign place, and many other aspects that characterize life away from home. In Tomizza's case, these considerations play a central role in his first novels and are further developed in his later works. For this reason, I will analyze the linguistic, stylistic, and narratological aspects of *Materada*, *La miglior vita* [Better Life], *La ragazza di Petrovia* [The Girl from Petrovia], *L'albero dei sogni* [The Tree of Dreams], *L'amicizia* [Friendship], and *Franziska*, as well as some of his more significant essays and articles. Although there are differences in plot, style, and perspective, these works approach exile in chronological sequence. Tomizza aims to separate and keep separated the moment before, during, and after exile to give a better idea of the process. *Materada* focuses on the decisive moments before the Istrian exile, presenting the population of a village overwhelmed by the urgent decision of whether to stay or move to Trieste. This novel shows the climate of increasing friction and even violence between those holding different exilic points of view and the progressive depopulation of the area. *La miglior vita*, centring on a succession of village priests, sketches the same initial moment, again describing the increasing tension. The second step is the trauma, the moment of detachment, and this is observed in *La ragazza di Petrovia*. In this novel there are two stories that alternate and finally intermingle. One of these concerns the girl of the title, who takes a coach to the Triestine refugee camp, still uncertain about her final choice. The mind of someone going through the process of exile is examined in detail, highlighting the mixture of identity. This element is pivotal in the story of Istria and surfaces again in *L'albero dei sogni*. The main character seeks to regain his lost identity first in Trieste and then in Belgrade, the two cities — one Italian, the other Yugoslavian — that correspond to his double belonging. This double exile (life abroad being the third phase) sheds light on the splitting of the character as a consequence of the paradoxes inherent in a frontier land, and suggests the impossibility of regaining a lost origin.

By separating the three stages, Tomizza is able to point up the moment at which two parameters, such as identity and monolingualism, are put under pressure. His characters experience the condition of being placed among different cultures and languages even before crossing the border and reaching the foreign land. In contrast to other experiences of exile in which it is the encounter or clash with another country and language that gives birth to a redefinition of the subject, there is here an exile before the exile.

Before exile Tomizza's characters explore an identity that is not only the sum of the Italian and the Croatian or Slovene components; it transcends definite boundaries, undergoing constant adjustments. Identity cannot be a certain attribution given by the territory, the family of origin, the language spoken, behaviours, or any parameter that can be attributed to a single culture. Any univocal and stable formulation is doomed to collapse because identity tends to coincide with a reshuffling that is constantly recurring. As Claudio Magris affirms in the short essay 'Identità ovvero incertezza': 'Le rappresentazioni autentiche di un'identità plurima, comunque incerta e contraddittoria, non sono mai definitorie' [The authentic representations of a plural identity, albeit uncertain and contradictory, are never definitive].[18] Also, Iain Chambers, in developing his notion of identity, dismantles any idea of completeness or wholeness independent of an ongoing process of construction and adaptation by the subject:

> Our sense of being, of identity and language, is experienced and extrapolated from movement: the 'I' does not pre-exist this movement and then go out into the world, the 'I' is constantly being formed and reformed in such movement in the world.[19]

The second parameter jeopardized before exile is monolingualism, as I will demonstrate in this analysis. Tomizza is an example of a bilingual or polyglot writer by birth who fully exploits the potential of multilingual synergies in his novels. His case recalls Elias Canetti, another writer whose background was characterized by remarkable forms of multilingualism. In his autobiography, *The Tongue Set Free: Remembrance of a European Childhood*, Canetti describes the linguistic richness of his youth in his native town of Ruschuk, a port on the Danube, where the variegated mix of ethnicities and cultures meant there was a coexistence of multiple languages. Stating the nationalities present, Canetti writes that:

> Aside from the Bulgarians [...] there were many Turks who lived in their own neighbourhood, and, next to it, was the neighbourhood of Sephardim, the Spanish Jews — our neighbourhood. There were Greeks, Albanians, Armenians, Gypsies. From the opposite side of the Danube came Romanians [...]. There were also some Russians here and there.[20]

The list of people who inhabited the area indicates that there may have been a mutual contamination of languages, of words, expressions, and idioms. This was certainly the case for Canetti and his family — the first children's song that he learnt was Spanish, the language spoken by his parents was German, one of his playmates taught him Bulgarian.

Like Canetti, Tomizza came from a zone shaped by many languages (Italian, Croatian, Slovene, and German words are present in his repertoire) that include some dialects, among which the Istro-Venetian and the Čakavian stand out. Furthermore, the area was also characterized by a linguistic mixing generated by the interaction of these languages, leading to the formulation of unique new words and expressions. This unpredictable mixture is explained by Tomizza who, in *Alle spalle di Trieste* [Behind Trieste], refers to children in the village of Materada as follows:

> E i loro genitori, nel litigare astratto, usano ancora non la lingua del *sì*, del *da*, né del *ja*, né dello *sta*, né del *ca*, ma dell'esclusivo materadese *zza* che, va un po' a pensarlo, si accosta al boemo e polacco *zzo*.[21]
>
> [And their parents, in their abstract fights, still use neither the language of *sì*, *da*, nor of *ja*, *sta* and *ca*, but the exclusive *zza* from Materada that, if you think about it, can be compared to the Bohemian and Polish *zzo*.]

The analysis of language gives us, therefore, a privileged perspective, because, better than any other, it reveals the ethnic and historical dynamics of a frontier land. Chapter 3 analyzes *Materada* and *La miglior vita*, the novels of Tomizza in which multilingualism plays a key role. Here I go further into the complex linguistic situation existing at the time in Istria and discuss the way in which it was transposed into a novel written in Italian. This examination takes advantage of the theoretical framework provided in Chapter 2, where I consider self-translation and multilingualism in this context. I also consider the distinction between frontier and border, as discussed by critics such as Anzaldùa, Zanini, Assenza, and Bertone. The aspects of a border area most relevant to this discussion, such as hybridity and subcultures, will be considered with reference to Bhabha, Young, Schöpflin, Robinson, and Pyrah and Fellerer. A more specific linguistic approach to the plurilingual condition and self-translation will be provided as well, while the notion of exilic trauma in relation to language will be developed through considerations of Caruth, LaCapra, Kaplan, Tabori, Murphy, Lagos-Pope, Glad, and Said.

In Chapter 3, I will also use two specific linguistic theoretical approaches: Pieter Muysken's *Bilingual Speech: A Typology of Code-mixing* and Gaetano Berruto's *Situazioni di plurilinguismo, commutazione di codice e mescolanza di sistemi*.[22] The former offers an understanding of the linguistic phenomena that govern bilingualism and it will be used along with Tomizza's essay 'Uno scrittore tra due dialetti di matrice linguistica diversa' to illustrate the Istrian situation. Tomizza gives an account of the complex linguistic scenario that he observed in his land, while Muysken helps to clarify the dynamics of languages when they come into contact with one another. Gaetano Berruto's analysis of multilingualism in literature offers a most useful tool when approaching the narrative of *Materada*. Using this theoretical basis, I will pay special attention to four linguistic processes: code-switching, code-mixing, hybridization, and interference. If the four processes mentioned are only the most obvious signs of the interference of a foreign language with the Italian narrative, there are also other signals that bear witness to the multilingual background. Besides more familiar ones, there are original solutions such as when the narrator declares that the language spoken is not Italian but rather an intersection of bilingualism and diglossia. Contaminations that more generally take place when the exile is abroad — the impact with another language, issues relating to bilingualism, and the relationships between languages — are already experienced in *Materada*.

It is evident that a writer like Tomizza who employs self-translation is consistently different from other authors. He puts the monolingual condition to the test, developing the potential of the encounter of two or more languages. He is challenged by different languages with the result that he overturns beliefs that work only for monolingual writers. Tomizza tests the monolingual condition of the 'native speaker', setting the context for a constant irruption of languages in everyday life. As Giulio Lepschy and Helena Sanson's statement confirms: 'It seems unsafe to believe that a condition of strict monolingualism, based on the familiarity with a single variety of a single language, is the norm of the majority of human beings'.[23] This is particularly so in a land where plurilingualism is the rule rather than the exception.

Chapter 4 deals with a series of issues concerning the trauma of exile. In Tomizza, exile is the specific moment at which one detaches oneself from one's own land. This closely circumscribed phase is experienced by Tomizza's characters as an 'impossible' decision given that, by favouring one side of a multiple identity to the detriment of the other, exile leads to an internal split. Trauma is an event that, for the subject, cannot be satisfactorily categorized or comprehended. Thanks to the contributions of Said, Friedrick, Radulescu, Caruth, and Brodsky, it will be possible to investigate the main character of *La ragazza di Petrovia*'s trauma in detail. It is unusual to have a cross-section of this moment available: in narratives of exile it is frequently omitted. Apart from Eva Hoffman's *Lost in Translation: A Life in a New Language*, a work that focuses extensively on the Polish author's own American exile, few other novels explore the actual departure and progressive distancing from the country of origin.[24] This switch divides the life of the exile into two phases; in *La ragazza di Petrovia*, the life of the central character, Giustina, splits into two very distinct entities. In a narrative composed of layers, Tomizza records her failed conversations aiming thus to mirror the inner development of her thoughts and her lack of interaction with the external world. In so doing we follow in detail her vexed decision as to whether to leave the village.

The necessity of moving to a different country is the origin of the inner fracture of the girl from Petrovia. The crucial characteristic of her exile is doubleness as a result of trauma, confirming André Aciman's statement: 'Exiles see double, feel double, are double'.[25] This phenomenon must be clarified — there are several forms of doubleness depending on the nature of the two components that shape the subject. By applying the approaches of Rank, Freud, and Fusillo I will focus my examination on Giustina's split movements to pinpoint the original features of her fracture. The fact that exile splits the girl into two shows that leaving one's native country means preserving at least one side of a double self. Rank and Freud, who both trace the origins of doubleness, explore this mechanism, suggesting that the fear of nullification drives the subject to redouble in order to have a greater chance of survival. As Edward Said suggests in his *Reflections on Exile*, exile leads people to experience a broken life but, at the same time, to have more angles of observation compared with people who have only experienced their original context.[26]

Chapter 4 also presents the double exile described in *L'albero dei sogni*. This can be viewed as an expansion of the concept of doubleness seen in the previous novel. Here Tomizza describes exiles to Trieste and Belgrade in which his protagonist is made a stranger twice over. Stefano's estrangement is explored through the device of a series of mirrors. Here, Luigi Pirandello's *Uno, nessuno, centomila* and Jacques

Lacan's formulations will help us investigate this fragmentation of a character. As suggested by Lacan, the image reflected in the surface of mirrors does not coincide with the identity of the subject, but rather with an estranged component that imposes a foreign and unpredictable dimension on it. The increasing number of mirrors in *L'albero dei sogni* marks Stefano's progressive alienation.

Chapter 5 focuses on two novels, *L'amicizia* and *Franziska*, that belong to the later part of Tomizza's career. Both exemplify the transition from remarkable forms of multilingualism to a narrative that is becoming more Italian. Now in exile, Tomizza seeks to get closer to his lost country by writing about the Slovene area beyond Trieste. In this later phase Tomizza employs indirect speech to present the phenomena of plurilingualism, as is evident in *L'amicizia*. I will suggest that Tomizza, in his interior self-translation (a specific type of self-translation which does not require the presence of an original text), applies a process of domestication to his works. In other words, he reduces the foreign element in favour of adaptation to the values of the target language.

Franziska also adds to our understanding of Tomizza's linguistic transition. In Chapter 5, I will seek to analyze the meaning of the titular character's broken Italian in relation to Tomizza's exile. Despite not being an autobiographical novel, *Franziska* touches upon the acquisition of a language, which it characterizes as a long and frustrating process. More than this though, in this novel political conflicts are presented through the linguistic problems experienced by the main character, a Slovene girl learning Italian. The mistakes she makes are comparable to those experienced by Nabokov's Pnin. The concept of 'un-literariness', or broken Italian of which Triestine writers such as Svevo have often been accused, is investigated to further characterize Tomizza's linguistic practice. Tomizza's text can be a challenge to the reader due to its hidden plurilingual processes, which do not make the reading of the Italian narrative a smooth experience. 'Un-literariness', positively interpreted, legitimizes written language that reflects the encounter or collision of two or more linguistic backgrounds and enables the further development of hybridity and linguistic creativity, leading to an expansion of the text.

The Conclusion considers the complex relationship between Tomizza and the trauma of exile. Having experienced this at first hand, he appears to process his exilic condition through writing. In his early novels, he is both a simple mouthpiece of the Istrian exile, describing the event through multiple viewpoints, and at the same time a character involved in the story. Nevertheless, he is also thinking through exile when he is not directly involved in the work. Tomizza seems to be always simultaneously included and excluded in his stories. Despite being an unutterable event, the trauma of exile had to be dealt with in the form of writing. This paradoxical condition, which will be supported by the theoretical framework of Caruth, Cavarero, and LaCapra, questions once more the linguistic choice made by the writer. Is dealing with the trauma of exile possible in translation — the language of the event and that of the narrative being foreign to one another?

Tomizza's life and works will now be introduced in the context of Triestine literature, which was his literary centre of gravity. By considering two great figures of Triestine literature, Scipio Slataper and Italo Svevo, it is possible to introduce a writer who can be considered their successor and one who further explored the issue of heterogeneous identities and languages in a frontier land.

Notes to the Introduction

1. Ivo Andrić, *Bosnian Chronicle* (London: Harvill, 1996), p. 262.
2. Ibid.
3. Ibid., p. 263.
4. Axel Englund and Anders Olsson (eds), *Languages of Exile: Migration and Multilingualism in Twentieth-century Literature* (Bern: Peter Lang, 2013), p. 1.
5. Ibid.
6. Nancy Berg, *Exile from Exile: Israeli Writers from Iraq* (Albany: University of New York Press, 1996), p. 6.
7. Paul Friedrich, 'European and Generic Exile', in *Realms of Exile: Nomadism, Diasporas and Eastern European Voices*, ed. by Domnica Radulescu (Lanham, MD: Lexington Books, 2002), pp. 159–83 (p. 179).
8. María-Inés Lagos-Pope (ed.), 'Introduction', in *Exile in Literature* (Lehigh, PA: Bucknell University Press, 1988), pp. 7–14 (p. 8).
9. Lloyd Kramer, *Threshold of a New World: Intellectuals and the Exile Experience in Paris, 1830–1848* (Ithaca, NY: Cornell University Press, 1988), p. 9.
10. Mary Besemeres, *Translating One's Self: Language and Selfhood in Cross-cultural Autobiography* (Oxford: Peter Lang, 2002), p. 10.
11. Yasemin Yildiz, *Beyond the Mother Tongue: The Postmonolingual Condition* (New York: Fordham University Press, 2011), p. 109.
12. Susan Levy and Alessandra Lemma, *The Perversion of Loss: Psychoanalytic Perspectives on Trauma* (London: Whurr, 2004), p. XV.
13. 'Slav' is an unsatisfactory definition that indicates a vast cosmos only connected by a similar ethno-linguistic core (which extends from Russia to Bulgaria) and which includes heterogeneous elements. However, it has widely been used by writers and critics, and by Fulvio Tomizza himself.
14. Linda Nochlin, 'Art and the Conditions of Exile: Men/Women, Emigration/Expatriation', in *Exile and Creativity: Signposts, Travelers, Outsiders, Backward Glances*, ed. by Susan Rubin Suleiman (Durham, NC: Duke University Press, 1998), pp. 37–58 (p. 37).
15. Nurrudin Farah, 'In Praise of Exile', in *Literature in Exile: Conference Transcripts and Papers*, ed. by John Glad (Durham, NC, & London: Duke University Press, 1990), pp. 64–77 (p. 72).
16. Danilo Kiš, *A Tomb for Boris Davidovich* (New York: Penguin, 1980), p. 3.
17. Anthony Pym, Miriam Shlesinger, and Zuzana Jettmarova (eds), *Sociocultural Aspects of Translating and Interpreting* (Amsterdam: John Benjamins, 2006), p. 118.
18. Claudio Magris, 'Identità ovvero incertezza', *Lettere italiane* (2003), pp. 519–27 (p. 522).
19. Iain Chambers, *Migrancy, Culture, Identity* (New York: Routledge, 1994), p. 24.
20. Elias Canetti, *The Tongue Set Free: Remembrance of a European Childhood* (London: Granta, 2011), p. 6.
21. Fulvio Tomizza, *Alle spalle di Trieste: scritti 1969–1994* (Milan: Bompiani, 1995), p. 139.
22. Pieter Muysken, *Bilingual Speech: A Typology of Code-mixing* (Cambridge: Cambridge University Press, 2000); Gaetano Berruto, 'Situazioni di plurilinguismo, commutazione di codice e mescolanza di sistemi', *Babylonia*, 6:1 (1998), 16–21.
23. Giulio Lepschy and Helena Sanson, 'Native speaker', in *Reflexivity: Critical Themes in the Italian Cultural Tradition: Essays by Members of the Italian Department at University College London*, ed. by Prue Shaw and John Took (Ravenna: Longo Editore, 2000), pp. 119–29 (p. 121).
24. Eva Hoffman, *Lost in Translation: A Life in a New Language* (London: Vintage, 1998), p. 91.
25. André Aciman, *Letters of Transit: Reflections on Exile, Identity, Language, and Loss* (New York: New Press, 2000), p. 13.

26. Edward Said, 'Reflections on Exile', in *Reflections on Exile and Other Essays* (Cambridge, MA: Harvard University Press, 2002), pp. 173–86.

CHAPTER 1

Istria: A Frontier Land

Trieste and Beyond

Despite the fact that Fulvio Tomizza is considered an Istrian writer, one who devoted his initial literary production to his homeland and showed a strong attachment to it throughout his life, his literary frame of reference is Triestine. Trieste is both the city to which he moved on being exiled from Istria after the Second World War and, above all, the place that played the decisive role in his literary training. Despite their proximity, Trieste and Istria are very different linguistically, historically, and geographically; crucially also the urban character of Trieste contrasts with the rural hinterland where Tomizza came from. Nevertheless, it is in Trieste — a city that over a period of a couple of centuries played a leading role in the Italian literary tradition — that Tomizza started writing, carrying on the literary heritage of the city.

In the book interview *Destino di frontiera* [Frontier Destiny], Tomizza characterizes this period very clearly, devoting an entire chapter to his affinity with Trieste and its literature. By exploring his relationship with the city, he admits that 'Ora, poi, la mia terra non è più solo l'Istria: lo è diventata anche Trieste' [Now, then, my land is no longer just Istria: it has also become Trieste].[1] Tomizza arrived in Trieste with many others looking for a new place to live. Most importantly for this analysis, Trieste historically attracted writers who belonged to the surrounding areas and who shared similar ideas and beliefs. Tomizza describes this condition as follows:

> Era naturale che qui si fosse creato un gruppo di scrittori intonati tra loro, la cui esperienza non era quella dei loro colleghi italiani, ma che avevano urgenza di affrontare ed esprimere dei problemi assillanti, come quello della loro nascita diversa o della loro origine addirittura incerta. Erano mezzi boemi come Slataper, mezzi ebrei come Saba o interamente ebrei come Italo Svevo, che si sentiva ugualmente partecipe del mondo italico e di quello germanico.[2]
>
> [It was natural that here was created a group of writers in tune with each other, whose experience was not that of their Italian colleagues, but who needed to face and express nagging problems, such as their diverse and even uncertain origins. They were half Bohemians like Slataper, half Jews like Saba or entirely Jews like Italo Svevo, who felt equally involved in the Italic and the Germanic world.]

This 'aria comune di reciproco rispetto nella diversità' [common air of mutual respect in diversity], which was evident both in language and identity, was what intrigued Tomizza, who had already been exposed in his homeland to a remarkable form of hybridity.[3] This condition is fundamental to his work and so a substantial consideration of the Triestine context is justified in introducing it.

'Triestine literature' has been a successful but also controversial definition that denotes the works of several poets and writers who were based in and around Trieste in the late-nineteenth and twentieth centuries. It is a complex category which includes figures such as Italo Svevo, Umberto Saba, Carlo Michelstaedter, Scipio Slataper, Giani Stuparich, Vladimir Bartol, and others who were able to connect different cultures and literary tendencies within their work, and, in so doing, transform Trieste into one of the key spaces of modern literature. Trieste, which stands at the furthermost edge of north-east Italy, wedged between the Adriatic and the rocky plateau of Karst, went in this period from being a marginal town without any cultural traditions to a unique literary centre.

Although the definition of 'Triestine literature' is not uncontroversial,[4] Pietro Pancrazi, who was the first critic to use the term, glimpses some traits which these writers appear to have in common:

> Esiste oggi una letteratura triestina? Mi pare certo. Non si pecca di rettorica o di regionalismo affermando che negli ultimi trent'anni si è rivelata a Trieste una famiglia di scrittori, poeti e prosatori, diversi ma in qualche modo consanguinei, segretamente intonati tra loro.[5]
>
> [Is there a Triestine literature today? It seems certain to me. No one is being overly rhetorical or regionalist by saying that over the past thirty years in Trieste there has emerged a family of writers, poets and prose writers, all different but in a way consanguineous, secretly attuned to one another.]

Among the elements that connect them is the situation of Trieste itself: a geographical arrangement complicated by a troubled history which had the consequence of the land becoming a melting pot of ethno-linguistic groups.

A major example of the Triestine 'essence' comes from the beginning of Slataper's *Il mio Carso* [My Karst].[6] In the clash between the evocation of three possible origins (Karst, Croatia, and Moravia) and the declaration of Italianness that follows, the writer implies that his background might not be considered homogeneous:

> Vorrei dirvi: Sono nato in Carso, in una casupola col tetto di paglia annerita dalle piove e dal fumo. [...] Vorrei dirvi: Sono nato in Croazia, nella grande foresta di roveri. [...] Vorrei dirvi: Sono nato nella pianura morava e correvo come una lepre per i lunghi solchi, levando le cornacchie crocidanti. [...] Vorrei ingannarvi, ma non mi credereste. Voi siete scaltri e sagaci. Voi capirete subito che sono un povero italiano che cerca d'imbarbarire le sue solitarie preoccupazioni.[7]
>
> [I would like to tell you: I was born on the Karst, in a hovel with a thatched roof blackened by rain and smoke. [...] I would like to tell you: I was born in Croatia, in the big oak forest. [...] I would like to tell you: I was born on the Moravian plain and ran like a hare up the long furrows, frightening the cawing crows. [...] I would like to fool you, but you would not believe me. You are cunning and wise. You would immediately understand that I am a poor Italian trying to make his solitary concerns seem primitive.]

Slataper's wandering among different provenances stops in the final admission that nullifies the three hypothetical ones. However, by referring to the prevalent Italian culture he takes a step back: 'È meglio ch'io confessi d'esservi fratello, anche se talvolta io vi guardi trasognato e lontano' [It is better to confess that I am your brother, although sometimes I look at you dreamy and distant].[8] Although the Italian element apparently defeats the others, different drives buffet the Triestine subject so that there is no easy identification with a single culture.

Slataper's non-simple belonging reinforces the thought that the Triestine soul may be a multiple one. In the struggle to find a barycentre, different components flow through the same individual, whose origins may not be uniform. The tensions that continually keep subjects from and at the same time let them get close to the different sides of their identity in an endless open process are even more evident in Slataper's statement: 'Tu sai che io sono slavo, tedesco e italiano' [You know that I am Slav, German and Italian].[9] This synthetic definition has been explained by Angelo Ara and Claudio Magris who derive from it the essence of 'Triestine literature':

> Slataper è slavo d'origine, come dice il suo nome,[10] ma staccato dal mondo slavo; è, per certi versi, tedesco di formazione, ma si sente diverso dai tedeschi, deve apprendere la loro lingua e alla fine se li ritroverà di fronte in guerra; è un italiano, ma in qualche modo un italiano particolare. La sua identità egli la può trovare nella letteratura ossia nell'espressione data al fantasma poetico della sua vita, al suo immaginario [...] Trieste, forse più di altre città, è letteratura, è la sua letteratura.[11]
>
> [Slataper is of Slavic origin, as his names says, but detached from the Slavic world; he is, in some ways, German by education, but he feels different from Germans, he must learn their language and he will ultimately find them opposite him in war; he is Italian, but in some ways he is an unusual Italian. He can find his identity in literature that is the expression given to the poetic ghost of his life, to his imaginary [...]. Trieste, maybe more than other cities, is literature, is its literature.]

Triestine writers have questioned identity in depth, insisting that one's 'origins' can only be the intersection of different cultures, which are usually experienced simultaneously. Despite the collision of backgrounds that runs the risk of favouring one part to the detriment of the other, putting the subject in an uncomfortable position, Trieste's double or triple soul has been an ideal background for literary innovation. This lack of univocal attribution, or rather the synergy of different contexts that resist associating themselves too closely in a single identity, has led some critics to define Trieste as a nationless place, a small compendium of the universe, a city of contrasts and paradoxes, a 'nowhere'.[12]

The discussion of Slataper when introducing Fulvio Tomizza is not accidental. As the poet Biagio Marin suggests, among the Triestine writers Slataper is the real predecessor of Tomizza. The latter, who reports the claim in his book interview *Destino di frontiera*, observes: 'Biagio Marin, che era amico suo ed è stato amico mio, non aveva dubbi: ne vedeva in me il continuatore. Diceva: "Scipio finisce dove comincia Fulvio"' [Biagio Marin, who was his and my friend, had no doubt:

he saw his successor in me. He said: 'Scipio ends where Fulvio begins'].[13] Slataper's troubled identity that includes, and transcends, the Italian spirit, but above all his opening up to the Slav world, a rare disposition among Italian writers, certainly enters into Tomizza's work.

The three segments of the Triestine world did not develop equally. Under Austro-Hungarian domination the German speaking component played a crucial role, establishing relationships that went beyond commercial exchange. Among the most pertinent aspects of this influence we could mention the introduction of psychoanalysis to the Italian literary scene with the figure of Ettore Schmitz (whose pseudonym 'Italo Svevo' was intended to emphasize a double belonging).[14] However, 'Triestine literature' seems to have generally omitted its Slav component. Indeed, as Gilbert Bosetti points out, only a few references can be traced back to it:

> Ne *La coscienza di Zeno*, che Svevo scrive mentre i fascisti italiani incendiano la casa della cultura slovena, l'io narrante ignora gli sloveni. Nel ciclo degli *Anni ciechi* [by Pier Antonio Quarantotti Gambini], gli unici personaggi sloveni sono la serva della gleba di casa e qualche rozzo *zagabrian*. Di slavi, nel mondo poetico di Saba, c'è solo la nutrice Beppa Sabaz.[15]

> [In *La coscienza di Zeno*, that Svevo writes while Italian fascists are burning the Slovene house of culture, the I ignores the Slovenes. In the *Anni ciechi* cycle, the only Slovene characters are the maid and some rough *zagabrian*. The only Slav, in Saba's poetic wold, is the wet nurse Beppa Sabaz.]

For a city that had been profoundly influenced by Slovenes, this omission is rather striking. The city, its hinterland, and part of the surrounding coast are inhabited by them, which suggests that they should have played an even more evident role than the German-speaking population. But obstacles of various natures have limited this:

> Con l'elemento slavo, con cui si vive gomito a gomito quotidianamente, i rapporti veri furono pressochè nulli, ostacolati dall'ignoranza della lingua, fenomeno costante, non solo nel periodo prebellico, ma ancora nel secondo dopoguerra, [...] e impediti dalla coscienza di una presunta superiorità non solo economica ma anche culturale.[16]

> [With the Slav element, with whom people live shoulder to shoulder, the real relationships were almost none, hindered by ignorance of the language, a constant phenomenon, not only during the pre-war period, but still in the second post-war period [...] and impeded by the awareness of a presumed superiority not only economic but also cultural.]

Slataper can be considered an exception. In Tomizza's words: 'Lo Slataper (Pennadoro), di lontana origine boema, aveva per primo chiamato fratello il contadino sloveno del Carso' [The Slataper (Goldenpen) of Bohemian origin, was the first to call the Slovene peasant of the Karst brother].[17] Nevertheless, Tomizza sketches him as an observer, without truly embodying the Slav spirit:

> La differenza sostanziale tra me e lui è che Slataper è un uomo della borghesia triestina. È sempre un cittadino che parla ed il suo è un approccio tutto cerebrale, mentre io appartengo a quel mondo. Nel Carso vede un grande

scenario. L'uomo ne *Il mio Carso* si vede poco. È sì invocato: 'Tu, s'ciavo, vieni, ti porterò'. Ma in realtà scompare, non esiste.[18]

[The main difference between me and him is that Slataper is a man of the Triestine bourgeoisie. He is always a citizen who speaks and his approach is cerebral, whereas I belong to that world. In the Karst he sees great scenery. Man in *Il mio Carso* is barely visible. He is beseeched: 'You, Slav, come, I'll take you'. But he actually disappears, he does not exist.]

In the Triestine literary tradition Tomizza is a third-generation writer who breaks down the barrier with the East. Coming from the hinterland of the Istrian peninsula, a land beyond Trieste where Italians and Croats (and Slovenes) encounter one another, meant being caught in between two cultures. Slataper began to fill this gap in Triestine culture but only laid out the path that would be fully explored by Tomizza:

Penso infatti di continuare la tradizione triestina senza ripeterla passivamente, ma anzi arricchendola di significati, esperienze e tendenze, che rispecchiano la nuova realtà di Trieste. A differenza dei triestini del passato, ma anche a completamento della loro opera, mi sono aperto al mondo slavo anziché a quello austro-tedesco.[19]

[I think of continuing the Triestine tradition without passively repeating it, but rather enriching it with meanings, experiences, and trends that mirror the new reality of Trieste. Unlike the Triestines of the past, but also in the completion of their work, I opened myself to the Slavic world instead of the Austro-German.]

Given that 'la frontiera triestina è e soprattutto era una frontiera con l'est' [the Triestine frontier is and above all was a frontier with the East], Tomizza should now be thought of as the figure who included the contiguous Slav world for the first time.[20]

Slataper, through his circling around and hinting at the issue of the Slav background, led to another of Tomizza's innovations. 'Triestine literature' has always questioned the diverging synergies of a multicultural city, putting identity under strain. The 'completion' mentioned by Tomizza refers to a development of these dynamics that were not fully exploited in the Triestine tradition. In his *Alle spalle di Trieste*, whose emblematic title sums up Tomizza's world, he specifies the essence of this 'completion':

Il piccolo mondo lasciato alle spalle si ridimensionava, ma ecco che per i suoi conflitti di sempre, l'ambiguità di fondo e gli umori più segreti, esso non differiva molto (o addirittura mi appariva più indicativo nella sua esasperazione) da quello di uno Slataper, di uno Stuparich o di un Quarantotti Gambini [...]. Ma come rappresentarlo se non con la deliberazione di continuare e completare un discorso che sembrava concluso e che fatalmente era rimasto invece sospeso? A distanza di cinquanta anni mi si offrivano, identiche e forse ancora più aspre, le loro ragioni di divisione, di lotta e di scelta.[21]

[The small world left behind was scaled down, but as to its constant conflicts, its basic ambiguity, and most secret moods, it was little different (it even appeared to me more symptomatic of its exasperation) from that of Slataper, Stuparich, or Quarantotti Gambini [...]. But how best to represent it, if not by deciding to continue and finalize an issue that seemed complete, that was inevitably deferred instead? Fifty years later identical and perhaps even more bitter reasons for division, struggle, and choice were offered to me.]

The Istrian provenance of the author offers him the chance to provide a new perspective on a hybrid land, where identity and language cannot be established clearly. To put it differently, Tomizza not only presented and developed the Slav cosmos that was suppressed in Triestine literature, he also considered matters relating specifically to his land where different cultures shaped, even more evidently than in Trieste, mixed identities. The Istrian subject is exposed to a series of issues, such as bilingualism and hybrid identity, but also to exile and this spurred Tomizza to explore his homeland in depth.

Tomizza does not consider 'Triestine literature' finished but still in progress: 'Trieste scopre ancora un terreno quasi vergine, uno spazio sostanzialmente inedito, dal quale dunque potrebbe venire qualcosa di nuovo' [Trieste still offers an almost virgin territory, a substantially unknown space, from which something new could come].[22] This would have been unthinkable if it were not for the fact that the writer himself belonged to that heterogeneous context overwhelmed by dramatic events. As Marco Neirotti points out: 'Questo dramma è molto più che il motivo dominante della narrativa dell'autore istriano: ne costituisce la ragione stessa, è la radice, la linfa del suo impegno di scrittore' [This drama is much more than the primary theme in the narrative of the Istrian author: it constitutes its reason for being, it is the root, the sap of his task as writer].[23] The historical and political context explored by Tomizza also goes beyond the Istrian exile, as it includes:

> The fragmentation and destruction of this multicultural community over the course of his life span: World War I, Fascism and the Italianization of the village, World War II, the German occupation, and finally Communism and the village becoming a part of Yugoslavia. The internal rupture of the community reaches its high point in the years immediately after World War II, when the village is assigned first to the Free Territory of Trieste and later to Yugoslavia and the question of whether to be pro-Italian or pro-Yugoslav divides even families and couples.[24]

For this reason, and to lay the groundwork for this analysis, I shall now focus on the peculiar characteristics of Tomizza's home country.

A Troubled History

Istria is the Adriatic peninsula where Fulvio Tomizza was born and where he based his most important works. Introducing this dry plateau that lies between the gulf of Trieste and the Kvarner area, he describes it as follows:

> La penisoletta a forma di foglia, che si insinua nel termine dell'Adriatico, si allontana da Trieste riproponendone per un buon tratto i fondali bassi, i fertili promontori gialli, le insenature paludose un tempo tutte occupate dai riquadri delle saline [...]. Con la punta di Salvore, fuori del golfo triestino e inserita nella Repubblica di Croazia, la costa rocciosa è premuta da un mare più azzurro e

gagliardo. La sormonta un manto di terra rossa propizio alla vite e all'ulivo, là dove la ricomparsa della pietraia non ne limiti la vegetazione a stenti roveri, al ginepro e ai cespugli spinosi del Carso.[25]

[The small leaf-shaped peninsula that insinuates itself into the top of the Adriatic, stretches out from Trieste offering a good stretch of shallow waters, fertile yellow headlands, marshy inlets once occupied by salt pans [...]. With the cape of Savudrija, out of the Gulf of Trieste and inserted in the Republic of Croatia, this rocky coast is buffetted by a blue and vigorous sea. It is surmounted by a covering of red earth favourable to vines and olive trees, where the vegetation of oaks, junipers, and thorny bushes of the Karst is unrestrained by intermittent stones.]

To begin to understand the peninsular one needs to consider its troubled history. Istria has a long, complicated past that has produced a stratification of civilizations, the influence of all of which is still detectable. Due to its strategic location and its being at the margins of different cultures, several populations have set out to conquer it since prehistoric times. Several invasions (including the Roman conquest of Epulon's kingdom) occurred up until the crucial settlement by Venice (1267) of the coastal towns of the region. This settlement facilitated commerce and freed the sea from pirates, but also accentuated the break between the Istrian coast and the mainland, and this was still a major issue in Tomizza's time. As the Istrian poet Lina Galli wrote:

Per poter navigare gl'Istriani avevano bisogno della protezione di Venezia [...]. Ogni città costiera formava ormai quasi una repubblica a sè, per nulla interessata alla sorte delle consorelle [...]. L'unità, ch'era esistita con Epulo e s'era rinsaldata con Roma [...] era ormai spezzata.[26]

[In order to sail the Istrians needed the protection of Venice [...]. Every coastal town built its own republic, not at all interested in the fate of its sisters [...]. The unit, that had existed with Epulon and was strengthened by Rome [...] was now broken.]

As with other Mediterranean settlements, the coastal zone only occasionally had dealings with the culture of the backcountry, which, from the sixth century, had been dominated by Slav populations. These populations come from the Carpathians.[27] Numerous Glagolitic inscriptions (the first Slav form of writing, spread by Cyril and Methodius) coexisting with Latin ones testify to their presence.[28] Tomizza took note of this double written heritage and drew an episode of his novel *La miglior vita* from Glagolitic inscriptions that he had his character Don Stipe discover next to some Venetian tombs:

Lo lasciai ritirarsi in chiesa per il rosario e, quando mi parve il momento di chiamarlo a cena, lo trovai ginocchioni in mezzo alla navata intento a ricopiare su un foglio non l'iscrizione ben marcata sulla tomba di Ràdovan, bensì gli strani segni semicancellati e racchiusi in un cerchio sulla lapide vicina, somiglianti a una fitta serie di rastrelli e forconi in miniatura. 'Caccia grossa' mi salutò alzandosi: 'un *glagolitico* assai interessante'.[29]

[I let him retire to the church for the rosary, and when it seemed time to call him for dinner, I found him on his knees in the middle of the aisle intent on copying on a sheet of paper not the well-marked inscription on Ràdovan's tomb but the strange half-erased signs enclosed in a circle on the nearby tombstone, resembling a dense series of rakes and pitchforks in miniature. 'A big-game hunting' he greeted me standing up: 'a very interesting *Glagolitic*'.]

The episode marks the history of a parish church that allowed two worlds to coexist and two different but complementary cultures to develop, giving birth to new mixtures. Tomizza, who often explores the relationships between Venice and the Slavs,[30] identifies the process of intermingling:

> Sommariamente si può asserire che nelle cittadine litoranee e interne della Serenissima, a dispetto delle epidemie, si perpetuava la presenza veneta, e che ai margini di esse s'insediavano sempre più numerosi ed alacri gli immigrati croati. [...] Va però subito aggiunto che la povertà e il rigore ancora feudale di quel territorio, andavano favorendo una continua infiltrazione nell'area veneta, dentro la quale i più intraprendenti coloni balcanici tendevano a venetizzarsi, fino ad accedere all'inurbamento.[31]

> [In summary, one can claim that in the towns of the coast and in the hinterland of the Serenissima, despite the plagues, the Venetian presence continued, and that numerous hard-working Croatian migrants settled on the margins. [...] However, we should add that the poverty and the still feudal rigour of that territory favoured a continuous infiltration into the Venetian area, within which the more enterprising Balkan settlers tended to become Venetian, in order to have access to urbanization.]

The two cultural and linguistic contexts that form the axis around which the history of this land revolves created a mixed area partially resembling the two, but determined by a fresh combination of elements. This 'grey zone' and its subtle dynamics have been considered by Nelida Milani, who argues that living in Istria meant:

> Vivere lungo la linea di unione fra due lingue e due culture che entrano in contatto e si confondono in una fascia grigia stratificata e sovrapposta, un territorio rimosso, quasi onirico nella sua reale irrealtà. [...] Il grigio è la bruma del non-luogo.[32]

> [To live along the line of union between two languages and two cultures that came into contact and mingled in a layered and overlapping grey band, a removed territory, almost dreamlike in its real unreality. [...] Grey is the mist of non-place.]

However, the peninsula is far from simply an area shared by different cultures. Given that it, as suggested by Predrag Matvejević's paradoxical statement, is 'island, peninsula, and hinterland all at once', there are many variables, such as the presence of internal borders, languages, and dialects, with greater or subtler forms of interaction.[33] The Italo-Croatian axis that lies at the heart of Istria represents only the most obvious perspective on the peninsula. In fact, Istria was depopulated and land was given to people from abroad several times over. Families from Dalmatia, Friuli, Tuscany, Albania, and Greece repopulated the area, developing further ethnic interactions. As Tomizza noted: 'Sulle soglie del Novecento non vi era famiglia in grado di vantare tutta intera una nazionalità' [On the threshold of the twentieth century there was no family who could boast a complete nationality].[34] The Austrian Empire, when it acquired the Istrian territory after the Treaty of Campoformio in 1797, had to deal with the difficulties of ruling a country which contained manifold cultural entities and which was under a constant risk of disintegration. The centrifugal forces that acted on it were explored by Joseph Roth in *The Emperor's Tomb*:

> I want to say that only for this crazy Europe of nation, states and nationalism does the obvious appear to be strange. In fact, it is the Slovenians, the Polish and Ruthenian Galicians, the Caftan Jews from Boryslav, the horse traders from Bacska, the Sarajevo Muslims, the Maronibraters from Mostar, who sing '*Gott erhalte (Kaiser Franz)*'. [...] The essence of Austria is not its centre but its periphery.[35]

Under the Austrian umbrella, different ethnicities fighting for independence created the explosive situation that led to the First World War. This moment marked the transition from Austrian to Italian administration, which, shortly afterwards, as a result of the rise of the Fascists, led to the breaking down of the relationship between the Latin and the Slav components.

When Istria became part of the Italian state in 1921, contrasts between Italians, Croats, and Slovenes became more significant. Under Fascism, Slavic languages were banned in public institutions such as courts, churches, schools, and the press. One of the most important examples of the repression of the Slovene minority was the fire at the Narodni dom in Trieste (Trieste National Hall). This multimodal building, which was the centre of the Slovene community in the city and included the Slovene theatre in Trieste as well as a hotel and other cultural associations, was burnt down in 1920 by Italian Fascists.[36] The increasing violence led thousands of Slovenes and Croats to move to more peaceful areas, especially when the Fascist government started expropriating their assets:

> In the newly acquired region of Venezia Giulia, the existence of large Slovene and Croat populations gave rise to a virulent Fascist movement, supported by the urban middle class and industrialists, who saw in Fascism an opportunity to advance their class interests and to affirm their own Italianness. The specificity of 'border Fascism' was made clear by Mussolini in his visit to Venezia Giulia in 1920. The task facing the Fascists there was, for Mussolini, 'more delicate, more sacred, more difficult, more necessary, the most necessary'. In their dealing with Slavs, an 'inferior and barbarous race,' the Italians would have to rely on 'the club'.[37]

This aggressive assimilation in border areas came with the idea of the superiority of the Italian nation and civilization, which also put relationships with Slovenes and Croats under pressure. The Blackshirts employed violence to eradicate other ethnicities and nullify the presence of minorities with the result that 'resistance intensified, and [...] Slovene-speakers [were] identified as non-Italian and anti-Fascist'.[38]

Following the Wehrmacht's invasion of Yugoslavia in 1941, Italy expanded its area of occupation, annexing other parts of Slovenia (including Ljubljana) and the majority of littoral Croatia. In these zones, during the Second World War, the Italians were helped in repressing the local population and partisan activities by the Croatian Fascist and ultranationalist movement of the Ustaše (Hrvatska revolucionarna organizacija, the Croatian Revolutionary Organization). The Ustaše, which aimed at the creation of an independent Croatian state, was a puppet of Nazi Germany. This oppression favoured the growth of anti-Italian sentiment within the Slovene and Croatian populations of Fascist Italy, and this sentiment exploded after Italy's capitulation in 1943 when Fascist collaborators were murdered by being thrown into the *foibe*, deep, natural sinkholes previously used by Fascist soldiers 'as open-air cemeteries for opponents to the regime'.[39] At the same time, the rising state of Yugoslavia, which was founded in the aftermath of World War II, was establishing a contrasting regime in the Julian areas. At the beginning of the Cold War until 1948 the new leader here, Josip Tito, sided with the Eastern bloc; his eventual split with Stalin led to a policy of neutrality. The new regime in Istria meant a climate of repression and terror that forced the vast majority of Italian residents to move abroad. The Fascist authorities were expelled and the National Liberation Committee of Istria endeavoured to 'free' Istria from the Italians and annex it to the Yugoslavia of Tito:

> Strengthened by its authority and by an 'entirely totalitarian' plan, from the beginning the Yugoslavs implemented a policy aimed at sweeping away all obstacles, particularly their political enemies. It is within this context that the second and most radical wave of violence against the Italians [...] went on for several months and took many different forms: summary court cases, spontaneous executions, and planned deportation to camps from which the majority never returned. There was a mixture of 'actions from below' and policies planned by the local communist political and military authorities.[40]

After World War II, Italians who chose Italy rather than continuing to live in communist Yugoslavia were called *optanti*, which can be translated as 'choosers', while they called themselves refugees or exiles. Their reasons for moving were to some extent economic but above all political, that is, the fear of reprisals and ethnic persecution. The option is described by Ballinger as follows:

> According to Article 19, all 'Italians' resident in the ceded territories (which included not just southern Istria, but also the Dodecanese islands and parts of the Valle d'Aosta) on or before 10 June 1940 had the legal right (though by no means the obligation) to choose Italian citizenship. The principal requirements of Italian-ness in the case of the option were Italian as the *lingua d'uso* (language of customary use) and *domicilio* (domicile) in Italy on the determined date. Opting for Italian citizenship required moving to the territorially reconfigured Italian state. Writing at the time of events, legal scholar Josef Kunz declared the option process 'theoretically correct and apt to avoid difficulties.' Determining Italian-ness on the ground proved no easy feat, however, either for Italian and Yugoslav governments deciding individual option cases or for the international organizations (United Nations Relief and Rehabilitation Administration or UNRRA and the International Refugee Organization or IRO) charged with determining whether individuals coming from the formerly Italian parts of Istria and Venezia Giulia were eligible for refugee relief. The national

indeterminacy of some of these refugees — populations that had become increasingly illegible within the bureaucratic apparatus of states — made them quite visible to the staff of the international agencies trying to figure out who counted as an individual displaced outside his or her 'home' country.[41]

A clear-cut division was not possible in a territory like Istria and the necessity to opt for one side rather than the other created many 'undetermined' individuals, who were often displaced and misunderstood. In this chaotic period, facing drastic changes imposed by the Yugoslavian regime, some Slovenes and Croats also moved to Trieste, despite the Italian government trying to obstruct the movement of a huge mass of Istrians to Italy:

> Il governo italiano cercava di non agevolare l'esodo. Si temeva che la fuga degli italiani e l'afflusso degli slavi, modificando la composizione etnica della regione potesse nuocere alle rivendicazioni italiane sulla Venezia Giulia durante le trattative alla conferenza di pace.[42]

> [The Italian government tried not to facilitate the exodus. It feared that the flight of the Italians and the influx of Slavs, by changing the ethnic composition of the region could be harmful to Italian claims on the Venezia Giulia during negotiations at the peace conference].

From the end of the war to 1955 around 200,000–300,000 persons left Istria, questioning in depth their sense of belonging, often without being able to find a suitable answer.

This change carried with it a frightening increase in violence and instability. Evidently, Trieste and Istria were facing an uncertain future. At that moment the Trieste area was supervised by Allied troops in order to stop a Yugoslav conquest of the city. The whole population of the region was deeply affected and as Ara and Magris write, one could easily have 'la sensazione di essere una pedina nella scacchiera internazionale' [the feeling of being a pawn on the international chessboard].[43] This tension resulting from the establishment of new borders, the descent of the iron curtain, and the application of so-called Real Socialism are the context in which Tomizza's works are constructed.

The Istrian exile of 1945 inspired writers such as Lina Galli, Pier Antonio Quarantotti Gambini, Giani Stuparich, and many others to develop the theme of the loss of homeland and displacement. However, the specificity of this exile emerges only in the works of a few writers, among whom Tomizza stands out. In describing Materada, the village in which Tomizza set his first novel, Marin discusses the troubled identity of a population struggling to clarify its sense of belonging before opting for a life elsewhere:

> Materada: un minuscolo borgo là sul margine delle due civiltà, l'italiana ascendente dal mare, la slava calante dal retroterra. Su quella linea, per molto tempo la pressione penetrativa dei due popoli aveva trovato un qualche equilibrio che neanche l'annessione dell'Istria all'Italia, aveva potuto mutare. [...] Due anime in contrasto erano spesso negli stessi individui, due linguaggi erano sulle loro bocche. E a volte la ingenuità propria degli slavi si scontrava con la maggiore complessità italiana; il senso di giustizia degli uni con l'accortezza degli altri. Ma come si sarebbero potuti separare? Che, in realtà erano una sola

> vita. Ma la guerra era venuta e aveva separato ciò che pareva inseparabile. Aveva tagliato nella carne viva, nella storia, la più reale e aveva separato gli italiani dagli slavi, la vita italiana dalla vita slava.[44]
>
> [Materada: a tiny village on the margin of two civilizations, the Italian ascending from the sea, and the Slav dropping from the hinterland. Along that line, for a long time the penetrating pressure of the two populations has found the perfect balance that not even the annexation of Istria to Italy could have altered. [...] Two contrasting spirits were often experienced within the same people, two languages spoken by the same mouth. Sometimes the ingenuity of the Slavs clashed with the greater Italian complexity; the sense of justice of the one with the canniness of the other. How could they have been separated? They were one life only. But war came and separated what seemed inseparable. It cut into the bare flesh, into history, and separated the Italians from the Slavs, Italian life from the Slav life.]

Not only did the unique characteristics of this land rule out any straightforward sense of identity, but once the decision to leave the country had been made, the balance was broken and the lost home could not be pieced back together. The special nature of Istria meant it was unlikely that its exiles would fit into another place: the mixture they were used to would no longer be available nor was it possible to recreate it.

Many critics have defined Tomizza as a frontier writer: 'Molti mi hanno definito scrittore di frontiera per antonomasia' [Several defined me as the borderland writer par excellence].[45] Starting from the review which appeared in *The Times Literary Supplement*, in which Isabel Quigly notes that 'Fulvio Tomizza is, quite literally, an Italian borderline case', his literary production has been associated with a land at the crossroads of different cultures.[46] But what does being a writer from the frontier mean? Tomizza offers a definition in an essay entitled 'Mi identifico con la frontiera':

> Dirò dunque che frontiera reale, frontiera 'per antonomasia', è per me quel territorio sempre conteso, e in definitiva sempre estraneo ai contendenti, che alla sommità dell'Adriatico si insinua tra Italia, Austria e Jugoslavia, nel quale si radicano il mio destino di uomo e la mia ricerca di narratore.[47]
>
> [I will say, then, that the real frontier, the frontier 'par excellence', is for me that contested territory, fundamentally always foreign to its disputants, that, at the top of the Adriatic, is wedged between Italy, Austria, and Yugoslavia, where both my human destiny and my researches as storyteller are rooted.]

From the time of Slataper, centrifugal forces have guided the Triestine subject beyond the Italian border, determining a culture at the margins, constantly turning to the 'elsewhere'. Tomizza gives a definition of writers who face the frontier condition, arguing that they always have one foot outside Italy and stressing the idea of an identity that can only be defined in contrast to more homogeneous ones:

> Tutti gli scrittori che qui sono nati e hanno operato, da Italo Svevo (classe 1861) a Claudio Magris (1939), volenti o nolenti, sono uomini e autori di tale Nord-Est da tenere un piede oltre i confini d'Italia, da mettersi a scrivere per proclamare o scoprire la loro italianità diversa se non esigua.[48]

[All writers who were born and worked here, from Italo Svevo (born 1861) to Claudio Magris (1939), willingly or not, are men and authors of the Northeast, who keep one foot beyond the borders of Italy and start writing to proclaim or discover their different, if not small, Italian spirit.]

Tomizza's formulation highlights the idea of a decentred subject, whose barycentre is inclined to other poles. If the frontier, which can also lead to very strongly demarcated identities, is the cornerstone around which Tomizza's works are built, how can it be defined? According to Magris:

> La frontiera è una striscia che divide e collega, un taglio aspro come una ferita che stenta a rimarginarsi, una zona di nessuno, un territorio misto, i cui abitanti sentono spesso di non appartenere veramente ad alcuna patria ben definita o almeno di non appartenerle con quella ovvia certezza con la quale ci si identifica, di solito, col proprio paese. Il figlio di una terra di confine sente talora incerta la propria nazionalità [...] ma la frontiera, la quale separa e spesso rende nemiche le genti che si mescolano e si scontrano sulla sua linea invisibile, anche unisce quelle stesse genti, che si riconoscono talora affini e vicine proprio in quel loro comune destino — che le madrepatrie non riescono a capire — in quel loro sentimento segreto d'inappartenenza, in quell'incertezza e in quell'indefinibilità della loro identità.[49]

[The frontier is a strip that divides and connects, a rough cut like a wound that is difficult to heal, a no man's land, a mixed area, where people often feel they do not really belong to any well-defined home or at least not with the obvious certainty with which one usually identifies with one's own country. The son of a borderland sometimes feels his nationality uncertain [...] but the frontier, which separates and often makes enemies of people who mingle and clash on its invisible line, also links those same people, who sometimes recognize themselves associated by a common destiny — that the motherlands fail to understand — in that secret feeling of not belonging and the uncertainty of their identity.]

Tomizza lives the double dimension of his frontier land. On the one hand, this nullifies any certain attribution, shaping a neutral space characterized by a sense of non-belonging that paradoxically unifies people: in these areas, as was the case in Tomizza's Istria, people may create new mixtures that bring them closer together. On the other hand, it could be a place of rivalry and hatred springing from disputes and the clashes of different cultures. Magris summarizes it as follows: 'La frontiera è duplice, ambigua; talora è un ponte per incontrare l'altro, talora una barriera per respingerlo' [The frontier is twofold, ambiguous; it is sometimes a bridge to meet the other, sometimes a barrier to reject it].[50] This theoretical framework relating to the borderland will be considered in the following chapter.

Fulvio Tomizza: Life and Early Works

Fulvio Tomizza was born in 1935 in Giurizzani (now Juricani), a small Istrian village a few kilometres from Umag. In contrast to the coastal town of Umag where the influence of Venice had prevailed for centuries, Giurizzani belonged to an Italo-Croatian mixed area. Tomizza highlights this unusual situation in an autobiographical passage, pointing out the crucial differences between his hybrid home village and more homogenous regions:

> Non è lontana più di sette chilometri dal centro costiero di Umago, nostra sede comunale, eppure conserva tutt'oggi il carattere di un'Istria assai diversa da quella ufficiale — veneta — che il lettore italiano avrà riconosciuto attraverso le pagine di Giani Stuparich e di Pier Antonio Quarantotti Gambini.[51]

> [It is no more than seven kilometres from the coastal town of Umag, our communal constituency, but it still retains the character of a very different Istria from the official one — Venetian — that the Italian reader has recognized through the pages of Giani Stuparich and Pier Antonio Quarantotti Gambini.]

The vicissitudes encountered by his family and the history of the village itself had a profound influence on the writer's life and work. Materada, the main village in the area, was founded by Tomizza's ancestor Zorzi Tomica, who escaped from Dalmatia, which at the time was being put under pressure by the Turks, and claimed lands which had been depopulated by the plague (the same plague, which had spread from the Venetian Republic, that Alessandro Manzoni described in *I promessi sposi* [The Betrothed]). In *Il sogno dalmata*, a novel in which Tomizza recreates the history of his homeland, he also draws attention to his Dalmatian origin: 'Tutti noi siamo di origine dalmata' [All of us are of Dalmatian origin].[52] He lingers over the mythical conquests of his ancestor Zorzi Tomica, picturing him in these terms:

> La tradizione familiare lo vuole bendato ad un occhio, sacrificato in circostanze che potevano essere delle più svariate e controverse. Aveva combattuto a fianco dei veneziani contro i Turchi, oppure con i corsari uscocchi scappati dai Turchi e assoldati dai veneziani? Aveva fatto parte della banda del Giurizza o era lui stesso l'implacabile Giurizza che seminava il terrore lungo le coste dalmate?[53]

> [The family tradition has him with a patch on one eye which had been sacrificed in circumstances that varied according to the teller: had he fought alongside the Venetians against the Turks, or fled from the Turks with the Uskok corsairs and been hired by the Venetians? Had he been part of the Giurizza gang or was he himself the implacable Giurizza that sowed terror along the Dalmatian coasts?]

The history of Zorzi Tomica foreshadows the cultural mixture eventually established in the area. This mixture was also recapitulated in Tomizza's family: his father was of the Italian middle class while his mother came from the countryside. The former was a wealthy landowner who was imprisoned by the Yugoslav authorities before his exile at the end of the war. He is an overwhelming and confrontational presence in Tomizza's life and works: the son breaks from, betrays, and is reconciled with him. In contrast, Tomizza hardly ever refers to his mother but her influence is no less important. She embodies a different culture and sometimes seems to be used as a device to underline this distance. Coming back to her usually signifies 'un oscuro ritorno alla parte materna, laboriosa e sbrigativa, alla ricerca anche del calore che originariamente doveva accompagnarsi a quei suoni sempre un po' bruschi' [an obscure return to the maternal side, industrious and curt, in the search for the warmth that was originally accompanied by sounds that were always a little brusque].[54] Tomizza's relationship with his mother is summarized in a statement contained in *I rapporti colpevoli* [Guilty Relationships]: 'Chini sul lavoro, quasi ci sfioravamo con le facce, l'uno specchio dell'altra, i due esseri più vicini e più lontani al mondo' [Bent over our work, our faces almost touched, one the mirror of the other, the two closest and most distant beings in the world].[55]

Tomizza's double belonging is far from being the harmonious sum of two different cultures and is experienced as a divided status generated by the political changes of the Second World War:

> Di educazione italiana che mi vedeva dalla parte degli avversari, ma come stordito dal pulsare giovanile di un sangue riscoperto differente, addirittura opposto, [...] mi trovavo tra due fuochi dentro alla nostra stessa frontiera, e questa lacerazione me la portavo dietro in famiglia e nella scuola, come una piaga segreta.[56]

> [The Italian education placed me on the side of the opponents, but as though dazed by the young pulse of a rediscovered different, even opposite, blood, [...] I found myself between two fires within our own border, and I brought this laceration into my family and to school, like a secret wound.]

Tomizza's youth was conditioned by various contradictions that led him to lean towards his Italian or Croatian sides at different moments. This peculiar situation is touched upon by his character Stefano Marcovich in the quasi-autobiographical novel *L'albero dei sogni*, when he describes his double existence. However, what may at first appear an advantageous condition runs the risk of turning into one which displaces the subject, hovering between two different cultures might mean losing both: 'Con due anime da salvare rischia sempre di perderle entrambe' [With two souls to be saved one always risks losing them both].[57] The risk could be still higher: being in between the Italian and Croatian cultures may mean being misunderstood by both:

> Amavo mio padre, che nel suo cuore aveva sempre optato per l'Italia, e soffrivo di vederlo perseguitato dagli jugoslavi... Andavo a Trieste col lasciapassare e là venivo considerato slavo perché provenivo dall'interno, tornavo a Materada e qui venivo considerato italiano. Era lo sbandamento, era il dramma della frontiera vissuto fino in fondo.[58]

> [I loved my father, who in his heart had always opted for Italy, and I suffered to see him persecuted by the Yugoslavs... I went to Trieste with a pass and there I was considered Slav because I came from the interior, I came back to Materada and I was considered Italian. It was like skidding from one to the other, it was the drama of the frontier lived to the full.]

Since going to his first school in Capodistria (now Koper) in 1945, Tomizza felt he was being pulled by two divergent sides that could not be reconciled ('mi sentivo diviso fra un mondo e un altro, fra un'ideologia e un'altra' [I felt torn between one world and another, and between one ideology and another]).[59] The two spheres progressively diverged until the day when the decision whether to remain in Istria or to move away had to be resolved.

When considering Tomizza's youth, it is evident that the decision to reduce a double culture to a single one was a crisis for him. The disintegration of his hybrid world, at the same time as a period of political instability and danger, undermined his ability to move freely between cultural poles and produced in him a confused and clouded spiritual condition. Once his father was released from prison in 1953, the entire family moved to Trieste where they opened a coffee shop; at the same time Tomizza was preparing for his high school diploma. Years of rapid change and vacillation followed: his father died (he had wanted to die in Istria), which meant that Tomizza had to make a series of crucial decisions.

After a cultural collaboration with radio Koper, Tomizza made the unusual decision to move to the Yugoslav capital Belgrade in 1955, where he was awarded a bursary at the city's Art Academy, and where he also attended the Faculty of Languages and Romance Literature: 'Ottenni una borsa di studio per l'accademia cinematografica di Belgrado. Nella capitale jugoslava vissi i più strani, alieni, ribaldi e tristi quattro mesi della mia vita' [I got a scholarship from the film academy in Belgrade. In the Yugoslav capital I lived the strangest, the most alien, delinquent and sad four months of my life].[60] Making the decision to move to the capital of what the Italian side of Istria considered the enemy gives a clue to his troubled spiritual state. A series of inextricable matters played a role in his choice:

> Contrariamente ai compagni i quali da Capodistria si trasferivano a Trieste governata allora dagli anglo-americani, io decisi di continuare gli studi in Jugoslavia, che da dieci anni amministrava 'provvisoriamente' il nostro territorio. [...] Dirò soltanto che, seppellito quell'estate mio padre che aveva saggiato il carcere del nuovo regime, e in sordo conflitto con gli stessi compagni di scuola per la mia origine contadina e in parte slava, intendevo punirmi e nel contempo farmi ancora più detestare ma anche compiangere.[61]
>
> [Contrary to my companions who were moving from Koper to a Trieste ruled by the Anglo-Americans, I decided to continue my studies in Yugoslavia, which for ten years 'provisionally' ruled our territory. [...] I will only say that, having buried that summer my father, who had been trying out the new regime's prison, in an unvoiced conflict with the same classmates over my peasant and partly Slav origin, I intended to punish myself and simultaneously become both even more detested and pitied too.]

The sense of displacement experienced by Tomizza in Trieste, a city which, despite being one of the most cosmopolitan of Italian cities, was at the time displaying its nationalistic side, developed further in Belgrade. It was very different here from the rural Croatian culture of Istria and Tomizza struggled to settle in. Alongside the many obstacles he encountered, of which the most significant were linguistic and political in nature, the arrival of extreme winter conditions also discouraged him from prolonging his stay:

> Si sfociava nei giardini e tra i tozzi bastioni della fortezza turca del Kalemegdan, eretta sul punto in cui la Sava sbocca nel Danubio. La lastra di ghiaccio che equiparava i due fiumi m'impediva di precisarne il corso, per cui non riuscivo a stabilire nemmeno in quale direzione si situasse la mia terra, sede di quel groviglio di affetti contrastanti che mi ero illuso di lasciare alle spalle.[62]

> [One ended up in the gardens and among the stocky bastions of the Turkish fortress of Kalemegdan, erected on the spot where the Sava flows into the Danube. The sheet of ice which levelled the two rivers prevented me from seeing their course, so I could not even determine in which direction my land was situated, that place of a tangle of conflicting emotions that I had the illusion of leaving behind.]

His stay in the Yugoslav capital did not last long; the final decision to attribute Istria definitively to Yugoslavia seems to have put further distance between Tomizza and Belgrade. However, he had not finished his Yugoslav parenthesis because he then moved to Ljubljana, where he worked as assistant director on the production of the film *Trenutki odločitve* [Moments of Decision] by František Čap, which was presented at the Venice Film Festival in 1955. Meanwhile, the troubles in Istria resulted in a second exile, which, ten years after the provisional Yugoslav settlement, led ever more people to abandon their homeland. The Istrian littoral remained empty and people collected their transportable goods to relocate to refugee camps in Trieste:

> Partì dal sessanta al settanta per cento della popolazione, con camion stracarichi di suppellettili e dell'entrata di quell'estate, nei carri tirati dai manzi come uscissero nei campi, semplicemente in corriera come si recassero dal dentista o dovunque il mezzo pubblico li avesse portati. Lasciavano le case spalancate a tutti i venti, oppure con la porta e le finestre sbarrate, quasi che l'ultima pestilenza non avesse rispettato uno solo della famiglia. Erano figli e pronipoti di una gente che soltanto a partire dalla mia giovinezza aveva appreso di essere italiana o di essere slava, e che poi un intrecciarsi di animosità e di istigazioni, apertesi proprio con quella scoperta forzata, con quella scelta ugualmente imposta, aveva obbligato a riconfermare la propria fede oppure a smentirla. (*MV*, p. 208)

> [Between sixty and seventy per cent of the population left on trucks loaded with furniture and the proceeds of the summer on carts pulled by oxen as if they had come straight from the fields, simply on buses as if they were going to the dentist or wherever else public transport had taken them. They left their houses wide open to the elements, or with the doors and windows boarded up, as if the last plague had not left even one family member alive. They were children and grandchildren of people who from my youth had learned to be either Italian or Slav, and whom a mixture of animosity and incitement, realized either through enforced discovery or equally imposed choice, had forced to either reaffirm or deny their faith.]

While Tomizza's mother and brother finally opted to live in Trieste, Tomizza was still hesitant and postponed his decision until the last minute when he too finally chose the Italian side. In the ambivalent declaration made in *Il sogno dalmata*, the distress of an 'impossible' choice was defined as follows:

> Allo scadere dei termini dell'esodo feci un ragionamento inverso: l'anima delle

> cose, dei luoghi, dei ricordi, si era trasferita di là, stava dall'altra parte. E partii, sapendo o soltanto temendo di collocarmi per sempre in uno spazio di mezzo, neutro e impervio, nel quale molte volte mi sarei sentito estraneo anche a me stesso.[63]

> [When the deadline for the exodus expired I made an inverse reasoning: the soul of things, places, memories, had moved there and were on the other side. And I left, knowing or only fearing to place myself forever in a neutral and impervious limbo, from which I would have felt estranged even from myself on many occasions.]

The confusion of the mid-1950s became precious material for Tomizza's writing. Exile seems to have inspired him to reflect upon the dramatic events in Istria and transform them into novels. He wrote three stories, winning the Premio Cinque Bettole of Bordighera in 1957, for which the jury was formed of Betocchi, Bo, Calvino, Tecchi, and Vigorelli. This was the year before he started writing his first novel *Materada*, which was published in 1960 (when Tomizza was only twenty-five) by Mondadori, being subjected to supervision by Elio Vittorini, Vittorio Sereni, and Niccolò Gallo. It deals with a hybrid world before a diaspora, in which people from Materada, who for centuries had formed a mixed Italo-Croat community, are forced to opt for only one side of their double soul. Besides the direct confrontation with the question of exile, Tomizza approaches topics such as living in a frontier land shaken by conflicts in an original way, putting down the first milestone in a cycle dedicated to the Istrian problem. This novel, as I will later explain, can be considered a 'self-translated' work, because Tomizza transfers the chaotic linguistic world of Istria into an Italian narrative.

Tomizza's first work created much interest and his career as a writer and journalist took off quickly as a result. Although its subject had been hidden and neglected over the years, the novel was received favourably by the critics. Paolo Milano in *L'Espresso* compared Tomizza to other writers, who also examined frontier issues:

> Le zone di frontiera con la loro popolazione mista, spesso contese e quindi drammatiche, sembrano propizie alla letteratura. Dei due giovani romanzieri tedeschi che si sono affacciati alla fama in anni recenti, l'uno, Günter Grass, è di Danzica, e l'altro, Uwe Johnson, ha dato per sfondo a un suo fortunato romanzo la città bifronte, la Berlino dei nostri giorni. I romanzi di questi due scrittori di confine sono sperimentali, nel senso tuttora vivo del termine; mentre *Materada* [...] è il libro di un nuovo narratore italiano, Fulvio Tomizza, nato e vissuto in una regione dell'Istria passata alla Jugoslavia.[64]

> [The frontier areas with their mixed population, often disputed and so dramatic, seem favourable to literature. Of the two young German novelists who have become famous in recent years, one, Günter Grass, is from Gdansk, and the other, Uwe Johnson, gave as background to his successful novel, the two-faced city that Berlin is these days. The novels of these two border writers are experimental, in the current sense of the term; while *Materada* [...] is the book of a new Italian narrator, Fulvio Tomizza, born and raised in an area of Istria given to Yugoslavia.]

In parallel, Tomizza's interest in theatre led him to write *Vera Verk*, which in 1962 was staged by the Teatro Stabile of Trieste and was produced later in Ljubljana and Zagreb. The director was Fulvio Tolusso and the play was also published in the magazine *Sipario*. This theatrical parenthesis did not stop Tomizza from publishing a new book, *La ragazza di Petrovia* (1963). This focused on two stories: the settlement of a family in a refugee camp, and that of a girl from Petrovia, who, while still uncertain of her future, crosses the border and is then killed when she changes her mind and decides to return to Istria. The structure of the work aims to weaken any coherent development of space and time approaching the condition of the exile. Apart from being one of the very few books in which the process of exile is closely analyzed (it is a sort of x-ray of this condition), *La ragazza di Petrovia* also brings the subject of borders to the fore. The friction between the frontier region and the borderline itself is at the core of the second story and it ends on the border which the girl does not recognize. This continues the theme of displacement, but above all the novel shows the unpredictability of the border — the girl does not know it when it appears, she does not expect it and the linguistic division is not distinct.

La quinta stagione [The Fifth Season] (1965) followed shortly thereafter. This work focuses on Istria during the Second World War as viewed through the eyes of a young boy, Stefano Markovich, an alter ego of the writer (this device is present in other of Tomizza's works). After *Materada* and *La ragazza di Petrovia*, *Il bosco di acacie* [The Acacia Grove] (1966) completed the exilic cycle, describing the difficulties encountered by a family who settle in some fields in Friuli and the sense of loss and laceration that typifies exile. This work is probably the most conventional part of the trilogy. Nevertheless, characters explore in depth their inability to live in the new country: 'Somiglia ma non è. Non è quello di prima, non lo sarà mai. Mi pare una terra di altri, che non sarà mai mia' [It looks like it but it is not. It is not the same as before, it never will be. It seems to me a land of others, it will never be mine].[65] These three novels form the *Trilogia istriana* [The Istrian Trilogy], which was published as such in 1967, and constitute the beginning of Tomizza's literary production.

In Trieste, the city in which he settled in 1956, Tomizza began to develop his thoughts on his exile. In *L'albero dei sogni*, he underlines the complex condition of Istrian inhabitants in relation to the escalation of violence and political change. The world of *Materada* is here experienced internally by one character, Stefano Marcovich (who is also the main character of *La quinta stagione*), who is trying to define himself but who can only declare that he is caught in the middle of two diverging cultures. He fashions a word that summarizes this condition: 'eènza'.[66] In *L'albero dei sogni*, Tomizza also deals with his dramatic years of indecision, the months spent in Trieste, Belgrade, and Ljubljana, the problematic reconciliation with Istria, and, above all, with his father. From beginning to end, the novel is marked by this figure, who seems to be the cause of twisted feelings that result in a sense of rebellion and at the same time guilt. The final part of the novel recaptures the nightmares that Marcovich has after the death of his father and describes his ultimate achievement of a sense of peace. This is done through a version of Aeneas's journey to the underworld looking for his father Anchises, which is the subject of the sixth book of the *Aeneid*. Tomizza's title and epigraph recall this episode, underlining the deceptive and dreamlike nature of the novel. As Claudio Casoli points out:

> Il titolo è suggerito da alcuni versi dell'Eneide, là dove è detto che i sogni ingannevoli hanno la loro sede tra gli annosi rami d'un grande e folto olmo. Di sogni e di bruschi risvegli è intessuto tutto il libro.[67]

> [The title is suggested by some verses of the Aeneid, where it is said that deceptive dreams are located between the age-old branches of a large and broad elm. The entire book is woven from dreams and sudden awakenings.]

The relationship between the unusual narrative made of gaps, openings, and omissions and Tomizza's life and his troubles is hinted at by Mario Petrucciani:

> Basta notare le interruzioni e le riprese tra un capitolo e l'altro, e, all'interno di uno stesso capitolo, i modi delle pause, degli stacchi tra un brano e l'altro. È sufficiente prestare un minimo di attenzione alla scrittura, contesto insieme di allusioni e di realismo, di lucida razionalità e di turbati sogni, per comprendere che il conflitto non si esaurisce nella sfera topografico-ambientale, o ideologica, o culturale, o politica. Questa, con le sue multiple implicazioni di respiro narrativo, costituisce soltanto il supporto di una antinomia più sotterranea e radicale, ma non districabile con tagli netti, e che quindi solo approssimativamente potrebbe ricondursi al conflitto tra sentimento e ragione, di fronte alle scelte ardue della coscienza.[68]

> [Just notice the interruptions and links between one chapter and another, and, within the same chapter, the breaks, divisions between one passage and another. It is enough to pay attention to the writing, the set of allusions and realism, lucid rationality and troubled dreams, to understand that the conflict is not confined by the topographical and environmental, ideological, cultural, or political sphere. This, with its multiple layers in the narrative, constitutes only the base of a more subtle and radical antinomy, that is not clearly extricable and therefore could only be roughly traced back to the conflict between feeling and reason, faced with the difficult choices of consciousness.]

L'albero dei sogni was awarded the Viareggio Prize in 1969 and Pier Paolo Pasolini wrote a review remarking on how a 'local' story could turn into a more universal one: Istria had become the quintessential hybrid region: 'Anche lì c'è un "paesaggio", il paesaggio istriano; ma poiché tale paesaggio è terra di nessuno, né italiano né slavo, ecco che esso perde la sua tranquillità provinciale, e si drammatizza' [Also there, there is a 'landscape', the Istrian landscape; but since this landscape is no man's land, neither Italian nor Slav, it loses its provincial tranquillity, and becomes dramatized].[69]

L'albero dei sogni appears to have generated two further works. On the one hand, the dreamlike atmosphere was carried on in *La torre capovolta* [The Overturned Tower] (1971), a book based on fragments that continues to deal with Istrian events. As Carlo Sgorlon observes:

> Ma per lo più è ancora in Istria che Tomizza soggiorna: ma un'Istria veduta dal di sotto, dalle radici, o attraverso lo spessore deformante del sogno. Se la realtà base è sempre la stessa, è cambiato lo strumento d'indagine. Tomizza analizza

spesso il suo inconscio, concede libera uscita agli incubi, i terrori, i complessi, i pensieri stravolti, i ricordi infantili, i sogni.[70]

[But above all it is still in Istria that Tomizza stays: but in an Istria viewed from below, from the roots, or through the distorted thickness of a dream. If the basic reality is always the same, the surveying tool is different. Tomizza often examines his unconscious, allows free expression to nightmares, terrors, complexes, distorted thoughts, childhood memories, dreams.]

On the other hand, *La città di Miriam* [Miriam's City] continues the treatment of Trieste found in *L'albero dei sogni* and that city becomes the protagonist of the new novel. A new phase in the life of the writer begins here, in which he discovers his relationship with Trieste, a relationship that is affected by those with his wife and father-in-law. In this novel, the writer describes these dynamics, as summarized by Enzo Siciliano: 'Con *La città di Miriam* egli ha spostato il fuoco dell'attenzione dalle proprie vicende istriane al diverso che per lui il medesimo profilo di Trieste delinea' [With *La città di Miriam*, he shifted the focus from his Istrian stories to different ones, that to him outline the very same profile of Trieste].[71] Before writing the novel *La miglior vita*, Tomizza's interest in the theatre led him to work on an adaptation of the play *Martin Kačur* by Ivan Cankar, a prominent Slovene writer.[72] Tomizza's version was staged both in Italian and Yugoslav cities, in an effort to improve the relationship between the two countries through culture.

La miglior vita (1977) concludes Tomizza's early literary production based on events in Istria. This novel recounts three hundred years of Istrian history from the point of view of a sacristan, Martin Crusich, who describes the various alternating conquests of his village and the dynamics of the Italo-Croatian relationship. He tells of events that take place in his parish, including deaths, which he terms 'passare a miglior vita' [passing to the better life], and this gives the book its title. *La miglior vita* summarizes Tomizza's previous works, treating the subject of the frontier land in an epic dimension. As suggested by Magris:

> L'epica — che è tradizione, racconto orale, cronaca oggettiva di sentimenti e di vicende, 'pietas' e coralità fraterna — è possibile soltanto là dove c'è il senso della frontiera, matrice per eccellenza di quella molteplicità variegata eppure unitaria che è il presupposto del raccontare. [...] Tomizza, scrittore epico e cantore di un mondo contadino di frontiera, contrappone a questa consapevolezza moderna dell'esilio un largo respiro narrativo, che si radica nella tradizione.[73]

> [The Epic — that is tradition, oral narration, the objective chronicling of feelings and events, 'pietas' and fraternal chorality — is possible only where there is the sense of the frontier, matrix par excellence of that varied and unitary multiplicity which is the presupposition of storytelling. [...] Tomizza, epic writer and poet of a rural frontier world, counterposes to this modern awareness of exile a broad narrative breath, which is rooted in tradition.]

The interest in history shown by Tomizza in this novel opened a new period in his production in which he treats historical figures facing the condition typical of frontier lands. Once the experience of exile had been dealt with, he expressed himself through other situations, sometimes linking his interest in history to religious figures. However, also in this case, as Vittorio Spinazzola writes in the review 'Lo scrittore? Diventa biografo', which refers to the novel *Il male viene dal nord: il romanzo del vescovo Vergerio* [Evil Comes from the North: The Novel of Bishop Vergerio], Tomizza's interest in biography uncovers material concerning the frontier: 'Il Vergerio si profila come il rappresentante emblematico di una gente di frontiera, da sempre votata a vivere in primissima persona il confronto e lo scontro fra movimenti di civiltà antagonistici' [Vergerio looms as the emblematic representative of frontier people, since always consacrated to live in the first person the confrontation and clash between movements of antagonistic civilizations].[74]

In parallel with these historical works, Tomizza published some book-length essays, such as *Alle spalle di Trieste* (1995), *Le mie estati letterarie* [My Literary Seasons] (2009), and a book-length interview, entitled *Destino di frontiera* (1992). This part of Tomizza's literary production is key to understanding the complexities of his background. He seems, in this period, to have become aware of the need to clarify some cardinal issues that had been ignored or misunderstood in Italy as well as in Istria.

In his final years, the 1990s, Tomizza produced hybrid works that lay between the essay and fiction. His life was lived to the full, a life in which writing coexisted with journalism, and which led him to travel quite a lot. A collection of his articles, including those that focused on his travels, is published under the title of *Adriatico e altre rotte: viaggi e reportages* [Adriatic and Other Routes: Travels and Reportages] (2007). Among the literary prizes he won were the Viareggio Prize (1969) and the Strega Prize (1977). He was also selected several times for the 'Selezione Campiello' and won the 'Austrian State Prize for European Literature' (1979), becoming an important authority on the cohabitation of populations in the Germanophone world. He was awarded a *Laurea honoris causa* in 1984 by the University of Trieste and his works are translated into several languages.[75]

The borders that remained a key feature throughout Tomizza's life finally turned into the one between life and death, as the writer hinted in *I rapporti colpevoli*: 'Mi trovavo come sempre in una terra di nessuno, adesso allargata a entrambi i territori ricompostisi dentro di me e ugualmente non invitanti. Il mio nuovo confine era collocato in verticale e una fitta nebbia ne nascondeva il valico' [I found myself as always in a no man's land, now enlarged to both territories, recomposed in me and equally uninviting. My new border was situated vertically and a thick fog hid the pass].[76] Tomizza died on 21 May 1999 and is now buried in the cemetery in Materada.

Tomizza Within the Italian and European Context

Although Tomizza introduced the issue of the borderland to Italian literature, and dealt with key contemporary matters such as hybridism, exile, and plurilingualism, he remains a significantly neglected writer. This is evident when approaching the secondary literature, which presents a fragmented analysis that does not cover his entire literary production. Even though this apparatus has been developing since the publication of his first novel, *Materada*, extended examinations have been lacking, and these have only begun to emerge in recent years. The current situation remains almost that which was denounced by Maria Claudia Bellucci in 1973:

> Su Fulvio Tomizza non esistono ancora libri di critica, e la fonte principale di informazioni sono gli articoli apparsi su quotidiani e riviste. Questi ovviamente non comprendono di regola esami di tutta l'opera dello scrittore istriano, limitandosi a registrare e commentare l'ultimo libro uscito; si tratta dunque di analisi frammentarie, che però permettono ugualmente di osservare le impressioni che i romanzi del Tomizza hanno suscitato nei vari commentatori.[77]

> [On Fulvio Tomizza there are still no books of criticism, and the main source of information are the articles published in newspapers and magazines. These of course do not include examinations of the entire work of the Istrian writer, merely recording and commenting on the last published book; this is a fragmentary analysis but it allows one to see the impressions that Tomizza's novels have aroused in the various commentators.]

Tomizza is mentioned in the most important introductions to and anthologies of Italian literature of the twentieth century both in Italy and abroad, but he is often not included within specific studies on borderlands and exile. For instance, he is considered by: Giulio Ferroni in *Profilo storico della letteratura italiana*; Giacinto Manacorda in *Storia della letteratura italiana contemporanea (1940–1975)*; Mario Petrucciani in *Segnali e archetipi della poesia: studi di letteratura contemporanea*; Roberto Damiani in *I contemporanei*; Cesare De Michelis in *Dizionario critico della letteratura italiana*; Giorgio Luti in *Il Novecento*; in *Storia letteraria d'Italia*; and Robert Gordon in *An Introduction to Twentieth-century Italian Literature*. Nevertheless, at the present time, when interest in migration and exile is perhaps at its peak, Tomizza is at risk of being overshadowed by more recent authors who deal with similar topics. For example, in the chapter, 'Frontier, Exile, and Migration in the Contemporary Italian Novel', written by Andrea Ciccarelli in *The Cambridge Companion to the Italian Novel*, his name does not even appear.

Several factors have led to this adverse situation for Tomizza, beginning with his origins at the margins of Italy, far from cultural and editorial centres. Because of their specific locations and history and their late annexation, Istria and Trieste have been little considered in Italy, as expressed in an anecdote reported by Tomizza in *I rapporti colpevoli*:

> Oggi, definitivamente, mi sono reso conto di far parte dell'assetto e del destino di quella terra, estranea perché incomprensibile, incomprensibile perché estranea, all'Italia. Nella rubrica 'Che tempo fa?' è risultato che la temperatura minima di Trieste ha superato di un grado quella massima. Può succedere, ma lo strano e il normale è che il diligentissimo meteorologo non l'abbia preso neppure in considerazione. Ha invece confermato scirocco con pioggia, mentre da noi soffia la bora e grosse stelle si fanno rapidamente largo nel cielo.[78]

> [Today, I finally realized that I was part of the layout and destiny of that land, alien because it is incomprehensible, incomprehensible because it is alien, of Italy. Under the column 'What is the weather like?' the minimum temperature of Trieste was said to exceed the maximum by one degree. It can happen, but

the unusual and completely normal thing is that the very diligent meteorologist did not even consider it. Instead he forecast sirocco with rain, while here blows the bora and big stars quickly spread out in the sky.]

For this reason, Anna Modena, in her essay 'L'esilio ininterrotto di Fulvio Tomizza', defines his condition as an 'endless exile in the isolation of Trieste'.[79] Apart from the actual exile that overwhelmed the author, a different form of isolation progressively affected his life, which became increasingly detached from lively cultural centres. As Tomizza underlines in an essay entitled 'Le mie estate letterarie': 'Non è certo casuale che tutti i miei 20 libri di narrativa, a eccezione di un paio, siano stati scritti d'estate, in campagna' [It is not a coincidence that all my 20 books of fiction, with the exception of a few, have been written in summer, in the countryside].[80]

This is only one of the possible explanations for the critical disregard to which Tomizza has been condemned. The second reason lies in the subjects approached by a writer who had the courage to deal with the Italian eastern front. By investigating recent territorial losses, the writer was touching a raw nerve, at least politically speaking. During the Cold War years, the Istro-Dalmatian issue was an embarrassment that needed to be forgotten, as recent historical criticism has started to describe.[81] Tomizza's approach to the loss of Istria, which took neither the Italian nor the Yugoslavian side, was an obstacle to the acknowledgment of his literary production. The questions concerning the frontier that imbue Tomizza's works may well have been too advanced for his times. In the 1960s, when Carlo Emilio Gadda wrote *La cognizione del dolore* [The Experience of Pain], Primo Levi *La tregua* [The Truce], Natalia Ginzburg *Lessico famigliare* [Family Sayings], and Beppe Fenoglio *Il partigiano Johnny* [Johnny the Partisan], pluriculturalism and plurilingualism, which are typical of borderlands, were not yet being explored. Even though all these novels deal with multilingualism, they do not explore the condition of being born among different civilizations, in an area where identity is constantly unclear. Elvio Guagnini states that the novel *Materada* introduces 'un discorso (sulla letteratura di frontiera, sull'interculturalità) del quale Tomizza è stato antesignano' [an issue (on border literature, on interculturalism) of which Tomizza was the forerunner].[82] Tomizza's works mark the border question in Italy, anticipating problematics which would only be discovered decades later. When Gordon faces the issue of multiculturalism in Italy, he immediately refers to the 'Italo-Slav writer Fulvio Tomizza'.[83] Italy has contributed strongly to the subject, due to the experience of massive emigration, the presence of minorities in Italy, and in recent times also migration, but Tomizza was the trailblazer.

Tomizza must be related to the Triestine context, given that 'Literary maps [...] are fundamental to our understanding of modern Italian literature'.[84] Usually, when dealing with writers from Trieste, the cultural-geographical reference cannot be omitted. As I have demonstrated at the beginning of this chapter, this key European borderland deeply influences its writers. Nevertheless, the geographical reference may also limit Tomizza, a writer who could certainly be located within the context of the second Italian novecento, but who also aspires to be inserted within the broader European one.[85] Several critics have attempted to locate Tomizza within

Italian literature. Marco Neirotti, Carmelo Aliberti, and Gian-Paolo Biasin, to mention a few, have compared the subject and the style of Tomizza's *Materada* with the work of writers such as Giovanni Verga, Beppe Fenoglio, and Cesare Pavese. In Neirotti's words:

> Tutto in *Materada* è impostato sul pensare, il parlare, l'agire della gente, sulle verità e genuinità di cose e persone. Al mondo contadino di una ricchissima letteratura (alla campagna molisana di Jovine, a quella sarda di Dessi, a quella piemontese di Fenoglio, Pavese e Arpino, a quella toscana di Tozzi), Tomizza aggiunge e contrappone un mondo contadino diverso perché di confine, schiacciato da un'esperienza unica. [...] Un accostamento che si può tentare, anche se da condurre con cautela, è quello che avvicina l'autore di *Materada* a Verga. [...] Comune con Verga è il radicato attaccamento alla terra, alla casa, alla famiglia, alla 'roba'.[86]

> [All in *Materada* is based on the thinking, speaking, acting of the people, on the truth and authenticity of things and persons. To the rich rural literature (the Molise countryside of Jovine, the Sardinian of Dessi, the Piedmont of Fenoglio, Pavese, and Arpino, the Tuscan of Tozzi), Tomizza adds and juxtaposes a different borderland world, crushed by a unique experience. [...] A combination that one can try, but this is to be conducted with caution, is to put the author of *Materada* close to Verga. [...] In common with Verga is the attachment to the land, the house, the family and 'stuff'.]

Tracing parallels between Tomizza and Verga in style, language, and narrative structure can be productive as I will show in Chapter 3 (for example, they employ a similar choral form). Nevertheless, Tomizza belongs to the second novecento and must be compared primarily to contemporary authors with whom he shares common traits. The central role played by land, and in particular by the rural Istrian element, may be related to Piedmontese writing such as that of Pavese, Fenoglio, Primo Levi, and Giovanni Arpino. Tomizza himself underlined his link with their background: 'C'è stato un incontro di due mondi, Piemontese e Istria, cultura del vino, tipi di economia vicini. Anche delle consonanze dialettali, almeno nell'uso di certi strumenti: certe botti che si chiamano *cavagni*, ad esempio' [There was a meeting of two worlds, Piedmont and Istria, wine culture, similar types of economy. Even between dialects, at least in the use of certain tools: some barrels that are called *cavagni*, for example].[87] He also acknowledges the importance of these authors to him, admitting that: 'Ho sempre detto che se non avessi letto Pavese non avrei mai scritto' [I have always said that if I had not read Pavese I would have never written].[88] From them, and in particular from Fenoglio and Pavese, he inherited an interest in dialects and plurilingualism, as well as the treatment, without the mediation of an urban perspective, of the troubled rural situation that was shaping the destiny of peasants. Life in the countryside, characterized by hard work and often a harsh destiny, links works like *Materada* and Fenoglio's *La malora* [Ruin]. *La malora*'s protagonist Agostino, and his story set in the Piedmontese area called Langhe, recalls the misfortunes of *Materada*'s Francesco. Even though the plots are different, both novels — strongly related to a life in the fields — are marked by an adverse destiny which characters are unable to overturn.

The influence of Levi on the work of Fulvio Tomizza is significant too. Levi was a model not only in terms of writing: 'Per me Primo Levi ha rappresentato un modello di uomo e di scrittore da seguire' [For me, Primo Levi represented a model of a man and a writer to follow].[89] The relationship between Levi and Tomizza was probably decisive in the progressive assimilation of Tomizza within the Jewish environment (more specifically within Trieste's Jewish elite). The two authors built a relationship of mutual esteem and consideration that influenced some important artistic decisions, as Ian Thompson points out:

> Meanwhile Levi was being fêted on all sides; his life in Turin took on a frantic pace as he answered post, met friends, attended book launches. In April Levi read his friend Fulvio Tomizza's new novel, *The better Life*: it was a revelation. Tomizza had incorporated Italo-Slovene dialect words into the writing. [...] The success of Tomizza's novel, which sold more than 400,000 copies in Italy, encouraged Levi to abandon his ailing carbo-chemistry sequel, *The Double Bond*, and push on with another long-planned project.[90]

Despite the differences between the two writers, the linguistic approach used by Tomizza and Levi led to the two authors influencing each other. Tomizza's essay 'Uno scrittore tra due dialetti di matrice linguistica diversa' can be directly related in structure and content to Levi's 'Argon', an essay which deals with the Jewish-Piedmontese idiom spoken by Jews in southern Piedmont.[91] This is evidence of a real connection between the two authors and a relationship of mutual inspiration (in this case, Tomizza inspired by Levi).

Leaving aside Piedmontese writers, let us consider another parallel that has been drawn in attempting to situate Tomizza within the Italian literary panorama. Given the importance that should be attributed to his writing of history, there are useful comparisons to be considered such as with Manzoni or Natalia Ginzburg. Tomizza's involvement with Istria led him towards a precise study of historical events that explains the conflicts and vicissitudes undergone there and in the surrounding area. On this basis, Marco Casagrande traces a parallel with Manzoni:

> I cardini della poetica di Manzoni si possono sintetizzare nei seguenti principi: fedeltà alla verità storica, elevata ad una dignità sacrale, che si traduce in uno scrupoloso e certosino lavoro di documentazione sulle fonti per riprodurre nella maniera più fedele possibile il clima di un'epoca, soprattutto nei particolari più minuti del quotidiano; su questo sfondo storico oggettivo il narratore ha licenza di inserire vicende o personaggi frutto di invenzione ma in armonia con il realismo che intende perseguire. Orbene anche Tomizza procede nella stessa direzione; gran parte dei suoi romanzi nascono da puntigliose ricerche d'archivio ed hanno come sfondo periodi od eventi storici scolpiti a chiare lettere.[92]

> [The cornerstones of Manzoni's poetry can be summarized by the following principles: fidelity to historical truth, elevated to a sacred dignity, which is translated into scrupulous and painstaking documentation of the sources in order to reproduce as faithfully as possible the climate of an era, especially in the smallest details of everyday life; against this objective historical background the narrator has the right to place events or characters that are the result of invention but in harmony with the realism that he intends to pursue. Tomizza

also proceeds in the same direction; most of his novels are generated by meticulous archival research and for background have periods or historical events that are clearly sculpted.]

This sort of deep archival investigation led Tomizza to a new literary phase, which his translator, Anne Jacobson Schutte, has defined as 'a type of writing very close to microhistory'.[93] The novels *La finzione di Maria* [Maria's Pretence], *Il male viene dal nord*, *Quando Dio uscì di chiesa* [When God Exited the Church], *L'ereditiera veneziana* [The Venetian Heiress], *Fughe incrociate* [Crossed Escapes], and *L'Abate Roys e il fatto innominabile* [Roys the Abbot and the Unnameable Fact] can all be defined as historical novels that combine extensive documentation with the ability to fascinate through an imaginative narrative. This new form certainly recalls Manzoni's traditional works but it has also been used by modern Italian writers such as Carlo Ginzburg in *Il formaggio e i vermi: il cosmo di un mugnaio del '500* [The Cheese and the Worms]; Natalia Ginzburg in *La famiglia Manzoni* [Manzoni's Family]; as well as Elsa Morante in *La Storia* [History] and Umberto Eco in *Il nome della rosa* [The Name of the Rose]. Nevertherless, within his historical novels, Tomizza also sought to deal with the contrasting vicissitudes of his land by picking characters who exemplify the troubled condition of the hybrid. The most remarkable example comes from *Il male viene dal nord*, which is dominated by the figure of Pier Paolo Vergerio, a bishop involved in the dispute between Lutheranism and Catholicism.

As with many other Triestine writers, Tomizza's literary production seems to fit better within the European context than the Italian one. This is a consequence of the influence played in the area by Central European culture. Svevo himself can be considered one of the fathers of European modernism, the roots of which belong more to the Germanic sphere than the Italian. Without the influence played by Freud, his masterpiece *La coscienza di Zeno* [Zeno's Conscience] would have been unthinkable. Elizabeth Mahler-Schächter, who contributed to the volume *Italo Svevo scrittore europeo*, states that:

> Per il suo particolareggiato approccio analitico alla questione tematica di fondo, per la sua apprensione, per il malessere e per la crisi in cui versava la borghesia, Italo Svevo appartiene chiaramente alla principale corrente della tradizione letteraria europea che annovera fra essi scrittori del calibro di Musil, Mann, Schnitzler, Proust e Kafka [...]. Svevo ha maggiore affinità con questi scrittori che con qualsiasi scrittore suo contemporaneo, fatta eccezione per Pirandello.[94]

> [For his detailed analytical approach to the basic context, for his apprehension, for the malaise and the crisis besetting the bourgeoisie, Italo Svevo clearly belongs to the mainstream of the European literary tradition that includes, among others, writers such as Musil, Mann, Schnitzler, Proust and Kafka [...]. Svevo has a greater affinity with these writers than with any of his contemporaries, except for Pirandello.]

Tomizza's literary production had a similar destiny: he shares much with Italian authors, but he must be located within a wider picture too. Indeed, he has been strongly influenced both by Central European writers and by those belonging to the ex-Yugoslavian area and even beyond that to Russian literature. Tomizza declares a strong connection with the Central European linguistic and cultural heritage and he exploits this throughout the fictional works, but he also has a vast knowledge of the area as it was at the time. In his travel writings, Tomizza has often underlined, he found inspiration in a common mentality, way of being, and origin. It follows that his works often contain stories that go beyond the borders of Italy. As I will show in my analysis, Tomizza's debt to the work of Ivan Cankar inevitably places him in a different context. For instance, Cankar's fight for justice and moral concerns has not interested Italian authors to a great extent, but it became an essential part of Tomizza's production. Cankar influenced Tomizza's literary path like no other writer, not even Andrić, with whom he shares his complex multicultural background.

Central Europe and the Balkans constitute a fruitful field of comparison for a writer like Tomizza, who even specifies the relationship between the two within his works:

> Ritenevo e ritengo di possedere scarsi titoli per figurare quale scrittore mitteleuropeo [...]. Ma, in virtù di quei dieci anni decisivi per la mia formazione vissuti in un'Istria passata a un nuovo sistema politico e a un'altra cultura, sentivo di cadere in una Mitteleuropa aggiornata, rimodellata, maggiormente estesa ai Paesi di lingua slava.[95]

> [I thought and think I have few titles to be seen as a Central European writer [...]. But, by virtue of those ten decisive years for my training lived in an Istria that had passed to a new political system and to a different culture, I felt I belonged to an updated, reshaped Central Europe, mostly extended to the countries of Slavic language.]

There is one further factor which should be mentioned. The issues treated by Tomizza are generated by the collapse of Istria at the time of the Second World War, but they concern a wider movement. Millions of people at the end of the conflict had to move after the redefinition of Eastern European borders. There were refugees escaping from Nazi Germany — one of them was indeed Levi, who describes his repatriation in *La tregua* — or from Stalin's Russia. There were also people who were expelled from their countries, above all in Central Europe. These populations have been defined by Crainz, Salvatici, and Pupo as 'naufraghi della pace' [castaways of peace] and the phenomenon can be called the tragedy of minorities.[96]

In this sense, the link Milano establishes between Tomizza, Günter Grass and Uwe Johnson seems appropriate. Grass can be considered an exilic writer, especially when he deals with Gdansk, the troubled Baltic city, which, between the World Wars, was the Free City of Danzig located between German East Prussia and the Polish corridor to the sea. In *Crabwalk*, he illustrates the dramatic conditions of this exile in his description of the sinking of the *Wilhelm Gustloff*, an ocean liner packed with refugees that was attacked by a Soviet submarine near the end of the war. Grass and Johnson are only two examples of authors who belong to exilic German literature, which is represented also by Christa Wolf, Ernst Wiechert, Wolfgang Koeppen, Arno Schmidt, Johannes Bobrowski, Siegfried Lenz, and Franz Fühmann. Even though most of these writers explored exile through memory and autobiography while Tomizza approached it by delving into psychoanalysis, plurilingualism, and the problem of non-simple borderlands, there is a sound basis upon which to build up connections between them. For his contribution to the literature of exile, Tomizza deserves a place among the European authors who dealt with post-war political redefinitions and their terrible repercussions. I would argue that this field of literature should be considered as a whole and no longer only within national boundaries.

Notes to Chapter 1

1. Fulvio Tomizza, *Destino di frontiera: dialogo con Riccardo Ferrante* (Genoa: Marietti, 1992), p. 23.
2. Ibid., p. 41.
3. Ibid., p. 47.
4. A critique of the idea of a 'Triestine literature' appears in Pier Antonio Quarantotti Gambini, *Il poeta innamorato* (Pordenone: Edizioni Studio Tesi, 1984), p. 166, and also in Tomizza, *Alle spalle di Trieste*, pp. 18–19.
5. Pietro Pancrazi, 'Scrittori triestini', *Corriere della Sera*, 16 June 1930, p. 3.
6. Slataper is one of the most famous writers from Trieste, considered, alongside Svevo, as the initiator of 'Triestine literature'. *Il mio Carso* is the most important work in his literary production.
7. Scipio Slataper, *Il mio Carso* (Milan: Il Saggiatore, 1970), pp. 11–12.
8. Ibid., p. 12.
9. Scipio Slataper, *Alle tre amiche* (Milan: Mondadori, 1958), p. 421.
10. Fulvio Tomizza gives an account of the origins of Slataper's surname: ' "Che cosa vuol dire Slataper?" rispose prontamente alla domanda troppo facile "Penna d'oro. Dal boemo *zlato pero*" ' ['What does Slataper mean?' He promptly answered to this too-easy question 'Golden pen. From the Bohemian *zlato pero*'] (*Alle spalle di Trieste*, p. 27).
11. Angelo Ara and Claudio Magris, *Trieste: un'identità di frontiera* (Turin: Einaudi, 2007), p. 15.
12. See Claudio Magris, *Microcosmi* (Milan: Garzanti, 1997), Jan Morris, *Trieste and the Meaning of Nowhere* (London: Faber & Faber, 2001), and Katia Pizzi, *A City in Search of an Author: The Literary Identity of Trieste* (London: Sheffield Academic Press, 2001).
13. Tomizza, *Destino di frontiera*, p. 25.
14. See Pierluigi Barrotta and Laura Lepschy, *Freud and Italian Culture* (Bern & Oxford: Peter Lang, 2008).
15. Gilbert Bosetti, 'La letteratura triestina: modello di cultura di frontiera', *Rivista di letteratura italiana*, 2–3 (2000), 159–90 (p. 165).
16. Sandra Arosio, *Scrittori di frontiera: Scipio Slataper, Giani e Carlo Stuparich* (Milan: Guerini scientifica, 1996), p. 21. See also Miran Košuta, *Scritture parallele: dialoghi di frontiera tra letteratura slovena e italiana* (Trieste: Lint, 1997).
17. Tomizza, *Alle spalle di Trieste*, p. 66.
18. Tomizza, *Destino di frontiera*, p. 26.
19. Antonio Di Benedetti, 'Fulvio Tomizza', *Corriere della Sera*, 7 July 1977, p. 3.
20. Claudio Magris, *Utopia e disincanto: saggi, 1974–1998* (Milan: Garzanti, 1999), p. 52.
21. Tomizza, *Alle spalle di Trieste*, p. 16.
22. Ibid., p. 21.
23. Marco Neirotti, *Invito alla lettura di Fulvio Tomizza* (Milan: Mursia, 1979), p. 18.
24. Susanne Knittel, *The Historical Uncanny: Disability, Ethnicity, and the Politics of Holocaust Memory* (New York: Fordham University Press, 2015), p. 267.
25. Tomizza, *Alle spalle di Trieste*, p. 125.
26. Lina Galli, *Il volto dell'Istria attraverso i secoli* (Trieste: Cappelli, 1959), p. 30.
27. For a perspective on Slavs, see Francis Conte, *The Slavs* (Boulder, CO: East European Monographs, 1995).

28. An introduction to the Glagolitic inscriptions can be found in Branko Fučić, *Croatian Glagolitic Epigraphy* (London: Stephen Osborne, 1999).
29. Fulvio Tomizza, *La miglior vita* (Milan: Rizzoli, 1977), pp. 40–41; hereafter referenced as *MV*.
30. The Veneto-Slav relationships are described by Larry Wolff, *Venice and the Slavs: The Discovery of Dalmatia in the Age of Enlightenment* (Stanford, CA: Stanford University Press, 2001).
31. Tomizza, *Alle spalle di Trieste*, p. 127.
32. Anna Maria Mori and Nelida Milani, *Bora* (Milan: Frassinelli, 1998), p. 44.
33. Predrag Matvejević, *Mediterranean: A Cultural Landscape* (Los Angeles: University of California Press, 1999), p. 30.
34. Fulvio Tomizza, *Il sogno dalmata* (Milan: Mondadori, 2001), p. 27.
35. Joseph Roth, *The Emperor's Tomb* (London: Hogarth Press, 1984), p. 17.
36. The Slovene writer Boris Pahor based his 1959 novel *Kres v pristanu* [The Fire in the Harbour] on this event.
37. Michael Ebner, *Ordinary Violence in Mussolini's Italy* (New York: Syracuse University, 2010), p. 27.
38. Glenda Sluga, *The Problem of Trieste and the Italo-Yugoslav Border: Difference, Identity, and Sovereignty in Twentieth-century Europe* (New York: SUNY Press, 2001), p. 50.
39. Pizzi, *A City in Search of an Author*, p. 91.
40. Gustav Corni, 'The Exodus of Italians from Istria and Dalmatia, 1945–56', in *The Disentanglement of Populations: Migration, Expulsion and Displacement in Postwar Europe 1944–1949*, ed. by Jessica Reinisch and Elizabeth White (Basingstoke: Palgrave, 2011), pp. 71–90 (p. 78).
41. Pamela Ballinger, 'History's "Illegibles": National Indeterminacy in Istria', *Austrian History Yearbook*, 43 (April 2012), 116–37 (p. 123).
42. Arrigo Petacco, *L'esodo. La tragedia negata degli italiani d'Istria, Dalmazia e Venezia Giulia* (Milan: Mondadori, 2000), p. 159.
43. Ara and Magris, *Trieste*, p. 94.
44. Biagio Marin, 'Materada', *Voce Giuliana*, 16 February 1961, p. 4.
45. Tomizza, *Alle spalle di Trieste*, p. 195.
46. Isabel Quigly, 'On the Borderline', *The Times Literary Supplement*, 15 October 1971, p. 1291.
47. Tomizza, *Alle spalle di Trieste*, p. 195.
48. Ibid., pp. 99–100.
49. Ara and Magris, *Trieste*, pp. 192–93.
50. Magris, *Utopia e disincanto*, p. 52.
51. Fulvio Tomizza, 'Autoritratto: uomo e scrittore di frontiera', *Novecento* (1984), pp. 140–43 (p. 141).
52. Tomizza, *Il sogno dalmata*, p. 16.
53. Ibid., p. 19.
54. Fulvio Tomizza, *L'albero dei sogni* (Milan: Mondadori, 1969), p. 52; hereafter referenced as *AS*.
55. Fulvio Tomizza, *I rapporti colpevoli* (Milan: Bompiani, 1992), p. 286.
56. Fulvio Tomizza, 'Autoritratto', *L'Approdo letterario*, 77–78 (1977), 221–30 (p. 225).
57. Silvana Castelli, 'L'eterno straniero di Tomizza', *Avanti*, 2 August 1969, p. 3.
58. Grazia Livi, 'Intervista', *Epoca*, 3 August 1969, p. 93.
59. Ibid.
60. Tomizza, *Il sogno dalmata*, p. 52.
61. Fulvio Tomizza, *La casa col mandorlo* (Milan: Mondadori, 2000), p. 9.
62. Ibid., p. 11.
63. Tomizza, *Il sogno dalmata*, p. 56.
64. Paolo Milano, 'Un lungo addio a Materada', *L'Espresso*, 15 January 1961, p. 17.
65. Fulvio Tomizza, *Il bosco di acacie* (Milan: Mondadori, 1966), p. 150.
66. Without giving a definition of it, Stefano applies the label 'eènza' to this state, in an attempt to explain the uncomfortable position of the Istrian subject. 'Eènza' (formed by 'ènza' which means 'condition', and the ambivalent 'e') describes the sense of estrangement characterizing this condition. For a detailed account of 'eènza', see Marianna Deganutti, 'Fulvio Tomizza's "eènza": hybridity as origin', in *Shifting and Shaping a National Identity: Migration Literature Today*, ed. by Grace Russo Bullaro and Elena Benelli (Leicester: Troubador, 2014) pp. 87–106.

67. Claudio Casoli, 'L'albero dei sogni di Fulvio Tomizza', *Città Nuova*, 10 September 1969, p. 35.
68. Mario Petrucciani, 'Fulvio Tomizza: la ragione e i sogni', *Rassegna di cultura e vita scolastica*, 1 (1970), 118–30 (p. 123).
69. Pier Paolo Pasolini, *Il Caos* (Rome: Editori riuniti, 1999), p. 190.
70. Carlo Sgorlon, 'La torre capovolta', *I quaderni della FACE*, 39 (1971), 20–25 (p. 21).
71. Enzo Siciliano, 'Una ladra racconta', *Il Mondo*, 12 May 1972, p. 21.
72. Ivan Cankar, *Kačur Martin: The Biography of An Idealist*, trans. by John K. Cox (Budapest & New York: Central European University Press, 2009).
73. Claudio Magris, 'Ritorno all'epica della frontiera', *Corriere della Sera*, 10 April 1977, p. 19.
74. Vittorio Spinazzola, 'Lo scrittore? Diventa biografo', *L'Unità*, 9 June 1984, p. 13.
75. An account of Tomizza's translated novels is given by Elvio Guagnini, Gianni Cimador, and Marta Moretto, *Fulvio Tomizza: destino di frontiera* (Trieste: Comune, 2009).
76. Tomizza, *I rapporti colpevoli*, p. 233.
77. Maria Claudia Bellucci, *L'itinerario narrativo di Fulvio Tomizza* (Brescia: Tesi, 1973), p. 5. See also Marianna Deganutti, 'Fulvio Tomizza: un autore da ripensare', *Cartevive*, 50 (2013), 4–33.
78. Tomizza, *I rapporti colpevoli*, p. 311.
79. Anna Modena, 'L'esilio ininterrotto di Fulvio Tomizza', in *Rileggendo Fulvio Tomizza*, ed. by Marianna Deganutti (Rome: Aracne, 2014), pp. 115–44 (p. 116).
80. Fulvio Tomizza, *Le mie estati letterarie* (Venice: Marsilio, 2009), p. 155.
81. Giancarlo Restelli (ed.), *Le foibe e l'esodo dei giuliano-dalmati: una storia rimossa* (Milan: Raccolto Edizioni, 2007).
82. Elvio Guagnini, *Una città d'autore: Trieste attraverso gli scrittori* (Reggio Emilia: Diabasis, 2009), p. 27.
83. Robert Gordon, *A Difficult Modernity: An Introduction to Twentieth-century Italian Literature* (London: Duckworth, 2005), p. 139.
84. Ibid., p. 23.
85. As stated by Elvio Guagnini, Tomizza is: 'uno degli scrittori di maggior rilievo del secondo Novecento italiano' [one of the most important writers of the second Italian novecento] ('Con quelle storie riusciva a polverizzare i confini', *Il Piccolo*, 16 May 2000, p. 49).
86. Neirotti, *Invito alla lettura di Fulvio Tomizza*, p. 46.
87. Tomizza, *Destino di frontiera*, p. 79.
88. Ibid.
89. Ibid., p. 81.
90. Ian Thomson, *Primo Levi: A Life* (New York: Metropolitan Books, 2003), p. 384.
91. For a comparison between the two essays see Marianna Deganutti, 'Il dialetto mistilingue di Levi e Tomizza', *Letteratura e dialetti*, 8 (2016), 75–85.
92. Marco Casagrande, 'Un narratore tra narrazione e modernità', *La Battana*, 135:3–8 (2000), 3–20 (p. 4).
93. Anne Jacobson Schutte, 'Tradurre Tomizza', in *Rileggendo Fulvio Tomizza*, ed. by Deganutti, pp. 313–20 (p. 314).
94. Elizabeth Mahler-Schächter, 'Svevo e Schnitzler: affinità culturali', in *Italo Svevo scrittore europeo: atti del convegno internazionale, Perugia, 21 marzo 1992*, ed. by N. Cacciaglia and L. Fava Guzzetta (Florence: Olschki, 1994), pp. 547–60 (p. 547).
95. Tomizza, *Alle spalle di Trieste*, p. 68.
96. Guido Crainz, Raoul Pupo, and Silvia Salvatici, *Naufraghi della pace: il 1945, i profughi e le memorie divise d'Europa* (Rome: Donizelli, 2008), p. VIII.

CHAPTER 2

Borderland, Language, and the Trauma of the Exile: A Theoretical Approach

The Subcultures of Borderlands

To better inform our approach to Tomizza's works, I will first make a theoretical investigation into key notions such as that of the 'borderland' or 'frontier', which are characterized by hybridity and multilingualism, and after that the concept of 'exile'. Although these elements may not seem strictly related — for instance, 'borderland' and 'exile' are rarely considered together — in this analysis of Tomizza's literary production they will be considered in relation to one another.

I will start with the notions of 'borderland' and 'frontier'. Even though they are often used interchangeably, the two must not be confused. According to the *OED*, a border is 'a line separating two countries, administrative divisions, or other areas'; a frontier is 'a line or border separating two countries', but may also refer to 'the extreme limit of settled land beyond which lies wilderness, especially in reference to the western US before Pacific settlement'. Following these definitions, the idea of border may overlap with that of the frontier because both concepts seem to indicate a line of separation between two entities, most commonly between two or more countries. Nevertheless, 'border' and 'frontier' are different notions that should be kept separate because the former always indicates a specific line determining the division between two adjacent spaces. A border marks a division, an incommensurable difference, that cannot be divided or modified without it ceasing to be what it is. Furthermore, it is a fixed line, which, most of the time, is expressed through barriers, stones, or bars and cannot be moved. On the other hand, a frontier focuses on land at the margins — indeed, is a strip rather than a line — which is flexible and more difficult to localize. Giorgio Bertone, who notices Calvino's ambiguous use of the notions of border and frontier, accurately distinguishes between the two:

> Tra una linea stabile [il confine] che divide in modo sempre uguale e che può costituire, certo, un ottimo punto di osservazione e riflessione, e una fascia [la frontiera] mobile che si sposta, avanza e indietreggia, ingloba e abbandona. Il confine, invece, ha in sé una carica, una forza *ad escludendum*. S'intende che le due categorie vengono qui assolutizzate.[1]

[Between a fixed line [the border] that divides in the same way and may of course constitute an excellent point of observation and reflection, and a mobile strip [the frontier] that moves, advances, and retreats, incorporates and abandons. The border, instead, has an excluding force within itself. It should be understood that the two categories are here made absolute.]

In his analysis of the meaning of borders Zanini develops the two notions further. The frontier, he says, is located at the end of one civilization beyond which begins an unknown territory that makes the individual 'foreign'.[2] This definition could be associated with the frontier of the American West described by Frederick Jackson Turner as a margin that marks the edge of free land, separating savagery from civilization.[3] More remarkable for our analysis of Tomizza is that, rather than a line, the frontier is defined as a strip which is constantly redefined by the relationships between different groups:

Il confine indica un limite comune, una separazione tra spazi contigui; è anche un modo per stabilire in via pacifica il diritto di proprietà di ognuno in un territorio conteso. La frontiera rappresenta invece la fine della terra, il limite ultimo oltre il quale avventurarsi significava andare al di là della superstizione contro il volere degli dei, oltre il giusto e il consentito, verso l'inconoscibile che ne avrebbe scatenato l'invidia. Varcare la frontiera, significa inoltrarsi dentro un territorio fatto di terre aspre, dure, difficili. Il fronte è quindi il luogo dove forze opposte si confrontano, spesso si scontrano, altre volte si incontrano, comunque entrano in crisi, abitato da mostri pericolosi contro cui dover combattere. Vuol dire uscire da uno spazio familiare, conosciuto, rassicurante, ed entrare in quello dell'incertezza. Questo passaggio, oltrepassare la frontiera, muta anche il carattere di un individuo: al di là di essa si diventa stranieri, emigranti, diversi non solo per gli altri ma talvolta anche per se stessi. [...] Questi punti non disegnano una linea, ma definiscono una fascia, una zona sfrangiata, più o meno larga in funzione dei rapporti che corrono tra una parte e l'altra della frontiera.[4]

[The border indicates a common limit, a separation between adjacent spaces; it is also a way to establish in a peaceful way the property rights of everyone in a disputed territory. The frontier represents the end of the land, the ultimate limit adventuring beyond which meant going against the superstition of the gods' will, what is right and allowed, towards the unknowable that would have triggered envy. Crossing the frontier means reaching a territory made of rugged, hard, and difficult lands. The front is a place where opposing forces are compared, often clash, sometimes meet, in any case enter into crisis, inhabited by dangerous monsters to fight. It means getting out of a familiar, known, reassuring space and entering into uncertainty. This step, crossing the border, also changes the character of an individual: beyond it, one becomes foreigner, migrant, different not only from the others but sometimes also from oneself. [...] These points do not draw a line, but define a strip, a fringed area, of greater or lesser width depending on the relationships existing between one side and the other of the frontier.]

Silvia Assenza, who compared the Triestine and the Sicilian borderlands, further underlines the dynamism existing in this type of area: 'L'origine della frontiera risiede nel movimento, poichè essa è mobile' [The origin of the frontier resides in the movement, since it is mobile].[5] The lack of clear definition and the mobility that typifies a frontier leads to the creation of mixed groups, which constantly interact with surrounding territories, reshaping the idea of an original sense of belonging: 'non mostrandosi come una linea che separa, che ripara dall'altro, dal diverso, la frontiera si configura piuttosto come uno spazio liminale in cui l'alterità sta sempre innanzi, o meglio dentro come sua stessa intima natura' [not appearing as a line that separates, that protects from the other, from the different, the frontier is configured rather as a liminal space in which otherness is always there already, or, better, inside as its own intimate nature].[6]

Even though Tomizza, as well as other authors from the same area, uses the words 'border' and 'frontier' interchangeably, he usually refers to the hybrid space of a frontier, whose elements cannot be easily classified and disentangled. In this respect, his framework seems to have many features in common with the American-Mexican *frontera* theorized by Gloria Anzaldùa in her work *Borderlands/La Frontera: The New Mestiza*. As Anzaldùa writes, frontiers and borders should not be mixed up, given that:

> Borders are set up to define the places that are safe and unsafe, to distinguish *us* from *them*. A border is a dividing line, a narrow strip along a steep edge. A borderland is a vague and undetermined place created by the emotional residue of an unnatural boundary. It is a constant state of transition. The prohibited and forbidden are its inhabitants.[7]

These liminal areas involve dual opposing meanings. On the one hand, they suggest the idea that a border divides two different entities: it is a definite line which cannot be debated. On the other hand, a frontier corresponds to a space located among two or more cultures, classes, races, mentalities, languages, and ideologies, and which is shaped by mixtures, or in Anzaldùa's terms, *mestizo*.

Borderlands are inhabited by people who often struggle to define themselves within their multiple identities and linguistic mixtures. What links the American-Mexican zone and Istria is the fact that the complex historico-political events that have given rise to these areas contribute to troubled relationships between bordering countries. The American-Mexican frontier is the result of colonial and neo-colonial vicissitudes imposed first by Spain and later by America, but also by the current political situation between the United States and Mexico. As I have pointed out in the previous chapter, the Istrian borderland is the result of the interaction between the Italian and the Slovene-Croatian civilizations, their peaceful exchanges and their dramatic oppositions.

The space of the borderland should, therefore, be conceived as an 'in-between' area that promotes mixtures and cultural-linguistic hybridization, or, rather, a privileged place where there is a meeting with the other. Anzaldùa delves further into mechanisms that determine the relationship between the self and the other, pinpointing the specific position of the frontier subject. Her idea of *mestizo* (the word she uses is *Chicana*, the chosen identity of some Mexican-Americans in the United States) deals with a new dimension of the self, which distances itself from its two poles of reference (the American and the Mexican) to shape a middle space.

The definition of her identity corresponds to a hybrid process, generated at the intersection (collision or sometimes integration) of elements:

> *Nosotros los Chicanos* straddle the Borderlands. On one side of us, we are constantly exposed to the Spanish of the Mexicans, on the other side we hear the Anglo's incessant clamoring so that we forget our language [...] Chicanos and other people of color suffer economically for not acculturating. This voluntary (yet forced) alienation makes for physiological conflict, a kind of dual identity — we do not identify with the Anglo-American cultural values and we do not totally identify with the Mexican cultural values. We are a synergy of two cultures with various degrees of Mexicanness or Angloness.[8]

The typical status of the inhabitants of a borderland is hybridity, a condition which is not simply the sum or subtraction of factors. Hybridity is a (rather unpredictable) redefinition of elements, involving dynamics that transcend purely geographical factors.

Given that Tomizza has explicitly defined himself as a hybrid subject — 'Ero italiano e slavo, in definitiva né italiano né slavo, ma "altro": un ibrido' [I was Italian and Slav, ultimately neither Italian nor Slav, but 'other': a hybrid] — I will now further investigate the meaning of hybridity using formulations such as those of Homi Bhabha and Robert Young, as well as recent investigations made by Robert Pyrah and Jan Fellerer.[9]

From the beginning of *The Location of Culture*, Bhabha focuses 'on those moments or processes that are produced in the articulation of cultural difference' disrupting pre-existing power relations.[10] He touches upon notions of inbetweenness, liminality, hybridity, marginality, syncretism, transit, and describes hybridity as 'the re-articulation, or translation, of elements that are neither the One nor the Other but something else besides which contests the terms and territories of both'.[11] When cultures come into contact they create an interstitial space, the so-called 'third' or 'in-between state', which may also be considered the space of 'liminality'. This third space goes beyond the frame of reference given by the boundaries of the original cultures:[12]

> The importance of hybridity is not to be able to trace two original moments from which the third emerges, rather hybridity to me is the 'third space' which enabled other positions to emerge. This third space displaces the histories that constitute it, and sets up new structures of authority, new political initiatives, which are inadequately understood through received wisdom [...]. Hybridity puts together the traces of certain other meanings or discourses. It does not give them the authority of being prior in the sense of being the original: they are prior only in the sense of being anterior. The process of hybridity gives rise to something different, something new and unrecognizable, a new area of negotiation of meaning and representation.[13]

When two or more cultures come into contact, they start shaping a process of hybridization, which can be described as a space in continual movement acknowledging the permeability existing between the self and the other in the formation of identity and culture. This 'third space', which subverts the realm of dualistic categories, corresponds to the ambiguous site par excellence, as cultural meaning and representation do not have any 'primordial unity or fixity'.[14] Nevertheless, it tends to include elements rather than excluding them, given that it 'initiates new signs of identity, and innovative sites of collaboration and contestation'.[15]

Hybridity may still appear to be a doubtful and abstract notion covering a wide range of cases and circumstances. For this reason, many scholars, such as Young, Paul Gilroy, Stuart Hall, Iain Chambers, or James Clifford have developed it further, breaking down pre-existing hierarchies and binary divisions (between colonizer/colonized, East/West, self/other, minority/majority etc.) and investigating transcultural features that derive from linguistic, political, and ethnic mixtures, most of the time as the result of diasporas or exile. Among these theoretical developments, a contribution that is important to the understanding of Tomizza's hybrid condition is made by Young, who divides intentional from unconscious hybridity. According to Young, who is strongly influenced by Mikhail Bakhtin's linguistic version of hybridity (which will be considered in the following section), intentional hybridity 'enables a contestatory activity, a politicized setting of cultural differences against each other dialogically'.[16] On the other hand, unconscious hybridity leads towards more inclusive mixtures (which can sometimes be represented by creolization and miscegenation); it is 'the imperceptible process whereby two or more cultures merge into a new mode'.[17] Tomizza's subject is unconscious hybridity, which employs fusions rather than politicized differentiations.

The approaches to hybridity mentioned here focus on post-colonialism with a predominant interest in non-white immigrants in Western contexts, migrations, diasporas, and cultural mixtures that emerge in second or third generations. To examine Tomizza's condition in more detail, a more contextualized approach is required that would contemplate the characteristics of hybrid identities in Eastern Central Europe and the Balkans. These terms are problematic and are mainly arrived at by including or excluding countries by their political and ideological contexts.[18] As George Schöpflin states, 'there are serious methodological problems in trying to define "Central Europe", just as there are with South-Eastern Europe'.[19] Central Europe — which today includes Austria, the Czech Republic, Germany, Hungary, Poland, Slovakia, Slovenia, Switzerland, and partially Croatia — presents unique features, which are described by Richard Robinson 'as a forest of historical complexity [...] a territory where peoples, cultures, languages are fantastically intertwined, where every place has several names and men change their citizenship as often as their shoes, an enchanted wood full of wizards and witches'.[20] This consideration is based on the fact that here:

> There is a constant tension between political borders and the boundaries of imagination and cultural memory [...] because the political frontiers themselves are 'ever-changing boundaries': they may deal out a harsh reality, but they are themselves transient, chimerical and disappear into memory.[21]

Istria fulfils the characteristics outlined by Robinson, but its location at the intersection of Central Europe and the Balkans demands additional consideration as there are issues specific to this second zone which require special attention. The

Balkans, or in Tomizza's case Yugoslavia, can be considered a hybrid place par excellence, as Jozo Tomasevich demonstrates:

> The new kingdom included five different nations: Serbs, Croats, Slovenes, Macedonians, and Montenegrins. [...] In addition to the five nations, the new state also had many national minorities. Germans, Hungarians, Albanians, and Turks were the most important. Italians, Romanians, Gypsies, and Ruthenes, as well as other minorities, were also present. The new state was also multiconfessional.[22]

Historically, the term was used to define radical separations happening in fluctuating countries, as underlined by Vesna Goldsworthy:

> The idea of the borderline represents one of the most persistent symbolic images of a peninsula which, throughout known history, has been defined by major divisions. The Eastern and the Western Roman Empires and their Christian successor Churches, the Islamic and the Christian worlds, the Communist and capitalist, all met and clashed in the Balkans. While the Balkans themselves could be represented as a multitude of (sometimes tragically overlapping) peripheries, where the cultural ripples created by the great imperial centres outside the peninsula clash to form interesting patterns even as they subside, individual Balkan identities were shaped over the centuries by the idea of a frontier existence on which they based their own sense of importance.[23]

The idea of the Balkans, as theorized by Maria Todorova in her work *Imagining the Balkans*, is the result of a process that transcends strict geographical reference, because it is 'saturated with a social and cultural meaning that expanded its signified far beyond its immediate and concrete meaning'.[24] To put it in a different way, the signifier here seems to distance the signified in a precarious correspondence between the two: the image of the Balkans derives from a process which is often constructed by way of narrating it. By recalling Benedict Anderson's 'constructivist' notions of 'imagined communities', the Balkans may be viewed as the product of cultural construction; they 'include and exclude meaning that are the bases of an identity'.[25] Once the definition is accepted, it becomes a 'myth-symbol complex that sacralises the construct', despite being unfaithful to reality.[26] Thus, imagined communities might easily foment nationalisms. Anderson proves that nationalism (and the identity of a certain community) is invented or 'imagined because the members of even the smallest nation will never know most of their fellow-members, meet them, or even hear of them, yet in the minds of each lives the image of their communion'.[27]

This brief outline of Eastern Central Europe and the Balkans serves only to problematize the geographical component, which is so significant for understanding Tomizza's ethnical, cultural, and linguistic land of origin. Although it is not possible here fully to engage theoretically with the effects that these geographical definitions have on writers who belong to a borderland located at the intersection of major European civilizations, it is enough to observe that those communities present features that might not be present in more homogeneous backgrounds. As a result, it is very difficult to discuss these matters in Western Europe without running the risk of being misinterpreted. For instance, to make use of a definition, such as Central

Europe or the Balkans for an area such Istria, is already making a specific political and ideological choice.

What matters here is that these lands sometimes struggle to find a coherent analysis from the point of view of the West, and they need tailored approaches that can take into account their complexity. For this reason, I will also explore Pyrah and Fellerer's account of the concept of 'subcultures' in reference to hybrid identities in Eastern Central Europe, with a focus on the case study L'viv-Lwów-Lemberg. Leaving aside the many parallels that may be drawn between this Ukrainian city, Istria, and Trieste, this redefinition of 'subcultures' — which is used to replace hybridity and hyphenation — goes beyond the limits of an ethnic-based examination. As Rogers Brubaker suggests, by dismantling more static nation-state narratives, 'ethnicity, race and nationality are fundamentally ways of perceiving, interpreting, and representing the social world. They are not things in the world, but perspectives on the world'.[28] In offering a new approach to the analysis of 'subcultures', Pyrah and Fellerer accept the challenges imposed by many other factors, such as 'a multitude of complications and historical anomalies that do not fit the patterns of migration, and the majority/minority ethnic dynamics more typical of Western Europe'.[29] These include: the shifting of borders, and populations that consequently move from being majorities to minorities; the presence of national, ethnic, and regional borders; different narratives of presence amid absence; all the nuances of a sense of belonging that cannot be considered as simple assimilation or self-preservation; and discussions of memory at the level of top-down/bottom-up or both at the same time. Their new formulation of subcultures — which differs from three previous ones[30] — aims at a more comprehensive and integrated analysis that considers varied parameters, and simultaneously analyzes types of identification and dynamics of culture and identity formations:

> Our contention is that a new definition of 'sub-cultures' might offer useful and subtle insights into the dynamics of cultural identity formation and disputation, specifically in the East-Central European context. It involves examining groups resisting full classification by the standard labels of 'majority', 'minority' or 'ethnic group'. The definition entails considering a complex interaction of factors through which their identity is expressed and contested, namely: (1) in a given geographical, political, social, regional, context; (2) over time; (3) through use of ritual and symbols, as well as cultural practice more broadly; (4) in language and forms of linguistic expression; (5) but also how it is channelled, or interacts with very specific, historical and contemporary discourses at both micro- and macro-levels: within a group; as determined by a national or other macro-context; within a particular 'minority' discourse (which may or may not be incorporated); and among individuals.[31]

Bearing in mind Pyrah and Fellerer's formulation, which is a better approach for territory where history, geography, politics, ethnicity, and different cultures and mentalities have shaped hybrid identities, Tomizza's Istria will also be considered in relation to those elements that otherwise risk remaining below the surface. In their words, 'subculture is a heuristic term, a tool, to understand forms of East-Central European hybrid cultural identities which are orthogonal and invisible to the prevalent terms of nation and minority'.³² These premises now facilitate the linguistic investigation of borderlands that should include the notions of mono-, autochthonous, bi-, and multilingualism as well as self-translation.

Language: Breaking Down the Monolingual Condition

In most cases, the bi- or multiculturalism that is typical of borderlands can be described as a mixture of languages which integrate or alternate with each other. Rather than attempting to clarify a notion which has been formulated many times without consensus, I shall focus on some useful criteria that will help us understand the linguistic investigation going on in Tomizza's works. After a brief definition of multilingualism and differentiating it from similar notions, I will look at other categories before considering self-translation, which also sheds an original light on Tomizza's literary practices.

Multilingualism has often been opposed to monolingualism, a notion which brings into the analysis the idea of the 'native speaker' and 'mother tongue'. Giulio Lepschy clarifies these as follows:

> A native speaker is the most recent expression, which acquires its centrality in linguistics during the twentieth century, in particular with Leonard Bloomfield (1933) and Noam Chomsky (1957). [...] Language is 'acquired' (rather than 'learnt') through a natural process of maturation which takes place in a 'critical period' during the first few years after birth.

Linguists have tried to test what happens if you are a native speaker of more than one language. The view which seems to prevail is that the first first language appears to be dominant, and a second and other first languages are subject to learning strategies which are shared with the adult learning of second or further languages, and are different from the acquisition of real first languages.

> Mother tongue is a much earlier designation which carries a heavier sociocultural baggage. [...] the label tends to have cultural and ideological suggestions. It seems to refer to the Weltanschauung, the world view.³³

This distinction between 'mother tongue' and 'native speaker' or 'native language' is articulated even more in an area that is politically unsettled:

> But what are we actually talking about when we use terms like 'mother tongue' or 'native language'? The question is particularly relevant in the case of a writer who comes from an area where language politics is an infected issue, and whose native language even changed its name during the writer's lifetime.³⁴

A monolingual person, who has usually been identified with the native speaker of a certain tongue, could therefore be defined as a person able to speak a single language without interaction with others. This definition has been criticized many times by scholars, critics, and writers, who have suggested that languages already contain so many foreign elements within themselves that monolingualism does not exist. In *Monolingualism of the Other*, Jacques Derrida writes:

> One never speaks just a single or singular language. When we try to speak

one language properly, we are always aware that there are some other ways by which we speak, or some foreign elements in the native language that we speak, therefore, there comes the saying in the traditional philology that one only speaks a single language, but one never speaks one language alone.[35]

The idea of monolingualism, then, cannot help to define multilingualism, which itself presents hints of ambiguity. From the beginning, this latter phenomenon has followed a changing course — writing in different languages was common for the cultural elite in seventeenth-century Europe before the rise of monolingualism; the twentieth century has been marked by a plurilingual boom, mostly because of exiles and diasporas. Its formulations have evolved significantly as John Edwards notes, recalling the most common definitions of multilingualism:

> In 1933 Bloomfield observed that bilingualism resulted from the addition of a perfectly learned foreign language to one's own [...] Weinrich (1953) simply defined bilingualism as the alternate use of two languages; in the same year, Haugen suggested that bilingualism began with the ability to produce complete and meaningful utterances in the second language.[36]

From this brief outline certain important factors emerge, such as the way in which different languages interact, the level of competence of the interlocutor, and the differences existing between languages or dialects; I will briefly consider them in relation to literary plurilingualism. Despite the development of the notion of bi- and plurilingualism over the century, the theory of literary plurilingualism has been developed only over the last few decades, and still needs further clarification. In the twentieth century, the term 'hybridity' extended beyond ethnicity to include the linguistic domain. Mikhail Bakhtin developed the idea of linguistic hybridity and the concepts of polyphony, dialogism, and heteroglossia, which are still in use nowadays. For him, linguistic hybridization corresponds to an ongoing process which combines two or more languages, dismantling the idea of unity:

> What is hybridization? It is a mixture of two social languages within the limits of a single utterance, an encounter, within the arena of an utterance, between two different linguistic consciousnesses, separated from one another by an epoch, by social differentiation or by some other factor.[37]

Bakhtin's idea of linguistic hybridity mainly focuses on an internal heterogeneity, while only more recent formulations have brought out fully the possible interactions between different codes. For instance, Furio Brugnolo underlines the fact that manifold languages are present within a certain text: 'poetic plurilingualism' is a process which consists in 'l'impegno simultaneo di due o più idiomi differenti, in successione o alternanza prestabilita, all'interno di un medesimo testo' [the simultaneous employment of two or more languages, one after the other or in a pre-established alternation, within the same poetic text].[38]

Taking the latter as a valid (but still generic) definition, I shall now focus on more detailed categories which might be helpful in the examination of literary plurilingualism. The specific mechanisms that come into play when languages interact will be considered in depth in the following chapter using Gaetano Berruto's theoretical framework. Without going into too much technical and detailed linguistic examination, let me just mention here that there exists a multiple interplay of languages, as suggested by Elwert:

> The degree of mixtures can be very different: it can be one single word, a sentence or an entire passage; it can be an occasional insertion, made only for some purposes, or a mixture can be the entire work; the introduction of a foreign and heterogeneous element can be made in an irregular way, according to a systematic process or undergo a specific rule.[39]

Despite the presence of some standard processes, which allows for a comparison of different types of multilingual texts, plurilingualism remains a complex phenomenon, which requires the consideration of many components.

For example, Rainier Grutman argues that plurilingualism (or to be more precise, heterolinguism) can be generated by different purposes, among which are realist, compositional, and aesthetic motivations.[40] The first aims at rendering a determined linguistic context at a given socio-historical moment. The second is part of a specific writing plan, which includes an accurate use of the language to rebuild a specific context. The last implies the insertion of fragments or references from a different literary tradition. Despite accepting the accuracy of this classification, Bisanti criticizes Grutman's list of the purposes of multilingualism claiming that it should be extended to truthfulness, the exotic touch, an ironic-parodistic function, the choice of a certain register, stylistic-expressive aims, etc.[41] The functions detailed by Bisanti broaden the potential of the phenomenon. With each specific purpose, the author determines the type of interaction needed between languages. As suggested by Pohl, the presentation of a language and a dialect (vertical bilingualism) or two languages (horizontal bilingualism) provides different viewpoints.[42] The former, which characterizes Tomizza's texts remarkably well, has also been formulated by Ferguson, who called it 'diglossia':

> Diglossia is a relatively stable language situation in which, in addition to the primary dialect of the language, which may include a standard or regional standard, there is a very divergent, highly codified, often grammatically more complex, super-imposed variety, the vehicle of a large and respected body of literature, heir of an earlier period or another speech community, which is learned largely by formal education and is used for most written purposes, but is not used in any sector of the community for ordinary conversation.[43]

Ferguson also details the functions which are usually associated with one language or the other, following a 'vertical' (high-low variety) distinction, as clarified by Charlotte Hoffmann:

> The High variety (H), used for sermons (in church or mosque), formal speeches and public lectures, news broadcasts, in official documents and written communication, most books and newspapers, and in poetry. The Low variety (L), on the other hand, is the usual medium for less formal situations, for purposes such as conversation with family, friends and colleagues, instructions to waiters, servants and workmen, informal radio and television programmes (e.g. soap), captions in political cartoons, and in personal letters and folk literature.[44]

This clarification is particularly relevant when referring to the Italian and Croatian linguistic situations in the period under discussion in this study, where diglossia was the rule rather than the exception. Furthermore, the Italian literary panorama has historically been unique in 'its persuasive dual literary canon, in Tuscan and in a myriad of dialects'.[45] While only occasionally within Western literary traditions have texts employed dialects or regional languages in parallel with the standard one, 'plurilingualism and its literary expressions are in fact a quintessential, fundamental aspect of Italian civilization'.[46] The specific political and social situation of Italy — in particular, the division of the country into different states and their late national unification — led to an 'endemic bilingualism of Latin and vernacular in the Middle Ages, and of a literary standard and dialects thereafter'.[47] Nevertheless, apart from limited examples such as Carlo Porta, Giuseppe Gioacchino Belli, Giovan Battista Basile, Eduardo De Filippo, and a few others, only in recent times has dialect become part of the Italian canon.[48] On the other hand, Serbo-Croatian (nowadays usually divided into two languages: Serbian and Croatian) had within itself three different dialects, Shtokavian, Čakavian, and Kajkavian, named after the different word employed for the interrogative pronoun 'what'. The Čakavian dialect is used in Istria, Kvarner, and northern Dalmatia (the littoral regions of Croatia) and is based on the Latin alphabet. Here diglossia — standard Croatian accompanies Čakavian, while the Istro-Venetian dialect was widely employed on the coast — is the common linguistic situation as Tomizza shows with many of his characters. The situation is more complicated though, as there are specific dialects or languages that integrate Čakavian and Istro-Venetian, such as is the case in Pula and Rovinji:

> In Pula, these everyday language practices involve the varieties of Istro-Venetian, Čakavian and the urban Pula Croatian vernacular [...]. At the same time, the everyday practices neither include standard Italian, which is the officially recognized minority language, nor standard Croatian as the state language; both standard Italian and Croatian are used only in very official and formal contexts.[49]

As suggested by Nelida Milani, the complexity of the situation in Istria may often lead to 'triglossia e bilinguismo, bilinguismo e doppia diglossia e trilinguismo' [Triglossia and bilingualism, bilingualism and double diglossia and trilingualism], for people who, respectively, also possess the Istro-romance language; two languages and two dialects; or three standard languages.[50]

There may be a higher or lower degree of interaction between languages for any given writer who uses more than one of them. As the nature of diglossia itself would suggest, there are different ways and modalities concerning the interaction of tongues in general communication, and even more so in a text where the decision to allow the interplay of languages is carefully considered. Turning to this aspect then, there are three main groups of bilingual writers. First the 'intraterritorial', an author who, despite the employment of foreign linguistic fragments, remains within the literary tradition of his main language.[51] This type of writer may use a different tongue consciously, when required by the subject, or as a form of experimentation (for example, Dadaists and Futurists). Second, the extraterritorial is a bilingual writer, who belongs to a literary tradition different from that of his or her mother-tongue. There may be many reasons for this change, commonly including exile, migration, and diaspora, that is, movements which often require a change of language (this was the case with Joseph Conrad). The last group is that made up of writers who have a double linguistic membership or affiliation, such as Tomizza. Vladimir Nabokov and Samuel Beckett are cases of writers who belong to a double literary tradition. This category is the most unusual because, as Mackey states: 'Rare are bilinguals who have an identical repertoire within the two languages'.[52] Whether the role played by another language is more or less important, the impact of a second code makes the writer aware of the chances offered by multilingualism. This is pointed out by Elizabeth Klosty Beaujour: 'Bilingualism confers a continuing advantage for tasks involving metalinguistic awareness, or separating word-sounds from word-meaning, generating synonyms, being sensitive to communicative needs, and perceiving new sounds'.[53]

The interaction of more than one language concerns another specific phenomenon, which is related to multilingualism: self-translation. The two notions are closely related, given that a writer or poet who decides to translate his own work must be bilingual. Moreover, 'While bilingualism is the most obvious necessary precondition, it is not the only one. As self-translators are not only speakers of two languages, but authors in two languages, this also means that they must have a cultural status in both language communities'.[54]

Self-translation has been defined by Popovič, a pioneer of the concept, as 'the translation of an original work into another language by the author himself'.[55] Although this definition pinpoints the process, it does not question a great variety of matters that characterize self-translation, such as the motivations which spur a writer to translate his works, the choice of language, the directionality of the translation, the absence of an original, and the reasons behind the choice to transpose a text into another language. It follows that, as Simona Anselmi points out, self-translation cannot be seen as a 'homogenous type of translation', nor can it be 'establish[ed] once [and] for all [...] because [it] itself is not a univocal phenomenon'.[56] What is commonly recognized in self-translation is the fact that the original dichotomy existing between the writer and the translator is nullified and the self-translator is an unusual figure or writer who is able to make changes when translating, given that he is the author of the original text.[57] In the case of self-translation the two activities of writing and translation, which are traditionally polarized, intermingle, and a privileged figure who straddles the writer and the translator is engendered 'in-between': 'Here the translator is the author, the translation is an original, the foreign is the domestic, and vice versa'.[58]

The reasons a writer might self-translate his works may be economic, commercial, ideological, or postcolonial. 'What matters most [...] is that exile has served to provoke self-translation among many different kinds of writers, each of whom thereby undertakes to remain in active relationship with the first literary language, its legacies and its readers'.[59] There could also be the necessity to reach a major culture or literary tradition behind the decision to self-translate a work: 'Numerous authors writing in minor languages translate their works into major languages to reach a wider audience and more prestigious literary markets'.[60] Where a bilingual or multilingual writer is able to pick freely the language of his works, inner motivations sometimes emerge that are more related to the fact that one language better fulfils certain requirements, or that a specific work is better represented through one language rather than the other.

The relationship between the original and the self-translated text has always interested scholars, who have sought to classify the way in which the two works are related to each other. For instance, Oustinoff suggests that there are different degrees of adhesion to the original text and, consequently, freedom to reinterpret the self-translated work in the target language and culture. This goes from the 'naturalisante' [naturalized] at one end of the scale to the 'décentrée' [decentred] and '(re)créatrice' [(re)creative] at the other.[61] Despite these differences, self-translation remains the result of a process of translation and is, therefore, a derived work. On the other hand, the writer has the chance to reshape his own text in the other language:

> A self-translation, just like any translation, is also another text, derived from a former original and, consequently, its reflected image. But the self-translated text is not something alien to the original from which it derives, nor does it come from the hand of another author we call the translator: in self-translations both original and translated text are brought forth by one and the same hand, and therefore the hoped-for faithful, specular image may appear as deformed and distorted as the author may fancy. Only the author retains the right to change, alter, deform or distort the reflected image of the original, and we could not in any way accuse the author of mistakes or inaccuracies, because the 'mirror' is not something foreign to him or her: the author is, de facto, the 'mirror' in which the original looks at itself.[62]

This process of adaptation to a different audience has been named 'refraction' by André Lefevere; this determines the relationship between the original and the self-translated work. This process of writing and self-translating leads the author to a dialogue, 'a reciprocity whereby one text supplements and/or depends on the other as both texts become, in fact, the head and tail of the same coin'.[63] It follows that, 'although self-translation has often been unquestioningly viewed as a second original, it cannot merely be seen as such, since a very close reading of the text originally composed clearly precedes the composition of the new text'.[64]

Scholars have recently developed many sub-categories to classify different types of self-translation. The most useful one in understanding Tomizza's approach is that theorized by Oustinoff and Jung, who explore the notion of 'interior' self-translation. This may mean the transfer from an 'inner language' of the author's mind to a written output. Interior self-translation can be viewed as a passage from fragmented inner material into an organized text and not from a written original text to its translation. The presence of the original (whether real or mental), of which we might only see the translation, is a key issue that a theory of self-translation cannot avoid, as pointed out by Susan Bassnett:

> The term 'self-translation' is problematic in several respects, but principally because it compels us to consider the problem of the existence of an original. The very definition of translation presupposes an original somewhere else, so when we talk about self-translation, the assumption is that there will be another previously composed text from which the second text can claim its origin.[65]

These various factors concerning both the act of writing and translation lead, with Tomizza, to texts that mirror the condition of exile.

The Trauma of the Exile

At the core of Tomizza's literary production is the notion of exile. The *OED* defines exile as the banishment or prolonged separation from one's native land. It is a condition which implies a rupture with a country of the origin — which is usually associated with being settled or at home — and means, as Lagos-Pope underlines, 'separation, banishment, withdrawal, expatriation, and displacement; its emotional expression is loss, usually manifested as nostalgia'.[66] Exile, in other words, represents a fracture between the self and its environment that involves significant changes in the definition of identity. Reasons for departure are various, while the stay abroad can be temporary or permanent. Exile has historically taken various forms, determining which are often the reasons that led to the detachment from one's own homeland:

> 1. Involuntary exile, usually political or punitive ('Isaiah', Ovid, Dante, Thibault, Charles d'Orléans, Byron, Mickiewicz, and all the moderns, such as Ionesco, Sempun, Cernuda, Kundera, Solzhenitsyn, etc., alas). And these can be further divided into those exiled for their books or their behaviour (Ovid, Byron, Mme de Stael, Victor Hugo, Wilde, Solzhenitsyn) and those who fled as private persons from political conditions or war.
> 2. Voluntary exile, usually called expatriation, for many more personal reasons: social, economic, sexual (e.g., Radclyffe Hall and the lesbian group in Paris in the twenties), or simple preference (Beerbohm retired in Rapallo, Ezra Pound choosing Italy).
>
> Involuntary exiles may tend to be unhappy, poor, bitter (like Gregory VII), nostalgic about the society left behind, self-righteous; voluntary exiles may tend to be happy, comfortable, satiric about the society left behind, self-righteous.[67]

One might suggest that the result is similar for involuntary and voluntary exiles, given that in both cases the subjects find themselves abroad establishing a different relationship with the home country: 'It does not make an essential difference whether he is expelled by physical force or whether he makes the decision to leave (himself) without such an immediate pressure'.[68] However, in the above passage, Christine Brooke-Rose promptly highlights the contrasting consequences of voluntary and involuntary exile. This experience which puts identity under pressure like no other can lead to a state of desperation or to a life full of new possibilities.

For instance, Ovid, who was permanently banished to Tomis (now Constanta, a coastal town on the Black Sea in Romania) represents this first model of exile. His works *Tristia* and *Epistulae ex Ponto* are the classic expressions of the pain of exile.

Caren Kaplan calls this phenomenon the 'nostalgia of the past; for home; and for a 'mother-tongue'.[69] Exile, however, has also been interpreted as a metaphysical condition rather than a real one, and one that opens the way to new stylistic, thematic, or linguistic opportunities. Far from being a painful condition, this second type of exile has been viewed as travelling into the unknown, a source of inspiration and freedom. In his work on twentieth-century Irish authors, George O'Brien has described it as 'a movement of the mind, a cultural reaction, a metonym for restlessness, disaffection, isolation and self-respect'.[70] Among many examples there is also Marcel Proust who 'each day begins with an experience as psychologically hazardous as Odysseus' ten-year wandering', and 'by locating his narrative in the world of dressing tables and mirrored bookcases rather than the classical topos of myth, is saying that exile is in some way integral to how we all experience ourselves'.[71] Metaphysical interpretations of exile are manifest above all in the twentieth century when events produced millions of exiles and refugees.

Although the distinction between voluntary and involuntary exile may produce an initial classification that helps in determining what is meant by exile in general, this notion is problematic when it tries to come to terms with the so-called 'will' of the exile. As pointed out by Marina Franco:

> It is usually assumed that political migration or exile refers to the situation of those who left the country, voluntarily or not, but in any case against their wishes, forced by political circumstances which affected them as members of a certain community. But how can the forced nature of those circumstances be defined? Is fear a defining characteristic?[72]

This question is particularly pertinent when we seek to define the 'will' of the Istrian exile, as the reasons behind the move can be difficult to pinpoint. For instance, some of the Istrian exiles defined themselves as refugees because they were forced to leave their country to escape persecution. The word 'refugee' better describes the fact of being forced to leave one's own country: '"Refugee" refers to a necessary territorial displacement and consequently relates to the term diaspora'.[73] Leaving was, in most cases, the only option available in order not to die in a *foiba*: 'In 1943 and 1945, hundreds, possibly thousands of Italians, both partisans and civilians, were imprisoned and subsequently thrown alive by Yugoslav partisans into various chasms in the Karst region and the hinterland of Trieste and Gorizia'.[74]

Despite the dangers, some Istrians belonging to the Italian community opted to remain and become Yugoslavian citizens. The difference between the two categories has been formulated by Pamela Ballinger: 'Whereas exiles described the sadness with which they left their homes and departed to an uncertain future, *rimasti* stressed the desolation of being left behind. The memories of *rimasti* often focus on those material traces of exodus which symbolize their internal desolation'.[75] Deciding to stay represented a significant change in the lives of the *rimasti* [remained], as they underwent a radical metamorphosis of their identities, which was visible in everyday life. The political and linguistic changes that modified the identity of Istria imposed on the *rimasti* a series of changes which deeply affected their existence. Anna Maria Mori and Nelida Milani wrote a book together in which they offered a parallel between the condition of the exile and that of the *rimasto*, who Milani describes in the following passage:

> Noi che siamo rimasti abbiamo dovuto adattarci psicologicamente alla situazione reale, e in ognuno di noi si notano tracce di questo adattamento. La metamorfosi degli esseri non si procura: accade. Si sono venuti formando gli 'italiani speciali', esseri umani nel cui io più profondo sono avvenute strane fusioni fra ciò che sono stati e ciò che sono diventati nel luogo in cui sono nati, qualcosa di simile a una redistribuzione di molecole sconfinate in geometrie impreviste. Nessuna forza al mondo potrebbe più riportarci allo stato pristino. [...] Che ne sanno gli esuli del nostro 'esilio interno', garantito unicamente dallo spazio casalingo? Non immaginano quanto ci sia costato, di amarezze da patire, di orgoglio da salvare, di conflitti da superare, e di tensioni, di contraddizioni, di accanimento, di sofferenza.[76]

> [We who stayed, had to adapt psychologically to the real situation, and on each of us are visible the traces of this adaptation. The metamorphosis of beings is not provoked: it happens. This generated the 'special Italians', human beings in whose innermost self there occurred weird mixes between what they were and what they had become in the place where they were born, something like a redistribution of boundless molecules in unexpected geometries. No force in the world could bring us to the previous state. [...] What do exiles know of our 'internal exile', guaranteed solely by the home space? They cannot imagine how much it cost, the bitterness of suffering, the pride to be saved, the conflicts to overcome, and tensions, contradictions, fury, and suffering.]

What Milani points out is the fact that, despite having remained in her hometown, she underwent an 'internal exile'. According to Lagos-Pope, 'in the twentieth century, totalitarian regimes have produced a different type of exile often called internal exile', which 'was developed in Germany to refer to those citizens who, even though they stayed in their country during the Nazi period, rejected and opposed National Socialism in a variety of ways'.[77] Despite the fact that internal exile has not always been accepted as a real exile, because 'there is no physical displacement, no uprootedness, and no separation from one's own culture, language, and history', it inflicted a strong sense of estrangement.[78] Around Milani, 'le cose e le case, le insegne e le vetrine, le edicole e i cartelloni perdono i loro nomi, come quando a una persona cadono i capelli e, costretta a mettersi la parrucca, non la riconosci più' [things and houses, signs and shop windows, kiosks and billboards lose their names, like when a person loses their hair and has to wear a wig, you do not you recognize him or her anymore].[79] The internal exile is puzzled by the transformations which take place all around: 'Passiamo attraverso una foresta di simboli che ci osservano con sguardi non familiari e davanti a noi si apre la voragine dell'interpretazione: cosa vorrà dire *mlijecni*? E *ljekarna*?' [We pass through a forest of symbols that observe us with unfamiliar looks and in front of us opens the chasm of interpretation: what does *mlijecni* [diary] mean? And *ljekarna* [pharmacy]?].[80] More specifically, Milani argues that 'si crea in te un altro essere, un altro te stesso che non ami, e che dovrai combattere' [it creates another being in you, another self that you do not love, and that you will have to fight].[81] When we compare internal exile to real exile the former seems to involve a similar degree of estrangement, even though it differs in the way that homeland is contemplated. The radical transformation of the country of origin means that it cannot be kept alive in the imagination of the internal exile. Jan Vladislav states that the idea of home — despite home being destroyed — always persists in the mind of the exile:

> A man's native village can be engulfed by the waters of a dam, a city can be razed to the ground by bombs, a landscape can be rendered unrecognizable by the creative as well as the destructive activity of man. But one thing never changes. We never stop carrying within us this meeting place with ourselves, with all our successive and abandoned selves, this place of recognition, of acceptance or rejection of ourselves and the rest of the world.[82]

The internal exile who observes dramatic changes in his country of origin, and for whom home becomes progressively a site of exile, may challenge this interpretation.

To further complicate the situation in Istria there was a 'counter-exile' from Italy to Yugoslavia of some thousands of people, many of whom were Italian workers deciding to move from Monfalcone to Istria after 1947 to follow their Communist ideals:

> Mentre l'esodo dall'Istria verso l'Italia inizia a profilarsi, nelle sue dimensioni sempre più ampie, si delineano infatti — quasi paradossalmente — spostamenti in direzione opposta. Sono mossi da molte ragioni: ad esempio dall'idea — molto diffusa fra chi vive con passione la speranza comunista — che il socialismo jugoslavo offra prospettive e futuro.[83]
>
> [While the exodus from Istria to Italy begins to take shape, in its increasingly large numbers, there are outlined — almost paradoxically — movements in the opposite direction. They are driven by many reasons: for example, the idea — very common among those who live with passion in Communist hope — that Yugoslav socialism offers prospects and future.]

Most of them could not find what they were looking for in Yugoslavia and risked being deported to Goli otok, Tito's concentration camp located on a desolate rocky island in the Kvarner. Some, however, settled and were able to develop their careers, such as the writer Giacomo Scotti.

To sum up, the Istrian exile challenges a strict binary division between voluntary and involuntary exile because there were at least three major motives involved, associated with the three main groupings: refugees, the *rimasti* or internal exiles, and the counter-exiles. Although a vast majority left fearing for their lives, there were those who decided to remain, and there were even Italians from Italy who moved to Yugoslavia. In other words, 'Exile, diaspora and refugee are generally considered to be terms related to forced dislocations, whereas immigrant and emigrant describe a person who migrates, immigrates, or emigrates by choice'.[84] Istrian exile in its heterogeneity contemplated both categories in both directions.

I will, therefore, take into consideration a wider spectrum of elements to fully account for the phenomenon of exile. The 'multidimensional' model theorized by Glad widens the perspective of our analysis of Tomizza, allowing for a more comprehensive approach to characters who do not submit to the simple rigid classification of 'exile':

> First of all, we could classify the author according to the circumstances under which he finds himself or herself abroad. Does he view his sojourn as temporary? Or is he an 'expatriate' — one who regards his new address as his 'current primary' residence, but who returns home from time to time? [...] next in this gradation is the 'involuntary émigré', who makes the decision to leave under coercion. Finally, we have the true 'exile', who is transported abroad against his will and is not permitted to return even for a visit. [...]
>
> Dimension no. 2 in this model has to do with production — the place of publication of the work. Did it take place in the writer's home country (legally or clandestinely), or did it roll off a foreign press?
>
> Production is followed by marketing, bringing us to dimension no. 3: who are the intended primary readers — those 'back home'? [...]
>
> Dimension no. 4: of what magnitude are the differences in the way of life of the host country from that of the country of origin — roughly comparable (Germany to Scandinavia), significantly different (Hungary to Austria), radically different (USSR to U.S.A.), or overwhelmingly different (Somalia to France)?
>
> Dimension no. 5: the language of the host country. Is it the same as that of the author's country of origin? If it is different, would he rather 'fight than switch'?
>
> Dimension no. 6 is the most emotional one — repatriation. If the option is available, does the writer accept or reject it?[85]

This model includes different elements, which helps locate a writer in relation to his motivations, choices, and the relationship between the countries of origin and destination. Exile from a frontier region typified by remarkable forms of hybridity inevitably produces more complicated figures, the understanding of whom requires the investigation of all of these factors. For instance, examining the differences that exist between the country of origin and the host country (dimension no. 4) is significant in understanding the impact, the 'magnitude' of the displacement, as is the cultural and linguistic gap (see also dimension no. 5). As Caren Kaplan suggests, exile is among the most remarkable 'practices of displacement'; it is the amputation of the self, but also a loss. Displacement emphasizes an 'in-betweenness' that is commonly generated by three elements:

> (1) an imaginary return home, often with a new vision of it, and intense rediscovery of the past and longing for it; (2) a clash with a new society and attempts to adjust to it; and (3) adjustment to a new society or, in the case of failure, marginalization and even death.[86]

Exile, which causes strong forms of displacement, should be viewed as an event that marks the division between a 'before' and an 'after' — this boundary usually makes an indelible mark on the life and works of a writer — deeply affecting the self. As suggested by Dino Cervigni:

> Physical removal or absence from one's country, however, invariably creates a peculiar inner condition in all exiles, who may live this imposed physical removal or absence in as many different ways as the different circumstances of their physical removal, the conditions of their host country, and the personal

and subjective reactions to their new ways of life may be. [...] Being in exile according to the strict sense of the word, therefore, affects not only the body but necessarily also the spirit of all those who undergo it.[87]

Exile could, therefore, be considered as the result of an original rupture or trauma — trauma here being conceived of as a wound which affects the mind rather than the body — which drives forms of estrangement and even alienation. Leon and Rebeca Grinberg link the experience of migration and exile to trauma, associating them with the idea of several traumatic events, called multiple cumulative traumas:

> Migration is not an isolated traumatic experience observable at the time of departure/separation from one's place of origin or at the time of arrival in the new, unknown place where the person will settle. Quite the contrary; in any migration a constellation of factors combine to produce anxiety and sorrow.[88]

The trauma of migration and exile begins before the departure from one's own land of origin and continues after the initial displacement: 'migration as a traumatic experience comes under the heading of what have been called cumulative traumas and tension traumas, in which the subject's reactions are not always expressed or visible, but the effects of such trauma run deep and last long'.[89] Exile, more than migration, is the result of expulsion and punishment that prevent, from the early stages, the return home; this reinforces the traumatic nature of the event.

Trauma studies in literature were established by Cathy Caruth's publication of *Unclaimed Experience: Trauma, Narrative and History* and Kali Tal's *Worlds of Hurt: Reading the Literatures of Trauma* in the 1990s. From an initial psychoanalytic post-structural approach, they opened up to semiotic and socio-political models that focused more on the role played by language in the definition of a trauma, which is relevant in the case of Tomizza. Trauma has been described by Laplanche and Pontalis as an 'event in the subject's life defined by its intensity, by the subject's incapacity to respond adequately, and by the upheaval and long-lasting effects that it brings about in the psychical organization'.[90] Taking inspiration from Freud and Lacan and their theories of the repressed and the sense of absence, in *Unclaimed Experience* Caruth underlines that 'trauma is not locatable in the simple violent or original event in an individual's past, but rather in the way that its very unassimilated nature — the way it is precisely not known in the first instance — returns to haunt the survivor later on'.[91] This definition stresses that trauma is an event that can neither be compared nor confused with others since it leaves a mark that cannot be easily removed. Caruth, as well as other early scholars of literary trauma, present trauma as an event that cannot be represented because it temporarily nullifies both consciousness and memory, which are replaced by a material that is 'dissociated from normal mental processes of cognition, cannot be known or represented but returns belatedly in the form of "flashbacks," traumatic nightmares, and other repetitive phenomena'.[92] Trauma, in other words, is an unsolved matter of the unconscious, which cannot be remembered or told linearly and coherently.

The event causing trauma is a fact that has never been experienced before as such, but at some point became part of the ('unprocessed' or 'unsymbolized') experience of the subject in the form of an enigma, which is difficult to process or rationalize.

For Caruth, 'the most direct seeing of a violent event may occur as an absolute inability to know it'.[93] By investigating the Lacanian concept of trauma in relation to language, Charles Shepherdson argues that a traumatic event:

> Occurs with a shock or suddenness that prevents it from entering the ordinary classificatory schemas of mental life, with the result that the traumatic event is confined to a sort of limbo, imprinted upon the subject without becoming part of the subject's 'experiences' and thus unable to find its place in a memorable narrative.[94]

Lacan's approach, to which Caruth's formulation is deeply connected, crafts an idea of trauma, as an absence deriving from extreme experiences, which have never been symbolically recognizable, making trauma a phenomenon deriving from an unknown origin. For this reason, 'the "event" of trauma, because it does not have a discursive form, can only be betrayed by efforts of narration and can only be truly witnessed as a break in the language itself'.[95] Through the narrative, trauma may be finally located in the past, without resurfacing again in the present. Bessel van der Kolk and Onno van der Hart also suggest that those experiences are unassimilable and can only be 'transformed into a narrative language', where they finally find their location.[96] Here lies the paradoxical nature of trauma, a phenomenon that is unrepresentable (and, therefore, beyond language) because it is an event that cannot be assimilated, but at the same time needs to be told and narrated in order not to return. In his essay on Kafka, George Steiner states that 'The world of Auschwitz lies outside speech as it lies outside reason. To speak of the *unspeakable* is to risk the survivance of language as creator and bearer of humane, rational truth. Words that are saturated with lies or atrocity do not easily resume life'.[97] This means that language struggles to express the 'magnitude' of traumatic experiences, because words are unable to convey the range of unspeakable events. Although the experience of the Holocaust and the Istrian exile cannot be compared, Edward Said warns about the lack of assimilability of exile, which in the twentieth century becomes 'neither aesthetically nor humanistically comprehensible'.[98] Thus he positions himself against critics who consider exile as potentially a pleasurable adventure, stressing the consequences of the exilic fracture: 'To think of the exile informing this literature as beneficially humanistic is to banalize its mutilations, the losses it inflicts on those who suffer them, the muteness with which it responds to any attempt to understand it as "good for us"'.[99]

Even though exile may have unspeakable aspects, it is an event that has been described innumerable times in literature. The advantage offered by the literary tool to express a trauma is that trauma must 'be spoken in a language that is always somehow literary: a language that defies, even as it claims, our understanding'.[100] A literary text provides a space in which the trauma can be re-processed, thought through, worked out. Kathryn Robson even suggests that:

> How trauma can be narrated is intrinsically literary, calling for us to map out the possibilities and limits of memory and narrative, as well as of language itself. Trauma defies our attempts to comprehend and to assimilate it, to 'come to terms' with it in any way.[101]

The 'special' relationship that exists between trauma and narration (in this case fiction) depends on the fact that the former only seems to exist when it is formulated employing language through a narrative.

Dominick LaCapra develops the idea of the way in which trauma should be written, underlining the most significant methods employed by historiography to deal with displacing experiences. He points out that 'Trauma is a disruptive experience that disarticulates the self and creates holes in existence; it has belated effects that are controlled only with difficulty and perhaps never fully mastered'.[102] Historiography has created specific frameworks and indispensable parameters to be used to make an account of an event of this type, while fiction, which is not simply based on facts, may take full advantage of the 'freedom' of a literary text. La Capra suggests that, despite the fact that fiction might involve truth claims, it treats real and non-real events in the same way: 'the more pertinent contrast between historiography and fiction might be on the level of events, where historians, as distinguished from writers of fiction, may not imbricate or treat in the same way actual events and ones they invent'.[103] History writing, as White observed, requires narrativization in order to transform events into a material to be told: 'one cannot historicize without narrativizing, because it is only by narrativization that a series of events can be transformed into a sequence, divided into periods, and represented as a process'.[104] Fiction, on the other hand, needs fictionalization and not simply narrativization.

What matters here is not to establish coherence between traumatic experiences and the truth of the historical event, but rather the potential offered by the literary text for the trauma to be worked out. Trauma always carries a dissociation and this can be explored through troubled representation: 'Working through trauma involves the effort to articulate and rearticulate affect and representation in a manner that may never transcend, but may to some viable extent counteract, a re-enactment, or acting out, of that disabling dissociation'.[105] In the fictional text, trauma finds a suitable space where even diverging and controversial drives can find expression (in a disruptive way). In effect, as suggested by Leigh Gilmore, 'speech of all sorts spills from the site of trauma'.[106] The trauma of the exile must be transformed (or 'translated') from a magmatic material which cannot be fully grasped into a text. As Josefin Holmström puts it:

> Trauma is not a compound experience, so to speak; if we frame it in literary terms (as has become increasingly in vogue among psychoanalysts over the last few decades) it is not a coherent plot but rather a fragment, a book with the 'chapters in our personal history' out of sequence, to borrow Pierre Janet's terminology.[107]

The space of the text is able to arrange disruptive forms, which Michael Seidel calls 'the larger strategies of representations', brought onto the stage by exile.[108] Fictional texts are the result of a process of selection and reworking by the writer, 'the organisation and expression of a tiny proportion of the available material'.[109] Apart from spatio-temporal dislocational phenomena (such as flashback and flash forwards etc.) that can upset the linearity of the narrative, there are also gaps, omissions, unexpected turns, blockages, and other narratological phenomena, of which the exilic text takes full advantage. Wolfang Iser, who has worked in depth on the role played by 'negativity' in the literary text, highlights the complex balance that exists between the sayable and the unsayable: 'Once we have encountered the limits of the sayable, we must acknowledge the existence of 'unsayable things', and, by means of a language somehow formed on being silent, articulate that which cannot be grasped'.[110] Negativity should not be conceived of as the loss of meaning, but rather, meaning's 'transformation':

> To account for such transformation in literary texts an approach is required that comes to grips with the sequential or temporal nature of the play movement itself. This movement turns the split signifier into a matrix for double meaning. In fact, only through play can difference as oscillation be manifested, because only play brings out the absent otherness that lies on the reverse side of all positions drawn into interaction. In the play of the text there is neither winning nor losing. Nor is there any fundamental change in the status of that which is absent.[111]

This process of transformation of meaning necessarily interacts with memory, which is itself a controversial notion especially when following trauma. Narrative memory is usually associated with the idea of coherence and comprehensiveness, while trauma is described as fragmented, disruptive, and intrusive. However, some critics, such as Caruth, have underlined the false dichotomy that exists between memory and trauma. Susan Brison writes that: 'The tendency to take certain memories — traumatic memories — as simply given, and retained as snapshots, exists in trauma theory', even though 'traumatic memory, like narrative memory, is articulated, selective, even malleable, in spite of the fact that the framing of such memory may not be under the survivor's conscious control'.[112] Traumatic memories are the result of a sophisticated construction, rather than an image retained from the moment of trauma. Caruth 'refers to traumatic experience, traumatic events, the traumatic re-experiencing of the event, the traumatic symptom, the traumatic occurrence, the traumatic nightmare, traumatic dreams and flashbacks', while 'not once, does she refer to traumatic memory or traumatic memories'.[113] The reason is that 'Caruth sees "traumatic memory" as oxymoronic, the traumatic being "defined, in part, by the way that it pushes memory away"'.[114] The exilic memory, which follows the trauma of the irreversible detachment from one's own homeland, could be seen as a narrative strategy, which allows 'continuity' in time for the displaced self.[115]

Apart from the shock of exile, trauma and memory in the Istrian case must deal with drastic political changes that might well have altered the position of the subject. This certainly plays a role in the building of a 'comprehensible story' of the traumatic event. If memory is something we produce as a subject sharing a culture, it is significant for the subject to feel part of a community. By jeopardizing the possibility for the subject to belong to a determined community, exile also affects the practice of creating and maintaining memory. Given that 'memory is an action: essentially it is the act of telling a story', the community helps it to build and maintain its stability.[116] Memories are obviously able to change over time, as they are the result of an active process of storytelling, which is itself a malleable practice.

The influence of a difficult political situation, though, should be considered when discussing the process of memory. This was the case in post-war Italy, which was troubled by a series of factors that have been summarized by Rosario Forlenza:

> The birth of democracy in Italy after World War II was preceded by disruptive historical events that potentially could have divided the nation and jeopardized its political transformation. Fascism had enjoyed the support of part of the community. The regime had been more or less active in the repression of opponents. Moreover, beginning in 1943 World War II had evolved into a brutal civil war. The war had been experienced in very different ways by the various sectors of the population.[117]

The result was a country where conflicting memories dictated different political choices and prevented the establishment of a unified national memory. Partisan fighters started forming a post-war society, even before the signing of the armistice, and played a role in new national and local governments. However, the presence of a strong Catholic Church, the American influence, and the Allied military occupation reduced the possibility for the political change promoted by the Left party (made of Communists and Socialists). For this reason, the post-war situation in Italy is based on divided memories, as outlined by John Foot:

> Italian memories have often been divided. Events have been interpreted in contrasting ways, and the facts themselves are often contested. It has proved extremely difficult, if not impossible, for any group — public or private — to create a consensus around the past, or around ways of remembering that past. Various groups — be they regional, ethnic, political — have demanded that their memories be acknowledged. Individual events as well as history itself have been understood in a bewildering variety of ways. The state and other public bodies have rarely been able to build durable and commonly agreed practices of commemoration. There has been no closure, no 'truth,' and little reconciliation.[118]

Divided memories constitute mental obstacles towards the other, impeding a real confrontation with the events of the past. This antagonistic approach has been particularly remarkable in a borderland such as Istria and Trieste, where multiple ethnicities — which, as has been shown, were already in most cases divided internally — struggled to reach such a confrontation. As pointed out by Ballinger:

> This landscape not only recalls past violence, however, but also becomes the contemporary sites of contestation. Indeed, the territoriality itself — today divided between the Italian, Slovene, and Croatian states and referred to by different names [...] appears to mirror what some have deemed the 'divided memory' (Rusconi 1995) of World War II.[119]

This state of affairs constitutes a paradox, given that a multicultural area, as Magris suggested in his definition of borderland, could also be conceived of as a land of exchange, where transnational memories can be generated. Katia Pizzi has underlined the potential of this 'extraordinary incubator, a furnace of cultural imbrications, a convergence and cross-road of transcultural exchanges', where 'global and local identities, the regional, the national and the international, the general and the particular, collided and crashed, but also potentially intersected in manners that would not have been possible elsewhere'.[120] As has happened many times in history, conflicts and tensions overwhelmed the possibility of working through a form of transnational memory:

> The multi-lingual and multi-cultural make-up of this region, its national and ethnic 'fluidity', its relative geographic remoteness from the 'official', the canonic centres of culture, almost naturally led to eclectic forms of cultural experimentalism. Significantly, the manners and features whereby innovative cultural forms and pro-European agendas prevailed here, were steeped in a social and political landscape increasingly mired in national, ethnic and class polarizations. An experience, in other words, which was more readily divisive, rather than conducive to transcultural approaches.[121]

Memory in these areas must deal with a different idea of border, as borders here correspond to socio-political entities that 'are no longer situated at the outer limit of territories; they are dispersed a little everywhere', troubling further the cohesion of the state and relationships between different countries.[122] This is particularly the case when borders are redefined due to exile.

Notes to Chapter 2

1. Giorgio Bertone, *Il confine del paesaggio: lettura di Francesco Biamonti* (Novara: Interlinea, 2006), p. 21.
2. Piero Zanini, *Significati del confine: i limiti naturali, storici, mentali* (Milan: Mondadori, 1997).
3. The American Frontier began with the European settlement on the Atlantic coast and progressively advanced towards the West, until the final conquest of the lands that became the states of California, Nevada, Utah, parts of Arizona, Colorado, New Mexico, and Wyoming. The historian Frederick Jackson Turner, who in *The Frontier in American History* theorized this frontier, immediately distinguished it from European ones: 'The American frontier is sharply distinguished from the European frontier — a fortified boundary line running through dense populations. The most significant thing about the American frontier is, that it lies at the hither edge of free land' (*The Frontier in American History* (New York: Krieger, 1976), p. 3).
4. Zanini, *Significati del confine*, pp. 10–12.
5. Silvia Assenza, *Il confine nella letteratura: la Sicilia e Trieste* (Acireale & Rome: Bonanno, 2012), p. 100.
6. Ibid., p. 102.
7. Gloria Anzaldùa, *Borderlands/La Frontera: The New Mestiza* (San Francisco: Aunt Lute Books, 2012), p. 3. See also Josiah McC. Heyman 'Culture Theory and the US-Mexico Border', in *A Companion to Border Studies*, ed. by Thomas M. Wilson and Hastings Donnan (Oxford: Blackwell, 2012), pp. 48–65.
8. Anzaldùa, *Borderlands/La Frontera*, p. 63.
9. Tomizza, *Alle spalle di Trieste*, p. 65.
10. Homi Bhabha, *The Location of Culture* (New York: Routledge, 1994), p. 1.
11. Ibid., p. 13.
12. This concept has been criticized by many scholars, as Bhabha seems indirectly to assert the uniform condition of the two original cultures. As Sten Pultz Moslund observes: 'In order to make his hybrid space and hybrid subject stand out as radically new and ground-breaking, Bhabha simply imposes a homogeneity on national cultures that was not there in the first place' (*Migration Literature and Hybridity: The Different Speeds of Transcultural Change* (Basingstoke: Palgrave Macmillan, 2010), p. 34).
13. Homi Bhabha, *Nation and Narration* (New York: Routledge, 1990), p. 211.
14. Bhabha, *The Location of Culture*, p. 37.

15. Ibid., p. 1.
16. Robert Young, *Colonial Desire: Hybridity in Theory, Culture and Race* (London & New York: Routledge, 1995), p. 22.
17. Ibid., p. 21.
18. For further developments of the notion, see Timothy Garton Ash, *The Uses of Adversity: Essays on the Fate of Central Europe* (London: Penguin, 1999), and 'Does Central Europe Exist?', *The New York Review of Books*, 9 October 1986, pp. 51–80; Lonnie Johnson, *Central Europe: Enemies, Neighbors, Friends* (New York: Oxford University Press, 1996); Larry Wolff, *Inventing Eastern Europe: The Map of Civilization on the Mind of the Enlightenment* (Stanford, CA: Stanford University Press, 1994); Robert John Weston Evans, 'Essay and Reflections: Frontiers and National Identities in Central Europe', *The International History Review*, 14:3 (August 1992), 480–502; Robin Okey, 'Central Europe/Eastern Europe: Behind the Definitions', *Past and Present*, 137 (November 1992), 102–33.
19. George Schöpflin, *The Dilemmas of Identity* (Tallinn: Tallinn University Press, 2010), p. 253.
20. Richard Robinson, *Narratives of the European Border: A History of Nowhere* (Basingstoke: Palgrave, 2007), pp. 2–3.
21. Ibid., p. 4.
22. Jozo Tomasevich, *War and Revolution in Yugoslavia, 1941–1945: Occupation and Collaboration* (Stanford, CA: Stanford University Press, 2001), p. 1.
23. Vesna Goldsworthy, *Inventing Ruritania: The Imperialism of the Imagination* (New Haven, CT, & London: Yale University Press, 1998), p. 7.
24. Maria Todorova, *Imagining the Balkans* (New York: Oxford University Press, 1997), p. 1.
25. Schöpflin, *The Dilemmas of Identity*, p. 253.
26. Ibid.
27. Benedict Anderson, *Imagined Communities: Reflections on the Origin and Spread of Nationalism* (London: Verso, 1983), p. 6.
28. Rogers Brubaker, *Ethnicity Without Groups* (Cambridge, MA: Harvard University Press, 2006), p. 17.
29. Robert Pyrah and Jan Fellerer, 'Redefining "sub-culture": A New Lens for Understanding Hybrid Cultural Identities in East-Central Europe with a Case Study from Early 20th Century L'viv-Lwów-Lemberg', *Nations and Nationalism*, 21:4 (October 2015), 700–20 (p. 706).
30. The first formulation started at the beginning of the twentieth century with the so-called 'Chicago School' and focused mainly on urban ethnography; the second is a semiotic-sociological based type that originated from the Birmingham Centre for Cultural Studies (CCS) in the 1960s–90s; the third 'Post-subculture' or 'After Subculture' employs a postmodern approach, which includes a more globalized viewpoint and more fluid identities.
31. Pyrah and Fellerer, 'A New Lens', pp. 702–03.
32. Ibid., p. 715.
33. Giulio Lepschy, 'Mother Tongues in the Middle Ages and Dante', in *Dante's Plurilingualism: Authority, Knowledge, Subjectivity*, ed. by Sara Fortuna, Manuele Gragnolati, and Jürgen Trabant (Oxford: Legenda, 2010), pp. 16–23 (p. 17).
34. Nico Israel, *Outlandish: Writing between Exile and Diaspora* (Stanford, CA: Stanford University Press, 2000), p. 57.
35. Jacques Derrida, *Monolingualism of the Other, or, The Prosthesis of Origin*, trans. by Patrick Mensah (Stanford, CA: Stanford University Press, 1998), p. 12.
36. John Edwards, 'Foundations of Bilingualism', in *The Handbook of Bilingualism*, ed. by Tej K. Bhatia and William C. Ritchie (Malden, MA: Blackwell Publishing, 2006), pp. 7–31 (p. 8).
37. Mikhail Bakhtin, *The Dialogic Imagination: Four Essays*, trans. by Caryl Emerson and Michael Holquist (Austin, TX: Austin University Press, 1981), p. 358.
38. Furio Brugnolo, *Plurilinguismo e lirica medievale: da Raimbaut de Vaqueiras a Dante* (Rome: Bulzoni, 1983), p. 5.
39. Wilhelm Theodor Elwert, 'Das zweisprachige Individuum und andere Aufsätze zur romanischen und allgemeinen Sprachwissenschaft', in *Studien zu den romanischen Sprachen und Literaturen*, 8 vols (Wiesbaden: Franz Steiner, 1967–79), VI, 234.

40. Rainier Grutman, 'Les Motivations de l'hétérolinguisme: réalisme, composition, esthétique', in *Eteroglossia e plurilinguismo letterario: atti del XVIII convegno interuniversitario di Bressanone*, ed. by Furio Brugnolo and Vincenzo Orioles (Rome: Il Calamo, 2002), pp. 329–49, and *Des langues qui résonnent: l'hétérolinguisme au XIX siècle québécois* (Saint-Laurent, Quebec: Fides, 1997).
41. Tatiana Bisanti, *L'opera plurilingue di Amelia Rosselli: un distorto, inesperto, espertissimo linguaggio* (Pisa: Edizioni ETS, 2007), p. 75.
42. J. Pohl, 'Bilingualismes', *Revue Roumaine de Linguistique*, 10 (1965), 343–49.
43. Charles Ferguson, 'Diglossia', *Word*, 15 (1959), 325–40 (p. 336).
44. Charlotte Hoffmann, *An Introduction to Bilingualism* (London & New York: Longman, 1991), p. 166.
45. Hermann Haller, *The Other Italy: The Literary Canon in Dialect* (Toronto: University of Toronto Press, 1999), p. 3.
46. Ibid.
47. Ibid.
48. For further clarification, see Walter Binni, *Storia letteraria delle regioni d'Italia* (Florence: Sadea-Sansoni, 1968), and Alfredo Stussi, *Lingua, dialetto e letteratura* (Turin: Einaudi, 1993).
49. Rosita Rindler Schjerve and Eva Vetter, *European Multilingualism: Current Perspectives and Challenges* (Bristol: Multilingual Matters, 2012), p. 108.
50. Nelida Milani, *La comunità italiana in Istria e a Fiume fra diglossia e bilinguismo* (Trieste: Università popolare; Rovigno: Unione degli Italiani dell'Istria e di Fiume, 1990), p. 41.
51. See François Grosjean, *Life with Two Languages: An Introduction to Bilingualism* (Cambridge, MA: Harvard University Press, 1982), p. 109.
52. William Mackey, 'Determining the Status and Function of Languages in Multinational Societies', in *Status and Function of Languages and Language Variety*, ed. by Ulrich Ammon (Berlin & New York: Walter de Gruyter, 1989), pp. 3–20 (p. 3).
53. Elizabeth Klosty Beaujour, *Alien Tongues: Bilingual Russian Writers of the 'First' Emigration* (Ithaca, NY: Cornell University Press, 1989), p. 16.
54. Verena Jung, *English-German Self-translation of Academic Texts and its Relevance for Translation Theory and Practice* (Frankfurt am Main: Peter Lang, 2002), p. 18.
55. Anton Popovič, *Dictionary for the Analysis of Literary Translation* (Edmonton: Department of Comparative Literature, University of Alberta, 1976), p. 19.
56. Simona Anselmi, *On Self-translation: An Exploration in Self-translators' Teloi and Strategies* (Milan: LED, 2012), p. 11. See also *Self-translation: Brokering Originality in Hybrid Culture*, ed. by Anthony Cordingley (London: Continuum, 2013).
57. See Michaël Oustinoff, *Bilinguisme d'écriture et auto-traduction: Julien Green, Samuel Beckett, Vladimir Nabokov* (Paris: L'Harmattan, 2001), p. 17.
58. Jan Hokenson and Marcella Munson, *The Bilingual Text: History and Theory of Literary Self-translation* (Manchester: St. Jerome, 2007), p. 161.
59. Jan Hokenson, 'History and the Self-translator', in *Self-translation*, ed. by Cordingley, pp. 39–60 (p. 56).
60. Anselmi, *On Self-translation*, p. 51.
61. Oustinoff, *Bilinguisme d'écriture et auto-traduction*, pp. 29–34.
62. Julio-César Santoyo, 'On Mirrors, Dynamics & Self-translations', in *Self-translation*, ed. by Cordingley, pp. 27–38 (p. 28).
63. Ibid., p. 31.
64. Jung, *English-German Self-translation of Academic Texts and its Relevance for Translation Theory and Practice*, p. 30.
65. Susan Bassnett, 'The Self-translator as Rewriter', in *Self-translation*, ed. by Cordingley, pp. 13–26 (p. 15).
66. Lagos-Pope, 'Introduction', in *Exile in Literature*, p. 15.
67. Christine Brooke-Rose, 'Exsul', in *Exile and Creativity*, ed. by Suleiman, pp. 9–24 (p. 11). See also Jin Ha, *The Writer as Migrant* (Chicago, IL: University of Chicago Press, 2008), and Zeng Hong, *The Semiotics of Exile in Literature* (New York: Palgrave Macmillan, 2010).
68. Paul Tabori, *The Anatomy of Exile: A Semantic and Historical Study* (London: Harrap, 1972), p. 37.

69. Caren Kaplan, *Questions of Travel: Postmodern Discourses of Displacement* (Durham, NC, & London: Duke University Press, 1996), p. 33.
70. George O'Brien, 'The Muse of Exile: Estrangement and Renewal in Modern Irish Literature', in *Exile in Literature*, ed. by Lagos-Pope, pp. 82–101 (p. 99).
71. Michael Murphy, *Poetry in Exile: A Study of the Poetry of W. H. Auden, Joseph Brodsky and George Szirtes* (London: Greenwich Exchange Press, 2004), p. x.
72. Quotations taken from Kate Averis, *Exile and Nomadism in French and Hispanic Women's Writing* (Oxford: Legenda, 2014), pp. 19–20.
73. Sophia McClennen, *The Dialectics of Exile: Nation, Time, Language, and Space in Hispanic Literatures* (West Lafayette, IN: Purdue University Press, 2004), p. 15.
74. Pizzi, *A City in Search of an Author*, p. 91.
75. Pamela Ballinger, *History in Exile: Memory and Identity at the Borders of the Balkans* (Princeton, NJ: Princeton University Press, 2002), p. 237.
76. Mori and Milani, *Bora*, pp. 11–12.
77. Lagos-Pope, 'Introduction', p. 10.
78. Ibid.
79. Mori and Milani, *Bora*, p. 84.
80. Ibid.
81. Ibid., p. 79.
82. Jan Vladislav, 'Exile, Responsibility, Destiny', in *Literature in Exile*, ed. by Glad, pp. 14–27 (p. 15).
83. Guido Crainz, *Il dolore e l'esilio: l'Istria e le memorie divise d'Europa* (Rome: Donzelli, 2005), p. 75.
84. McClennen, *The Dialectics of Exile*, p. 15.
85. John Glad (ed.), 'Preface', in *Literature in Exile*, pp. vii–xiii (pp. x–xi).
86. Mykola Soroka, *Faces of Displacement: The Writings of Volodymyr Vynnychenko* (Montreal & Ithaca, NY: McGill-Queen's University Press, 2012), p. 7.
87. Dino Cervigni, 'Exile Literature', *Annali di italianistica*, 20 (2001), 11–14 (p. 12).
88. Leon Grinberg and Rebeca Grinberg, *Psychoanalytic Perspectives on Migration and Exile* (New Haven, CT: Yale University Press, 2004), p. 12.
89. Ibid.
90. Jean Laplanche and Jean-Bertrand Pontalis, *The Language of Psycho-Analysis*, trans. by Donald Nicholson-Smith (London: Hogarth Press, 1973), p. 465.
91. Cathy Caruth, *Unclaimed Experience: Trauma, Narrative and History* (Baltimore, MD: Johns Hopkins University Press, 1996), p. 4. See also Michelle Balaev, *Contemporary Approaches in Literary Trauma Theory* (Basingstoke: Palgrave Macmillan, 2014), and Jean-Michel Ganteau and Susana Onega Jaén, *Contemporary Trauma Narratives: Liminality and the Ethics of Form* (New York: Routledge, 2014).
92. Ruth Leys, *Trauma: A Genealogy* (Chicago, IL: University of Chicago Press, 2000), p. 266.
93. Caruth, *Unclaimed Experience*, p. 92.
94. Charles Shepherdson, *Lacan and the Limits of Language* (New York: Fordham University Press, 2008), pp. 91–92.
95. Ibid.
96. Bessel van der Kolk and Onno van der Hart, 'The Intrusive Past: The Flexibility of Memory and the Engraving of Trauma', in *Trauma: Explorations in Memory*, ed. by Cathy Caruth (Baltimore, MD: Johns Hopkins University Press, 1995), pp. 158–82 (p. 176). See also Paul Antze and Michael Lambek, *Tense Past: Cultural Essays in Trauma and Memory* (New York & London: Routledge, 1996), Richard McNally, *Remembering Trauma* (Cambridge, MA, & London: Belknap Press, 2003).
97. George Steiner, *Language and Science* (New York: Atheneum, 1967), p. 123. To know more about the establishment of the parameter of Auschwitz, see Daniel Levy and Natan Sznaider, 'Memory Unbound: The Holocaust and the Formation of Cosmopolitan Memory', *European Journal of Social Theory*, 5:1 (2002), 87–106.
98. Said, 'Reflections on Exile', p. 174.

99. Ibid.
100. Caruth, *Unclaimed Experience*, p. 5.
101. Kathryn Robson, *Writing Wounds: The Inscription of Trauma in Post-1968 French Women's Lifewriting* (Amsterdam: Rodopi, 2004), p. 13.
102. Dominick LaCapra, *Writing History, Writing Trauma* (Baltimore, MD: Johns Hopkins University Press, 2001), p. 41.
103. Ibid., p. 14.
104. Hayden White, 'Historical Discourse and Literary Writing', in *Tropes for the Past: Hayden White and the History/Literature Debate*, ed. by Kuisma Korhonen (Amsterdam: Rodopi, 2006), pp. 25–34 (p. 30).
105. LaCapra, *Writing History, Writing Trauma*, p. 42.
106. Leigh Gilmore, *The Limits of Autobiography: Trauma and Testimony* (Ithaca, NY, & London: Cornell University Press, 2001), p. 102.
107. Josefin Holmström, '"Born into absence": Trauma and Narration in W. G. Sebald, Anne Michaels and Pat Barker', *Bristol Journal of English Studies*, 2 (2012), 1–18 (p. 2).
108. Michael Seidel, *Exile and the Narrative Imagination* (New Haven, CT: Yale University Press, 1986), p. xii.
109. Nicoletta Simborowski, *Secrets and Puzzles: Silence and the Unsaid in Contemporary Italian Writing* (Oxford: European Humanities Research Centre, 2003), p. 1.
110. Sanford Budick and Wolfgang Iser (eds), *Languages of the Unsayable: The Play of Negativity in Literature and Literary Theory* (New York: Columbia University Press, 1989), p. xii.
111. Ibid.
112. Susan Brison, *Aftermath: Violence and the Remaking of a Self* (Princeton, NJ: Princeton University Press, 2002), p. 15.
113. Gary Weissman, *Fantasies of Witnessing: Postwar Efforts to Experience the Holocaust* (Ithaca, NY: Cornell University Press, 2004), pp. 133–34.
114. Ibid.
115. Roger Porter, *Self-Same Songs: Autobiographical Performances and Reflections* (Lincoln: University of Nebraska Publisher, 2002), p. 18.
116. Van der Kolk and van der Hart, 'The Intrusive Past', p. 175.
117. Rosario Forlenza, 'Sacrificial Memory and Political Legitimacy in Postwar Italy: Reliving and Remembering World War II', *History and Memory*, 24:2 (2012), 73–116 (p. 73).
118. John Foot, *Italy's Divided Memory* (New York: Palgrave Macmillan, 2009), p. 1.
119. Ballinger, *History in Exile*, p. 21.
120. Katia Pizzi, 'Triestine Literature between Slovenia and Italy: A Case of Missed Transculturalism?', *Primerjalna književnost*, 36 (2013), 145–54 (pp. 145–46).
121. Ibid.
122. Étienne Balibar, 'World Borders, Political Borders', trans. by Erin M. Williams, *PMLA*, 117:1 (2002), 71–78 (p. 73).

CHAPTER 3

Before Exile:
Bilingualism and Self-translation
in *Materada* and *La miglior vita*

The Hybrid Language in the Spotlight

As I have demonstrated in the previous chapters, the Istrian diaspora displays unusual characteristics that undermine the conventional view of the exilic experience. Given its composite background, Istria cannot support the idea of a homeland in the sense of a uniform place where people share the same language, culture, and background. In Istria, life before exile was already characterized by an Italo-Croatian mixture in which the clash of different cultures and languages took place on a daily basis.

Among Tomizza's literary works, *Materada* and *La miglior vita* are remarkable for the composite nature of their setting: the Istrian peninsula, which is examined in the years of increasing tension before the massive exile of the Italians (from the mid-1940s to the end of the 1950s), emerges as kaleidoscopic. It is no accident that Tomizza's first novel is celebrated as the quintessential 'romanzo di frontiera' [frontier novel] as it explores a land on the margins shaken several times by different forms of cultural mixing and border changes that made a 'pure' culture impossible. As Guagnini suggests, '*Materada* è il libro che inaugura e avvalora, in Italia, un discorso moderno sulla letteratura "di frontiera" nel suo senso più pertinente' [*Materada* is the book that inaugurates and confirms, in Italy, a modern discourse on 'frontier' literature in its most pertinent sense].[1] Although the novel offers several features which highlight the complex nature of Tomizza's country, its most important contribution is its extraordinary language. *La miglior vita* covers a more extended period, but it inherits from *Materada* the mirroring of the vexed ethno-linguistic situation in its linguistic mechanisms.

Language is the centre of gravity of these two novels. The very particular character of the idiom Tomizza employs becomes evident to the reader as the sophisticated linguistic mix of the setting is transferred to the Italian narrative. To give voice to his homeland, he creates a structure that aims to reproduce subtle linguistic dynamics that are then used to show the relationship between characters, narrator, and reader. It is through this complicated linguistic framework that characters reveal their identity, weigh up their choices, and fluctuate between their double origins; it is also through this that the narrator mediates dialogue, translating idioms or leaving foreign words and sentences untranslated.

In this chapter, I will investigate the language of *Materada* and *La miglior vita* and the strategies adopted by Tomizza in his texts to mirror the multilingualism of his homeland. Having introduced the central aspects of the novel, I will consider Tomizza's essay 'Uno scrittore tra due dialetti di matrice linguistica diversa', which deals with the Istrian intersection of bilingualism and diglossia. This analysis leads to a consideration of a 'self-translated' novel, or rather, a work that not only intermingles languages, but is also open to the translation of Croatian and Istro-Venetian dialects into Italian. Several linguistic processes such as code-switching, code-mixing, hybridization, and interference will be considered, as will the original solutions contrived by Tomizza.

Materada tells the story of an Istrian village where life is progressively disrupted by the approaching possibility of exile. It can be placed in a phase in Tomizza's life when he was deeply influenced by the Slovene writer Ivan Cankar (1876–1918), often regarded as one of the greatest Slovene writers. What struck Tomizza most about Cankar was his ability to recreate a rural world made up of morals and sensations similar to his own. He notes a similar anxiety for justice and the same religious controversies and sense of destiny. Tomizza recounts how he first felt the impact of Cankar during an hour of Slovene language at his secondary school, saying that it was one of the 'punti cardinali della mia giovinezza' [cardinal points of my youth]:[2]

> Un giorno il timido, impacciato professore ci lesse una novella di Ivan Cankar [...]. Forse nessun'altra pagina di autori ben più grandi mi ha colpito tanto, e nel profondo, facendo quasi una radiografia della mia anima. Sentivo che quel modo di scrivere, quel modo di accostarsi a certi problemi e a certi sussulti della coscienza, era fatto su mia misura.[3]
>
> [One day the shy, awkward teacher read us a story by Ivan Cankar [...]. Perhaps no other page even of greater authors has struck me so much, and so deeply, creating almost an x-ray of my soul. I felt that that way of writing, that way of approaching certain problems and jolts of consciousness, was done in exactly my terms.]

Cankar's influence is clearly detectable in *Materada*, a work which takes inspiration from one of his most famous novels, *Hlapec Jernej in njegova pravica* [The Servant Jernej and His Justice].[4] Tomizza makes this clear:

> Circolava in lingua italiana, quasi esclusivamente nell'area giuliana, la traduzione di *Il servo Bortolo e il suo diritto* [...]. Cankar tornava a incantarmi, e ad agitarmi, per l'estrema adesione al suo mondo, nel quale il mio si rifletteva non poco [...]. Per di più riscontravo nel piccolo universo cankariano un'interiorità complessa, violenta e umile insieme, asciutta e nel contempo carica di tensione religiosa ed esistenziale, che imponeva un linguaggio icastico quanto ricco di oscure vibrazioni, di una solennità quasi biblica. Avevo iniziato a scrivere *Materada*.[5]
>
> [The translation of *The Servant Jernej and His Justice* circulated in the Italian language, almost exclusively in the Julian area [...]. Cankar returned to enchant and excite me in his extreme absorption in his world, in which mine was

> reflected not just a little [...]. Moreover I observed in the small Cankar universe a complex, violent, and humble interiority, dry and at the same time full of religious and existential tensions that imposed a figurative language rich in dark vibrations and an almost biblical solemnity. I started writing *Materada*.]

Cankar's novel focuses on the story of the peasant Jernej who fights to gain rights to the fields in which he has worked his entire life. He is determined to obtain justice because the owner of the estate profited from his work without giving him either a decent salary or any form of pension. When Jernej becomes old and is left with nothing he begins to fight desperately against the owner. Meeting with no success he decides to go and meet the Viennese Emperor in person. However, his journey to the Austrian capital leads to a deep sense of exclusion and failure.

There are parallels to be found in the plots of Tomizza's and Cankar's novels as both involve a fight for justice and the experience of exile. As importantly, both works have a rural setting that is characterized by an attachment to the land. Even though Cankar's investigation into the peasant's background and perspectives deals with a period earlier than that of *Materada* (while Cankar's Slovenia was still under Austrian domination, Tomizza's Istrian village had switched from Italian to socialist Yugoslav), Tomizza inherits the Slav world view and values of Cankar's novel.

The importance attributed to the possession of land is explored in *Materada* through the story of Francesco Coslovich and his family, who struggle to obtain their rights to the estate that they should have inherited from their ageing uncle. The novel begins with Francesco's discovery of the uncle's will, an event that triggers a long dispute that runs parallel to the worsening of the political situation (that is, the annexation of the Istrian peninsula by Yugoslavia, the subsequent souring of the relationship between the two countries and the massive exile of the Italian population):

> E pensai che quella era stata la guerra, la guerra per tutti. Ma che dopo c'era stata un'altra guerra, riservata a noi soli, la quale aveva avuto anch'essa i suoi morti, i suoi dolori, ed aveva avuto inizio proprio quando tutto il mondo gridava alla pace e alla liberazione; quando i partigiani erano usciti dai boschi, avevano sfilato per le vie di Buje e di Umago lanciando all'aria i berretti, e si era istituito il nuovo regime.[6]

> [And I thought that was the war, the war for everyone. But after it came another war, reserved only for us, that also had its dead, its pain, and began just when the whole world proclaimed peace and liberation; when the partisans came out from the woods, they marched through the streets of Buje and Umag launching their caps into the air, and the new regime was established.]

The new regime imposes strict rules in Istria as well as drastic political changes, and this reduces the amount of land that Francesco stands to receive. Although *Materada* portrays the vicissitudes of a particular Istrian village, the novel opens up a wider perspective, as the troubles that Francesco faces will affect many villages and towns. Once Francesco and his family have given up the idea of taking the ageing uncle to court, the work gives more space to conversations and encounters that progressively converge on the impossibility of remaining in Istria and then the final decision to move. Like Francesco, many of his countrymen seek to reach Trieste, carrying only transportable goods and abandoning their properties. In an atmosphere of progressive tension, the fact of exile begins to materialize in the community, reaching its climax in a final Mass that takes place without a priest.

The story revolves around the issue of land. In a similar way to Cankar's novel, land summarizes the perspectives and the identities of characters, helping them to affirm their sense of belonging, but it is also the most stable thing available in life in a frontier region. Being caught in between cultures means fluctuating between different cultural backgrounds and languages, among uncertain borders and attributions. With land, the novel's characters find something to which they can always refer despite the troubles that afflict them, even when, as happens with Francesco and his family, they leave their village.

Materada continues Cankar's theme of attachment to the land, but Tomizza's novel assumes a new plural perspective. As suggested by the title, the work is based not on the experience of a single character but on a village, which is, as it were, put on stage to display its multicultural character. *Materada* has often been described as a 'choral' novel, that is, one in which a plurality of viewpoints, emerging from various episodes of dialogue, represents a community as a whole. It has also been noted that the great number of secondary characters, who are sometimes only mentioned or are but partially drawn, contributes to a sense of the collectivity. As Geno Pampaloni writes: 'I personaggi non sono, come individui, molto rilevati e lavorati psicologicamente, ma si integrano con naturalezza nell'ambiente e nella collettività. Ed è proprio questo il risultato maggiore, e più interessante, del romanzo' [The characters are not, as individuals, very prominent or psychologically worked, but they are integrated naturally into the environment and the community. And this is really the greatest and most interesting achievement of the novel].[7] The novel embodies the troubles of a village, which is recreated through the voices of its inhabitants. In this sense, *Materada* inherits the famed 'chorality' of Verga's *Malavoglia*, which follows the principle of allowing an entire village to emerge and act as the protagonist of the work.

Despite Francesco being the narrator of the story, in *Materada* an entire village takes centre stage. However, this 'chorality' is challenged by the use of the first person and by the centrifugal force of exile that scatters characters. The first impression given to the reader is of a fragmented chorus, made up of different perspectives which flow through the narrative, creating tension and collisions. Indeed, characters surface in the narrative, contrasting with each other, making objections and raising their opinions. For example, when the people power comes to force Francesco's uncle to give land to his nephews, several characters interact violently:

> 'Buonasera, signori' disse. 'Cosa c'è di nuovo?'. Tutti si alzarono in piedi. 'Scendete' disse Vanja. 'Abbiamo qualcosa da dirvi'. Ma lui non si fidava, e guardava in viso uno per uno. 'Posso ascoltare anche da qui. E poi, tolti questi quattro galantuomini, non so chi voi siate per dovervi rispondere'. 'Avete troppe arie, zietto' fece quello degli Affari interni. Intervenne Franjo, gli andò incontro e disse: 'Niente di male, barba. Siamo venuti per parlare da uomini'.

> Lo tirò giù in cucina. C'era silenzio e molta tensione. Guardai le donne, i figli che osservavano quella scena a bocca aperta, e aprii la porta del tinello. (*M*, pp. 90–91)
>
> ['Good evening, Sirs,' he said, 'What's new?' All rose to their feet. 'Sit,' said Vanya. 'We have something to tell you'. But he did not trust them, and looked into their faces one by one. 'I can hear from here. And then, apart from four gentlemen, I do not know who you are to have to answer to'. 'You are too full of yourself, Uncle' said the one from Internal Affairs. Franjo intervened, went to him and said: 'Nothing bad, *barba*. We came to talk like men'. He brought him down to the kitchen. There was silence and a lot of tension. I looked at the women, the children who were watching that scene with awe, and opened the door of the servant's quarters.]

Most of the time, pieces of dialogue emphasize the frustration of characters who are overcome by events; their anger is expressed in quick interactions as well as longer discussions involving friends and relatives. Their little world has been torn apart by rifts that cannot be avoided. As Roberto Damiani writes: '*Materada* respirava un'aria inconsueta di coerenza problematica e eccitava una partecipazione viva e sanguigna [...] indicava decisa il contrappunto di un coro d'interessi agitati da un contesto storico e politico avaro di chiarezza. Un coro, appunto' [*Materada* breathed an unusual air of problematic coherence and aroused a lively and visceral involvement [...] it set out firmly the counterpoint of a chorus of excited interests from a historical and political context devoid of clarity. A chorus, precisely].[8]

However, the fragmentation created by *Materada*'s chorus, which also gives space to historical digressions, achieves a final harmony, thanks to a balance between involvement and neutrality:

> Apposta in questi due romanzi (*Materada* e *La ragazza di Petrovia*) ho voluto impersonificare esclusivamente il ruolo del cantore attento e a volte commosso; del cantastorie, se si vuole, cittadino beninteso di quella terra e quindi parte anonima di un coro. Ricorda i Fratelli Karamazov? Ad un certo punto, al processo di Mitja, stranamente Dostoevskij introduce la prima persona, viene a parlare del 'nostro distretto'. Un accorgimento tecnico di grande efficacia che è bastato a restituire una dimensione reale, partecipe, così prepotentemente russa, alla tragica vicenda dei Karamazov; e proprio dopo aver portato fatti e personaggi ai limiti dell'irrealtà, o addirittura, dell'inverosimiglianza. Io ho voluto mantenere appunto una narrazione obiettiva ma vincolata ai colori e ai sapori particolarissimi del mio 'distretto', che almeno giovanilmente non sentivo molto estraneo all'anonimo 'distretto' della Grande Russia dell'Ottocento.[9]
>
> [Deliberately in these two novels (*Materada* and *La ragazza di Petrovia*) I wanted to represent exclusively the role of the attentive and sometimes moved poet; of the storyteller, if you want, a citizen of that land and therefore an anonymous part of a choir. Does it remember the Brothers Karamazov? At one point, at the trial of Mitja, Dostoevsky oddly introduces the first person, he speaks of 'our district'. A highly effective technical device that gave a sense of reality, so overwhelmingly Russian, which participated in the tragic story of the Karamazov; and right after bringing facts and characters to the limits of unreality, or rather, to unlikelihood. I just wanted to keep an objective narration, but one constrained by the colours and flavours of my special

'district', that, at least in my youth, I did not feel very alien from the anonymous 'district' of the Great Russia of the nineteenth century.]

The novel is composed around dialogues that bind the entire village into the novel, while at the same time the thoughts of the central character Francesco intermingle with the narrator who relates the story neutrally and allows a great variety of secondary characters to emerge. This harks back to the technique on display in Verga's *Malavoglia* as described by Guido Baldi where the narrator is described as a 'narratore camaleontico' [chameleon narrator].[10] The narrator here becoming independent from the writer in a process called the 'artificio della regressione' [artifice of regression] of the author.[11] The aim is to allow characters to freely express their behaviours, beliefs, ideologies, and ways of thinking.

The multiple perspectives in this world find their own representation, moving in parallel to Francesco's train of thought as he also mulls over the novel behaviour of his compatriots and contemplates the newly-established regime, while at the same time the narrator describes the situations and characters, interrupting them to provide a context for the reader. Therefore, if the first person seems to distance Francesco from the chorus, on the other hand, the mediation of the narrator allows this character to become part of it: 'Dal coro (non a caso il romanzo si concludeva con una liturgia dal significato straziante) la voce di un testimone' [From the choir (it is not by chance that the novel ends with a heart-rending liturgy) the voice of a witness].[12] Francesco manages to draw his own space in the chorus, being clearly recognizable among the others, but he also is subject to the same conditions. *Materada*'s secret is its compositional power: singular and plural experiences are combined, there is an amalgamation of moments of introspection and conversation, and all this under the pressing dynamics of the story of a collapsing world.

Materada's chorus fulfils another aim: it draws attention to language which reveals more, and in a more profound and original manner, of the dramatic situation. The predominance in the text of unmediated dialogue allows for the possibility of inserting the language spoken by characters directly, thus foregrounding the multilingual character of Istria. As I will point out in this chapter, in *Materada* language unveils the complex dynamics of ethnic and political fluctuations and mixtures. As Guagnini suggests: 'Vanno anche ricordate sia la particolare attenzione alla lingua usata dai personaggi nelle varie circostanze sia le notazioni linguistiche che devono permettere al lettore di ricostruire la complessità del contesto anche da questo punto di vista' [Let us remember both the particular attention to the language used by characters in the various circumstances and the linguistic notations that should enable the reader to reconstruct the complexity of the context also from this point of view].[13]

La miglior vita, Tomizza's fresco of the Istrian land seen through the character of a sacristan, Martin Crusich, also underlines the complexity of the Italo-Croatian linguistic situation but on an extended temporal scale. In the sequence of priests described by Crusich, which follows historical and political developments, the important role played by language emerges. The choice of language made by a priest is itself a declaration of identity and belonging that influences the train of events in the parish. Among the chorus of voices, there are opposing figures such as the Venetian Don Ferdinando representing the Italian community and the Polish Don Kuzma who leans more to the Slav side. But there is above all a more conciliatory priest, a key character within the novel, who represents a model of behaviour for Crusich: Don Stipe. The identity of the priests is strongly characterized by their origin, and this is usually expressed through the language they use during mass, when talking to secondary characters, or when making notes in their diary. From these choices surface traces of conflict. The following example illustrates both how the language may easily switch within the same context, and how its use determines a specific point of view, not devoid of political consequences.[14] Here, the sacristan reads a page of diary written by Don Stipe:

> Non mi raccontò del gruppo di studenti scalmanati che per poco non lo avevano aggredito. Lo lessi nel suo diario, lo sguardo caduto sulle grida trascritte in italiano, non in dialetto: 'Dagli al prete schiavo, acchiappiamo la canaglia!'. E sotto aveva annotato nella propria lingua: 'Anche la vecchia portinaia del provvidenziale palazzo nel quale mi ero rifugiato notò che vestivo da sacerdote slavo, eppure mi accolse nel proprio sgabuzzino quando già mormoravo fra me: Signore, la Tua volontà sia fatta, non la mia'. (*MV*, pp. 68–69)

> [He did not tell me about the rowdy group of students who had nearly attacked him. I read it in his diary, my gaze fell on the shouts transcribed in Italian, not in dialect: 'Beat up the Slav priest, let us grab the rogue!'. Underneath he wrote in his own language: 'Even the old concierge of the providential building in which I sheltered noticed that I dressed like a Slav priest, but harboured me in his closet when I was already murmuring to myself: Lord, thy will be done, not mine'.]

Tomizza takes advantage of the implications linguistic choices have in his land, shaping a texture which maintains the chorality of *Materada*. Language in both works becomes a sophisticated tool, which is the result of in-depth investigations made by the writer, as suggested by Mario Lunetta:

> L'elemento più vistoso del raccontare Fulvio Tomizza [...] che si rivela, un libro dopo l'altro e in ogni libro di più, il più costante amore e il più gelosamente tesaurizzato patrimonio dello scrittore istriano, nutrito e goduto con affezione più che strumentale, certo al di là delle cose che è delegata a comunicare.[15]

> [The most eye-catching element of Fulvio Tomizza's storytelling [...] which reveals itself, one book after the other and even more in each book, is the most constant love and most jealously treasured heritage of the Istrian writer, nurtured and enjoyed with a more than self-serving affection, certainly beyond things that it is empowered to communicate.]

To give an idea of *Materada* and *La miglior vita*'s complexity, the idiom used in the world of the novels is built up from two dialects (the Istro-Venetian and the Čakavian) based on languages that do not share the same matrix (Italian and Croatian). This linguistic underground is filtered through the Italian language, which has been chosen to recount the story, but which is, in turn, deeply contaminated by these hidden elements. In other words, although the language chosen by Tomizza is Italian, the linguistic underground (including the structure and the syntax) seems to arise from others. This approach leads to the consideration of *Materada* and *La miglior vita* as 'self-translated' novels. I will now consider Istria's intersection of bilingualism and dialects, before analyzing *Materada*'s special linguistic phenomena.

'Uno scrittore tra due dialetti di matrice linguistica diversa'

Although the essay 'Uno scrittore tra due dialetti di matrice linguistica diversa', which is included in the collection *Alle spalle di Trieste* (1995), was published more than thirty years after *Materada* (1960), it helps us here as the basis for a linguistic understanding of the novel.[16] Tomizza's purpose in the essay is to set out clearly the linguistic landscape of Istria, to make the processes behind the languages used in his novels available to his readers. By investigating these mechanisms, he explores bilingualism in literature and, above all, focuses on the unusual phenomenon of the mixing of dialects drawn from two different languages. To be more precise, the writer's literary production is based on a convergence of languages that are wedged into the Italian narrative, as I will now show.

Let us begin by setting out the coordinates on which Tomizza's essay is based. As its title suggests, the question concerning a writer who is caught between two dialects taken from languages that do not share the same matrix can be located within two categories: on the one hand, the phenomenon of dialects in literature; on the other hand, bilingualism (or multilingualism). The first category in which *Materada*'s linguistic dimension is grounded is dialect. Characters express themselves in their Italo-Croatian dialect, while standard languages are considered alien. In his early works, when Tomizza focuses on Istria, he tries to employ dialect more or less directly, seeking to mirror the 'real face' of his land. The interaction of dialects within a standard language positions Tomizza in the Italian literary tradition of the novecento, which from Verga onwards started to include dialect in literature. In common with Verga, but also with Gadda, Pavese, and many others, Tomizza has a leaning towards dialect due to its immediate adherence to a specific place and culture, which standard languages are barely able to touch.

The second category that defines Tomizza's work is bilingualism, which refers to writers who use a second language in their works, as described in Chapter 2. These languages can be parallel, that is, ones that a writer has learnt from birth (such as Steiner, Nabokov etc.), or a language that is acquired as foreign and used for writing (such as Eva Hoffman, Milan Kundera, Joseph Brodsky, Joseph Conrad etc.).[17] 'Uno scrittore tra due dialetti di matrice linguistica diversa' recalls the first chapter of Levi's *Il sistema periodico*, in which the author from Piedmont gives an account of the linguistic interactions between the local dialect and the Jewish language, providing several clarifying examples. Following the same structure, Tomizza offers a detailed explanation of how the languages are used in *Materada* (and in his initial literary production), starting with a clear geographical reference. His language is evidently influenced by the context in which he was born and lived before exile; it is not a mixture of languages that one can learn, combine, and apply, rather it is the result of the unique circumstances of the Adriatic peninsula, where the Veneto dialect which is prevalent on the Istrian coast interacts with the Croatian dialect of the hinterland: 'Questo idioma popolare attinge liberamente dall'italiano (attraverso il familiare dialetto veneto) e, in misura pressoché uguale, dal croato e dallo sloveno' (S, p. 183) [This popular language draws freely from Italian (through the familiar Venetian dialect) and, in almost equal measure, from the Croatian and Slovene]. This situation originates from the historical stratifications of Istria, that have progressively formed a linguistic blend:

> Dalla penetrazione della lingua ufficiale della Serenissima, si ebbe un apporto di idioma veneto che alterò l'originaria parlata croato-slovena. Il successivo passaggio del territorio all'impero austroungarico [...] accrebbe la fusione della popolazione eterogenea, fino a sommergere le rispettive origini, e promosse un'ulteriore contaminazione delle lingue nazionali. Per cui all'antica parlata 'illirica', sostenuta anche dai riti officiati nella medesima lingua, ma che peraltro già accoglieva numerose voci e forme idiomatiche venete, si affiancò un dialetto alternativo di radice veneta, talmente insufficiente da doversi esso pure appoggiare alle due lingue slave. (S, pp. 184–85)

> [From the penetration of the official language of the Serenissima came the contribution of the Venetian dialect that altered the original Croato-Slovene parlance. The following passage of the territory to the Austro-Hungarian Empire [...] increased the fusion of the heterogeneous population, to the point of submerging their origins, and promoted further contamination of the national languages. Up alongside the old 'Illyrian' parlance, supported by the rites conducted in the same language, that moreover upheld numerous vocables and idiomatic Venetian forms, came an alternative dialect of Venetian root, so inadequate that it also had to be supported by the two Slavic languages.]

The succession of conquests, but also the encounter and overlapping of the Italian and the Croatian spheres, describes a marginal land that has created its own specific linguistic expression. In Tomizza's words, that population 'assai spesso premuta dalle conflittualità etniche della frontiera, ha saputo scavarsi nel tempo un alveo proprio di espressione linguistica' (S, p. 183) [very often borne down on by ethnic conflicts of the frontier, has been able to dig its own channel of expression over time]. He observes that, despite the conflicts, migrations, and cultural fractures that typified the area, Istria developed its own unique language. In *Materada*'s village and its surroundings, the Italo-Croatian union seems to have found an even more remarkable hybrid form. If the towns of the Istrian coast are imbued with Venetian culture and dialect, while in the backcountry the Croatian element prevails, Tomizza's village is positioned right in the middle:

> L'area in esame ha quale centro la parrocchia di Materada con la sua ventina di frazioni nutrite o ridotte a una sola casa. [...] Al di là di queste borgate ci si scontra col veneto dei centri costieri ed anche interni quali Buje, oppure con lo slavo delle campagne più addentrate che si rivela maggiormente sensibile o al 'čakavo' croato o alla lingua slovena. (S, p. 184)

> [The area in question has at its centre the parish of Materada with its twenty hamlets fed or reduced to a single house. [...] Beyond these villages one encounters the Venetian coastal towns as well as others such as internal Buje,

or the Slav of the innermost countryside, who proves to be more sensitive to the 'Čakavian' Croatian or Slovene.]

Materada's inhabitants communicate choosing one dialect or the other, according to the context and the interlocutors. However, despite being kept separate, the two dialects may from time to time converge, displaying mixtures. The reason behind this phenomenon can be traced back to the proximity of the two languages, but also to their 'poverty', which leads them to interact, reciprocally 'borrowing' words and expressions, to fill gaps. As Tomizza points out, 'Pur articolata in due espressioni linguistiche, la parlata di *Materada* resta povera, ridotta all'osso' (S, p. 188) [While articulated in two linguistic expressions, the parlance of *Materada* remains poor, cut to the bone]. He also gives characterizations that strongly mark the two different linguistic domains. The Croatian dialect seems to reflect the rural condition of the inhabitants of the countryside, their relationship with hard work in the fields, abandoned goods, plants, herbs, and wild animals. However, in comparison to the Croatian or the Slovene standard languages, the dialect lacks some crucial words, for example 'wood':

> La (parlata) slava possiede maggiori riserve per definire le cose dimesse, i lavori più duri [...]; per indicare le piante, le erbe e gli animali selvatici, senza tuttavia mostrare di conoscere lo sloveno *gòzd* né il croato *šùma* [...]. Ciò comproverebbe la massiccia provenienza di questa gente dalla deserta Dalmazia, dove l'aspra vegetazione [...] non riesce a infittirsi né ad elevarsi in un bosco. (S, p. 188)
>
> [The Slavic (parlance) possesses larger reserves for defining humble things, hardest jobs [...]; for indicating plants, herbs and animals of the woodlands, without appearing to know the Slovene *gòzd* or the Croatian *šùma* [...]. This would prove the large number of people who have come from the deserted Dalmatia, where the rough vegetation [...] cannot thicken or rise to a forest.]

Far from being a homogeneous linguistic idiom, this dialect has two standard languages of reference: Croatian, which is prevalent, and Slovene. Although Tomizza groups their dialects together under the Slav category, Materada is a village in which people speak a Croatian-based dialect mixed with Slovene words. On several occasions the writer underlines this, referring to Materada's population as:

> Una specie di sottominoranza destinata a rimanere sempre tale, che usava indifferentemente il dialetto veneto e il dialetto slavo, non dico sloveno né croato, perché entrambe le parlate erano da noi mescolate e in quell'area oggi sotto la Repubblica di Croazia si dice *dèlati* in luogo di *ráditi, hiša* anziché *kuća, das* invece di *kiša*.[18]
>
> [A kind of sub-minority destined to remain always such, that used without preference the Venetian and Slavic dialects, I do not say the Slovene or Croatian, because they were both mixed by us and in that area today under the Republic of Croatia people say *dèlati* instead of *ráditi, hiša* instead of *kuća, das* instead of *kiša*.]

The Istro-Venetian dialect can also be defined as 'poor', but it mirrors the maritime traditions of coastal Istria and a life sustained by commerce on the sea. This dialect is more apt to define domestic tools and the world of maritime commerce:

> Il veneto, dal canto suo, spadroneggia nella denominazione degli utensili domestici, degli strumenti di lavori più affrancati, nella navigazione e nei commerci: *stagnàda* (dall'italiano *stagnata* per calderone), *bòrca* (per barca), *cariùla* (per carriola), *cazziùla* (per cazzuola, dei muratori), *magasìn* (per magazzino), *sensiàl* (per sensale), *butìga* (per bottega) eccetera. [...] Sorprende la scarsità di verbi nella parlata italiana. (S, pp. 188–89)
>
> [The Venetian, meanwhile, dominates in the denomination of household utensils, the more advanced work tools, navigation, and commerce: *stagnàda* (from Italian *stagnata* for cauldron), *bòrca* (boat), *cariùla* (hand-cart), *cazziùla* (a bricklayer's trowel), *magasìn* (store), *sensiàl* (matchmaker), *butìga* (workshop) etc. [...] The scarcity of verbs in the Italian parlance is surprising.]

This consideration recalls the Slovene writer Alojz Rebula's statement: '[Qualche traduttore] potrebbe, forse, a esempio, aver trovato il sostantivo e l'aggettivo sloveno meno ricco di quello italiano, il verbo sloveno, invece, forse più espressivo'. [[Some translators] might, perhaps, for example, have found the Slovene noun and adjective less rich than the Italian, the Slovene verb, however, perhaps more meaningful].[19] Arising from the coexistence of two languages and cultures in the same territory, the two dialects seem to have found, at Materada, their complement. The rural and the maritime idioms represent the double soul of a land, each offering linguistic features that represent their sphere. Taken individually, they are not able to cover the range of a standard language, they need to be combined to make a whole.

Tomizza's essay offers several examples that illustrate the interaction between the two languages which forms the framework on which his works are built. He presents the idea of two languages that are more suitable to deal with one domain rather than another but also discusses other mechanisms, which I shall now examine. The first might be generated by the 'gaps' present in one language, which can be filled with words taken from the other. By employing Muysken's analysis, which specifically focuses on bilingual speech, Tomizza's essay includes 'borrowings', which can be defined as the process of 'entering alien elements into a lexicon. It is not always the case, however, that borrowing can be seen as a form of simple vocabulary extension'.[20] Cases of borrowings from Istro-Venetian that are incorporated in 'Slav' sentences are '*barèta* (in italiano berrètto e in veneto barèta); *bòzza* (in italiano bòccia e in veneto bòzza-bòssa, per bottiglia)' (S, p. 186) [*barèta* (in Italian berrètto and in Venetian barèta [for beret]); *bòzza* (in Italian bòccia and in Venetian bòzza-bòssa, for bottle)]. Tomizza also shows the opposite mechanism: 'Esempi di termini croati e sloveni che il dialetto di radice veneta annovera come suoi: *òreh* (nelle due lingue slave *òreh* = noce)' (S, p. 186) [Examples of Croatian and Slovene terms that the Venetian dialect includes: *òreh* (in the two Slavic languages *òreh* = walnut)].

The Istrian double dialect frequently simply borrows words from the other language and sometimes the original pattern is maintained, but most of the time the new context transforms it. Tomizza lingers over nouns that are taken and adapted from the Istro-Venetian dialect and placed into the Croatian one through 'insertion', the introduction of a constituent into a construction of the leading language:

> Nel dialetto di radice croato-slovena si registrano molto frequentemente delle

> espressioni venete [...] spesso condotte alla pronuncia e alla contratta costruzione slava, quasi per camuffarne la naturale acquisizione (in realtà per cercare di conformarle alla parlata slava). Esempi presi alla rinfusa: *got* (in italiano *gotto*, nel veneto *goto* = bicchiere); *pirùn* (dal veneto *piròn* = forchetta); *piàt* (italiano *piatto*, veneto *piato*); *luz* (l'italiano *luce* e il veneto *luse* vengono accostati allo sloveno *luč*); *lanzùn* (in italiano *lenzuolo* e in veneto *linziòl*); *cussìn* (*cuscino* e *cussin*) ecc. (S, p. 186)

> [In the Croato-Slovene dialect Venetian expressions frequently appear [...] often changed to the Slavic pronunciation and construction, almost to camouflage the original provenance (actually to try to make them conform to the Slavic parlance). Examples taken randomly: *got* (in Italian *gotto*, Venetian *goto* = glass); *pirùn* (from Venetian *piròn* = fork); *piàt* (Italian *piatto*, Venetian *piato*); *luz* (Italian *luce* and Venetian *luse* are compared to the Slovene *luč*); *lanzùn* (Italian *lenzuolo* and Venetian *linziòl*); *cussìn* (*cuscino* e *cussin*) etc.]

He also considers the 'insertion' of words from the Croatian dialect into the Istro-Venetian one:

> Esempi di termini croati e sloveni che il dialetto di radice veneta annovera come suoi, più inasprendoli che non addolcendoli: *lèscagn* o la metatesi *lèsgnac* (in croato *lijèska* e in sloveno *lèska* = nocciolo); *scrgat* corrisponde a *cicala* (dal croato *škrgut* e dallo sloveno *škrgat* che significano *stridore*, scambio evidente tra causa ed effetto); *pizùrca* (dal croato *pečùrka* = *fungo* in genere); *bràsda* (in croato *bražda* = solco); *còsa* (dal croato *kòza* = capra); *rèbaz* (in croato *vràbac* = passero) ecc. (S, pp. 186–87)

> [Examples of Croatian and Slovene terms that the Venetian dialect includes, sharpening them more than softening them: *lèscagn* or the metathesis *lèsgnac* (Croatian *lijèska* and Slovene *lèska* = hazelnut); *scrgat* corresponds to cicada (from Croatian *škrgut* and Slovene *škrgat* that mean screeching, obvious exchange between cause and effect); *pizùrca* (Croatian *pečùrka* = generic mushroom); *bràsda* (Croatian *bražda* = furrow); *còsa* (Croatian *kòza* = goat); *rèbaz* (Croatian *vràbac* = sparrow) etc.]

This process, which usually concerns the insertion of nouns, leads to the generation of some unique new expressions when it involves adjectives or verbs. For instance, as Tomizza illustrates: 'Non mancano gli accoppiamenti misti di aggettivo e sostantivo, sia in un dialetto che nell'altro: *brùta svigna* (brutto porco) o l'affettuoso *mio sin* (figlio mio) o il sospirato *dìzzna piova* (benedetta pioggia!)' (S, p. 187) [There are also mixed pairs of adjective and noun, either in one dialect or the other: *brùta svigna* (dirty swine) or the tender *mio sin* (my son) or the sighed *dìzzna piova* (blessed rain!)]. Verbs undergo the same process. Referring to the example he provides to show the lack of verbs in the Istro-Venetian dialect, he explains the solution adopted:

> Sorprende la scarsità dei verbi nella parlata italiana, per i quali è dunque d'obbligo ricorrere all'infinito slavo, troncato, e facendoli precedere dal servile 'fare': *me se fa smìlit* (mi impietosisce), *el me ga fato smùtit* (mi ha confuso), *go fato scus* (ho tirato fuori), *i se fa zìmbat* (si lasciano penzolare, dall'albero) [...]. In qualche caso il verbo italiano è coniugato nella forma croata: *zza-pensos?* (che cosa pensi?). (S, p. 189)

> [It is surprising the scarcity of verbs in the Italian parlance, which necessitates resorting to the Slavic infinitive, truncated, and preceded by the modal 'fare' (do): *me se fa smìlit* (I am moved to pity), *el me ga fato smùtit* (it confused me), *go fato scus* (I pulled out), *i se fa zìmbat* (are left dangling from the tree) [...]. In some cases the Italian verb is conjugated in the Croatian form: *zza- pensos?* (what do you think?).]

This last consideration seems to recall Muysken's notion of 'congruent lexicalization', which occurs when 'two languages partially share their processing systems' and 'material from different lexical inventories' flow into 'a shared grammatical structure'.[21] In contrast to mere insertion, 'congruent lexicalization' steps up the process of contamination between the two languages, as some words that share the same root in Istro-Venetian and Čakavian may turn into new combinations. This is the case with the following: '*missiàr* (dall'italiano *mèscere* e dagli slavi *mèšati*) o [...] *ùlika* (dall'italiano *ulivo* e dal croato *ùljika*), *laco* (rispettivamente *lago* e *lòkva*, per stagno), *ciaculàr* (dall'italiano chiacchierare, dal veneto *ciaculàr* e dal croato-dalmata *čakulàt*)' (S, p. 187) [*missiàr* (from Italian *mèscere* and Slav *mèšati* [mix]) or [...] *ùlika* (from Italian *ulivo* and Croatian *ùljika* [street]), *laco* (respectively *lago* and *lòkva* [pond]), *ciaculàr* (from Italian chatting, Venetian *ciaculàr* and Croato-Dalmatian *čakulàt*)].

The relationship between the two dialects is based on processes that shape internally their lexical, morphosyntactic, semantic, and grammatical features. The result is that the two parallel tongues may flow alongside one another, but also combine. The interaction between them seems to be a function of historical events and daily contaminations, but also casual circumstances and needs. Tomizza gives an account of phenomena that can be clearly categorized even though the coexistence of the two dialects has also generated unpredictable situations, as with the following:

> L'enigmatico *sèlin* (= sempre), che non esiste in alcuna altra lingua né in nessun dialetto nemmeno d'Istria, ed è certamente di derivazione albanese, ispirato forse dal lungo regno dei sultani Selìm e Solimano che si avvicendarono al trono di Turchia per 150 anni' (S, p. 187)

> [The enigmatic *sèlin* (= always), which does not exist in any other language or in any dialect even in Istria, and is certainly of Albanian origin, inspired perhaps by the long reign of the sultans Selìm and Suleiman who followed one another on the Turkish throne for 150 years].

The linguistic mixture described by Tomizza derives from two languages in contact, which, in his analysis, are compared to two branches of a river that intermingle. This metaphor suggests the birth of a new language out of the previous two, a sort of hybrid language that would symbolize an Italo-Croatian union. Tomizza's wish for this has not been achieved, but it illustrates the unique linguistic pattern of a mixed land:

> Questi due corsi, che quasi di continuo s'intreccianomescolando le loro povere acque, inducono talvolta a pensare che essi non fungevano da canale di scolo tra le differenti parlate nazionali, bensì venivano a costituire una terza via, la quale, se incoraggiata dall'esterno e divenuta consapevole nel suo interno, avrebbe potuto rappresentare una soluzione linguistica italo-slava. (S, p. 185)

> [These two courses, which almost continuously intertwine mingling their poor waters, sometimes seem to suggest that they might not act as the gutter between the different national languages, but come to be a third way, which, if encouraged by the outside and by awareness within, could have been an Italo-Slavic linguistic solution.]

In his essay, Tomizza describes the language spoken by Materada's inhabitants showing a fragmentation that is not present in standard languages. Sudden switches and mixtures may lead to a mode of speech that makes approximation and even mistakes likely, and this weighs on the linguistic context that Tomizza must deal with. Bearing in mind the series of processes already examined, it is evident that he cannot avoid a series of difficulties, such as the question of which language to adopt in his works.

If different languages shape the background of a writer, there inevitably comes the choice of the language or languages to employ in his work: when it comes to the act of writing clarification is needed. Writers who are bilingual or multilingual by birth must, to a greater extent than those who have acquired a second language at a later stage, consider and choose the language that they wish to use. As Jane Miller suggests, this becomes a 'deliberate choice, based on the writer's sense that a particular language embodies particular traditions of thought and culture which make it preferable [...] presumably to any other language'.[22]

When faced with a choice of languages, Tomizza reflects on his situation. The story he is planning to write must find a language — albeit a hybrid language — to begin. In his words:

> Nell'accingermi a raccontare questa storia [...] avvertivo il desiderio di ricomporre sia pure in extremis la concordia perduta, di denunciare gli affronti subiti, ma anche di far conoscere al mondo il tragico paradosso di una comunità in parte semi-taliana e in maggioranza semi-slava che nello scontro frontale tra i due Paesi da cui aveva avuto origine trovava la sua definitiva dispersione. E scelsi la lingua che conoscevo meglio e che più agevolmente mi sarebbe diventata letteraria. (S, p. 192)

> [In preparing myself to tell this story [...] I felt the desire to recompose albeit in extremis the lost harmony, to denounce the insults suffered, but also to let the world know the tragic paradox of a community in part semi-Italian and for its most part semi-Slav, that in the head-on confrontation between the two countries from which it originated it found its final dispersion. And I chose the language I knew best and that would more easily become literary.]

By picking Italian, Tomizza shows that for bilingual writers, the relationship between languages is always unbalanced, or at least asymmetrical, and that both are in danger of being overwhelmed. One of the languages always runs the risk of oppressing the other or others, favouring a specific point of view or adapting to a certain context better; the literary barycentre of the bilingual writer is difficult to find. As noted by Julien Green, an American writer who used both French and English: 'There cannot be a perfect balance between two languages, two ways of feeling, which is not tipped to one side or another by one's interior being'.[23]

Tomizza's decision to adopt Italian instead of Croatian involves a new linguistic orientation. He is aware of the daily contamination of languages in his repertoire: 'Su ognuno di noi, e su di me, mistilingue, in particolare, grava la compresenza nel colloquiare quotidiano di un'altra lingua o di più lingue' [On each of us, and on me, mixed-language, in particular, weighs the presence in everyday conversation of another or more languages].[24] Therefore, he is not only worried about the difficulty of representing his background; in seeking to offer a comprehensive representation of his land, he is at risk of being misinterpreted, because his bilingualism may affect the language that he uses. There might follow from this a lack of understanding of his condition:

> Un *errore* di grammatica o di sintassi, peccato veniale in altre parti d'Italia, qui diventa un *orrore* [...] da noi invece inducono a temere di appoggiarci inconsapevolmente a un'altra lingua, tedesca o slava, la prima al massimo criticata per la sua pesantezza, la seconda rifiutata con sdegno o messa in ridicolo tutt'oggi.[25]

> [A grammar or syntax *error*, venial sin in other parts of Italy, here becomes a *horror* [...] for us instead it leads to a fear of unknowingly leaning on another language, German or Slavic, the first at most criticized for its heaviness, the second rejected with scorn or ridiculed even today.]

A tangible acknowledgment of the phenomenon described here is found in Tomizza's correspondence with editors at Mondadori. Elio Vittorini, who enjoyed *Materada* and gave only marginal suggestions, was, on the other hand, concerned about the language. As he writes in a letter to Tomizza on 18 March 1959:

> Il compito di questa mia lettera è quello di indicarglieli (difetti di stile e di struttura) con la maggior precisione possibile. Difetti di stile: i più facilmente eliminabili, perché basta che lei sottoponga il testo ad una attenta revisione. [...] Ma, in genere, sono errori di grammatica o di lingua che lei deve correggere. Esempio in italiano non si può dire 'ne metteva fuori un pochi per comprare', ma 'ne metteva fuori pochi' o 'ne metteva fuori un po''; oppure 'feci di motto a mia moglie', riferito ad un gesto, non è esatto (meglio dire 'Feci segno a mia moglie'); né si può dire 'voleva che io andari' ma 'voleva che io andassi'. Come vede, piccoli difetti che lasciano inalterata la sostanza del testo.[26]

> [The task of this letter is to indicate them (style and structure defects) with the greatest possible precision. Style defects: the easiest to remove, as long as you carefully revise the text. [...] But, in general, it is grammar or language mistakes that you should correct. For example, in Italian you cannot say 'ne metteva fuori un pochi per comprare', but 'ne metteva fuori pochi' or 'ne metteva fuori un po''; or, 'feci di motto a mia moglie', referring to a gesture, is not correct (better to say 'Feci segno a mia moglie'); nor can you say 'voleva che io andari' but 'voleva che io andassi'. As you see, small defects that leave unchanged the substance of the text.]

In the process of revising the novel, Tomizza had to modify a language that presents difficulties for the Italian reader. He was aware of the asperities of his situation: 'Valendomi dei suggerimenti dell'illustre Vittorini, ho cercato di apportare delle modifiche intese a eliminare gli aspetti negativi, specialmente riferibili a certe espressioni regionalistiche usate in un'area troppo angusta per acquistare validità linguistica' [Availing myself of the suggestions of the illustrious Vittorini, I tried to make some changes designed to eliminate the negative aspects, especially those related to certain regional expressions used in an area that is too small to offer linguistic validity].[27] Tomizza knows that as in Svevo's case, being a 'giuliano' writer meant facing this linguistic question. His task became to balance, on the one hand, his desire to mediate the context in which *Materada* is set and, on the other, the requirements of his editor. Although the Italian he uses in his letters, as well as that which he will later employ in his novels, is certainly not deformed by this problem, he had doubts about certain expressions and sought to improve his text.

However, Tomizza also seems determined not to lose the unique character of his subject and the varied richness of his bilingualism. He insists on using what he defines, in a letter to Mondadori, as certain 'irrepressible' words: 'allego un breve elenco di insopprimibili vocaboli regionali dell'uso vivo e di vocaboli importati con la occupazione jugoslava, entrambi corredati da brevi noticine' [I attach a short list of irrepressible regional words of current use and of words imported with the Yugoslav occupation, both accompanied by brief notes].[28] Even more remarkable, given this situation, is an example of switching from an Italian word to the corresponding Istro-Venetian one, which clearly illustrates the intention of the writer to be faithful to his background. Without considering the potential difficulty encountered by the reader, in *Materada*'s first manuscript, the word 'zio' [uncle] in the sentence 'Come vi sentite zio?' [How are you uncle?] is transformed to 'barba'.[29] The dynamics described here sum up *Materada*'s linguistic background. To pull together the threads of his novel, Tomizza must somehow find a way of dealing with this world of intermingling dialects and bilingualism.

Materada: A 'Self-translated' Novel

The description of the Italo-Croatian mixture in the essay 'Uno scrittore tra due dialetti di matrice linguistica diversa' anticipates the expressive potential of the encounter or clash of languages that are fully explored in *Materada* and *La miglior vita*. *Materada* puts into practice the theory developed in the essay and explores the potential of 'self-translation'. The language Tomizza chooses is Italian, which is not the same as the linguistic basis of the work, that is, the language which is spoken in the village, which surfaces only from time to time in the narrative. Italian, in most cases, is given the job of 'translating' it. The result is an atypical novel, challenged by a language that does not coincide with the one conceived by the author to portray its subject. I shall now consider the linguistic peculiarity of *Materada*. By applying Berruto's model, I will try to offer an exhaustive framework of *Materada*'s literary bilingualism (showing examples of code-switching, code-mixing, hybridization, and interference). I will also illustrate specific devices that typify the novel, such as the system of indicators created by Tomizza to specify the language in use. In general, the Croatian dialect is what Francesco speaks at home, with his uncle and family, in conversations with friends, when he defines himself and deals with important issues. Standard Croatian is considered a foreign language, avoided by the local population, as is standard Italian. On the other hand, the Istro-Venetian dialect is widespread in daily conversation and is complementary to the Croatian one.

The most evident phenomenon in *Materada* is code-switching: the 'switching' from one language to another on an inter-phrasal level. In these cases, languages, maintaining their own syntax and grammar, almost alternate. For example, Gelmo is the owner of a local bar who adapts himself to the changing times, in which speaking Croatian can be an advantage. He is characterized by a wandering between Croatian and Italian and this represents the first marked break in the Italian narrative of the novel. He receives his guests using a language in which he is not confident — he is used to talking mainly in the Istro-Venetian dialect. Francesco and his friends stare at him to encourage him to speak Italian:

> Gelmo correva da un tavolo all'altro, si dava un gran da fare. 'Molim ljepo, drugui, izvolite!' (Prego tanto, compagni, favorite). Aveva imparato queste quattro parole di croato e le usava con ogni persona foresta che era di passaggio a bersi il quarto; poi cominciò a usarle un po' con tutti, non so se per burla o perché secondo lui non c'era da fidarsi più di nessuno. [...] Ed ora, come un vecchio grammofono che non sa più quello che suona, disse anche a noi due che aspettavamo al banco: 'Molim, drugui, izvolite!'. Io gli diedi un'occhiata, ma senza nessuna intenzione (anche se lo slavo che ora parlava lui era una cosa e quello che parlavamo noi in famiglia era un'altra), ed egli cambiò disco. 'Allora, Franz mio, come va?' disse in italiano. (*M*, pp. 20–21)
>
> [Gelmo ran from one table to another, he had a lot to do. '*Molim ljepo, drugui, izvolite!*' (Please, friends, help yourself). He had learned these four words of Croatian and used them with anyone who was passing through the village and had just stopped for a drink; then he began to use them a bit with everyone, I do not know whether in jest or because according to him he could not trust anyone anymore. [...] And now, like an old gramophone that no longer knows what it plays, he even told the two of us while we waited at the counter: '*Molim, drugui, izvolite!*' I gave him a look, but without malice (although the Slav he spoke was one thing and the one we talked in our family was another), and he changed topic. 'So, my Franz, how are you?' he said in Italian.]

Another crucial example is given by the Serbian official in charge of checking the transportable goods of people like Milio who have opted to move to Trieste. In this case, the dialogue does not occur in Italian: 'Poi gli chiede: "*Hočete i cipele?*" (Volete anche le scarpe?). L'altro lo fissava duro. "*I cipele*" (Anche le scarpe). [...] "*Dosta!*" (Basta!) disse il serbo [...] "*Sad idemo*" disse. "*Žuri me se*" (Adesso andiamo; ho fretta)' (*M*, p. 153–54) [Then he asks: '*Hočete i cipele?*' (Do you want shoes too?). The other stared at him hard. '*I cipele*' (Also the shoes). [...] '*Dosta!*' (Enough!) said the Serb [...] '*Sad idemo*' he said. '*Žuri me se*' (Now let us go; I am in a hurry)].

In the novel, code-switching is not limited to Croatian (and Slovene) insertions, there are also occasions of sentences in the Istro-Venetian dialect being placed in the Italian narrative. For instance, Barba Nin, a principal character to whom Francesco addresses his doubts about moving away from his home country, usually employs Slovene, but he also sings Istro-Venetian songs: 'E si mise a canterellare "*no la me vol più ben (...) La prega Dio che crepo e inveze stago ben*"' (*M*, p. 125) [And started humming '*no la me vol più ben (...) La prega Dio che crepo e inveze stago ben*']. Songs are mainly reported in this dialect, as are typical expressions or sayings. When Francesco arrives at the village of Buje to meet the judges who might help him obtain the land from his uncle, he is reminded of an old saying that emphasizes the nature of the fortification of the place: 'Vi arrivai che era appena l'alba, sudato, con le gambe rotte, perché il paese è arrampicato in cima a un'altura e giustamente cantavano i nostri vecchi "*sta Buje in sentinela dal monte suo zentil!*"' (*M*, p. 65) [I arrived, and it was barely dawn, sweaty, with tired legs, because the village is perched atop a hill and rightly our elders sang '*sta Buje in sentinela dal monte suo zentil!*'].

It is evident that insertions of Croatian, Slovene, and the Istro-Venetian dialects into the Italian make a break in the narrative. When characters are shown to be using standard languages, the switch may be perceived as a linguistic rupture, it is an intrusion in a context based on dialects. Even more noticeable is that the use of standard Croatian is considered alien because it assumes a political meaning. This is the case with Gelmo and the Serbian officer who support the new regime. Language here becomes a flag to assert or to deny identity, as Robert Greenberg says of the Balkans: 'These language choices are subjective and politically motivated'.[30] In contrast, the Istro-Venetian insertions help to orientate the reader, adding a folkloristic trait to the work. Songs and sayings underline the peculiarity of the village and its surroundings, without creating friction. In both cases, the narrator faces the impossibility of translating them into Italian, without losing the effect of estrangement or a colourful touch.

Materada is also strongly characterized by code-mixing, which is a similar process on a smaller scale, consisting of insertions of foreign syntagms, and not of entire phrases. In Istria this seems to happen especially in lexical terms. From the beginning, the novel is crossed by dialogues in which words appear that do not belong to the Italian language. Istro-Venetian dialect words, like *barba* [uncle], *pinze* [a Veneto cake], *piova* [rain], *cavedagna* [chair], *balla* [drunk], *brache* [trousers], and *gnagna* [aunt] are included in the text (*M*, pp. 8, 16, 139, 87, 43, 128, 122). These words may require an explanation from the writer which, most of the time, Tomizza provides in annotations (notes in the text and footnotes both appear in Tomizza's books). To give an idea of the use of the Istro-Venetian dialect in the Italian narrative, let us consider the word *barba*. When Francesco is concerned about his uncle's will, he calls the old man 'barba', which in standard Italian means 'beard', while in the dialect it signifies 'uncle':

> Mi avvicinai un poco al letto. 'Barba' gli dissi. Aprì lentamente gli occhi celesti che adesso erano annebbiati, non più furbi e maligni come altre volte quando lo prendeva la paralisi o diceva di star male e appena sentiva salir qualcuno per le scale respirava con maggior affanno. 'Barba' dissi più forte, con voce che tremava. 'Barba Tio, barba'. (*M*, p. 8)

> [I came closer to the bed. '*Barba*' I said to him. He slowly opened his blue eyes that were now blurred, no longer cunning and devilish as at other times when paralysis overcame him, or he used to say he was unwell, and began breathing more heavily as soon as he could hear someone coming up the stairs. '*Barba*' I said louder, tremulously. '*Barba Tio, barba*'.]

The repetition of the word *barba* (four times in the space of a few lines), in addition to the emphasis placed on the term, serves to alert the reader. The specific word used brings additional illumination to the scene. In this case, *barba* conveys a sense of authority that *zio* does not possess.

Code-mixing is not only based on the insertion of words taken from the Italian dialect. Once the reader becomes familiar with the Istro-Venetian linguistic context, the narrative inserts words taken from Croatian, like *skupčina* [assembly], *sudac* [judge], *zdravo* [hi], *zadruga* [collective], and *kolo* [a dance]; and from the Croatian dialect, like *colarich* [an Istrian common bandit] (M, pp. 48, 66, 87, 38, 51, 69). Also, the inclusion of Croatian words involves political consequences, as can be observed in the following passage. Francesco calls the barman 'gospod' (meaning 'sir' or 'lord', but the word contains the meaning of 'owner', and ownership was against the new rules imposed by the regime) and the barman is irritated by the expression: 'Posai la birra davanti a lui, battendo forte sul tavolo. "Eccoti la birra, *gospòd*" dissi; e lui prontamente rispose: "*gospòd*? Non ci sono più *gospòdi*; li abbiamo spediti tutti a Trieste. *Gospòd* semmai sei tu che l'hai pagata"' (M, p. 54) [I put the beer in front of him, banging the table loudly. 'Here is your beer, *gospòd*', I said; and he promptly replied: '*gospòd*? There are no more *gospòdi*; We sent them all to Trieste. If anyone is *Gospòd* it is you that paid for it'].

The Italian of the narrative is progressively 'corroded' by terms from different languages that burst on the scene in spontaneous dialogue, or as terms indicating specific meanings. This is the case with words like *graie* or *druži* (M, pp. 24, 13). The former means 'fence' and refers to streets and field divisions in the novel, pinpointing the meaning of the situation more clearly than the corresponding Italian word could: 'Le "graie" (dallo sloveno "odgràjati", cingere) che delimitano le nostre strade di ghiaia, mal sopportano di venir chiamate "siepi"' [The 'graie' (from Slovene 'odgràjati', enclosing) that surround our gravel roads, cannot bear to be called 'fences'].[31] A similar phenomenon is also the case with the word *druži*, which is the name used by Italians to refer to Yugoslav people, but which is not taken from the nominative; rather it is the 'Italianization' of the vocative: '*druži*: termine acconciato all'italiana dal vocativo croato *druže* (o compagno), e applicato per estensione agli occupatori' (M, p. 13) [*druži*: word adapted to the Italian from the Croatian vocative *druže* (or companion), and applied by extension to the occupiers].

Apart from hybridization, there are also linguistic interferences in the morpho-syntax of the Italian narrative, which clearly indicate foreign influences. The outward signs of this are when expressions or sentences seem to be translated from a different language, or when dialogue contains apparent mistakes or odd syntax: 'Ti hanno insegnato bene, i nostri capi, come è da comportarsi' (M, p. 23) [Your bosses have taught you well how to behave]. Other linguistic contaminations, which derive from the dialect, appear in expressions like 'una persona veramente studiata' (M, p. 66) [a very studied person] or 'più parte impiegati' (M, p. 141) [for the most part employed].

The Italian narrative 'covers' the linguistic underground of the novel, which only surfaces occasionally as we have seen in the processes analyzed here. Nevertheless, Tomizza creates a more obvious device to testify to the presence of different languages within and behind the Italian language: from time to time the narrator specifies that the language used by characters is not the one which appears in the text. The initial conversation between Francesco and his uncle (which involves many other secondary characters) suddenly turns out to have been a dialogue spoken in a Croatian dialect, when the former specifies that they were speaking '*po našu*', 'in our own': 'Come sempre in caso di affari e di cose importanti, parlammo in slavo: *po našu* (alla nostra), come si usa dire dalle nostre parti' (*M*, p. 19) [As always in the case of business and important things, we spoke in Slavic: *po našu* (at ours), as we say in our place].

Francesco draws attention to the fact that characters are talking in the Croatian dialect, pointing out that the entire conversation has been translated into Italian; this provides an important interpretative key to the reader. He states that the animated conversation has been spoken in a different tongue to that used in the text, but also that serious issues, like business and major topics, are not discussed in Italian. Moreover, if the use of Istro-Venetian terms warns the reader of a discrepancy between the language of the narrative and that of the conversation being reported, '*po našu*' announces an even larger gap, because Italian does not even share the same linguistic matrix with the Croatian dialect:

> Tant'è vero che il protagonista del romanzo *Materada* a un certo punto della vicenda narra di essersi accostato alla moglie e di averle parlato '*po našu*', alla nostra. Con ciò egli intendeva significare di essere risalito con la consorte, nell'intimità della casa, alla prima e vera fonte del loro esprimersi, che non consentiva reticenze né abbellimenti né infingimenti. Per me autore allora ventitreenne, quel '*po našu*', era stato come un avvertimento col quale dichiaravo che fino a quel momento la narrazione di quei luoghi e di quei personaggi era stata resa attraverso una lingua il più possibile aderente alla nostra parlata, ma che restava ad ogni modo un'espressione esterna, voluta dal di fuori. Segnalavo al lettore che quella trama familiare e collettiva, di problemi e di passioni, aveva un suo svolgimento più interno, dentro un tessuto linguistico immediato che la plasmava e la scandiva con aderenza e ritmo più appropriato e più incalzante di quanto non apparisse dalla mia fervida e scrupolosa traduzione. Non mi restava altro da fare se non denunciare la mia impossibilità di essere maggiormente fedele alla materia narrata, anche perché mi servivo di una sola delle matrici linguistiche che ispiravano quel dialetto e nemmeno assunta nella più familiare versione veneta. (*S*, pp. 190–91)

> [Thus, the protagonist of the novel *Materada* at some point in the story says that he approached his wife and talked to her '*po našu*' (at ours). With this he meant to return with his wife, in the privacy of their home, to the first and true source of their expression, which did not allow either embellishment or pretence. For me, a twenty-three-year-old author, '*po našu*' was like a warning declaring that until then the narrative of those places and characters had been made through a language as close as possible to our parlance, but that remained in any case an external expression, demanded by the outside. I pointed out to the reader that the collective drama of problems and passions of the family had its innermost development in an immediate linguistic fabric, that shaped and articulated it

adhering to a more appropriate and relentless pace than it looked from my fervent and scrupulous translation. I had nothing else to do if not denounce my inability to be more faithful to the topic told, also because I was only using one linguistic device which inspired that dialect, which was not even used in the more colloquial Venetian version.]

Although 'po našu' indicates a linguistic fracture to the reader, Tomizza is aware of and anxious about the difficulty of staying close to the world in which the novel is set. The Italian narrative has the potential to submerge this world, which Carlo Sgorlon has described as follows: 'spesso questa gente di Materada ha nomi croati, linguaggio croato, e sente come proprio il mondo slavo' [these people from Materada often have Croatian names, Croatian language, and feel as their own the Slav world].[32] For this reason, when the opportunity arises, Tomizza seeks to reaffirm the Croatian nature of the dialogue that otherwise would have been constantly at risk of being swamped by the prevalence of Italian in the narrative. The narrator underlines that characters are talking in the Croatian dialect several times, and includes important details, aiming to recreate the missing context. For example, when the judge tries to convince Francesco's uncle to give land to his nephew: 'Già si alzava, ci accompagnava alla porta e in un ultimo tentativo diceva allo zio, sforzandosi di parlare nel nostro dialetto: "Pensateci, barba Tio"' (M, p. 73) [Already he got up, accompanied us to the door and in a last attempt said to his uncle, trying to speak our dialect: 'Think about it, *barba* Tio']; or when Francesco, facing the changes imposed by the emerging regime, describes his position, reaffirming the tongue spoken: 'E io invece?... avevo indosso quegli stracci da quattro soldi, tipo sacco, che lo zio aveva comperato alla *zadruga*, e le scarpe grosse che potevano andar bene dieci anni prima. Inoltre a casa mia si parlava lo slavo' (M, pp. 38–39) [And me on the contrary?... I was wearing these cheap rags, like a sack, which uncle had bought at the *zadruga*, and big shoes that could have been alright ten years before. In addition in my house we spoke Slavic].

Despite these general rules, there are cases in which the language used becomes almost unpredictable. When Rozzan and Milio are discussing the possibility of leaving the country, they alternate between the two tongues in order to emphasize their different points of view. Once again, the narrator mediates languages, translating them into Italian: '"Allora solo a te è permesso?" e parlava in slavo. "Non sei mica il più bello. Scusami tanto, e a me chi mi tiene se voglio andarmene, per esempio?" "Questo lo saprai tu' disse in italiano"' (M, p. 43) ['So only you are allowed?' and he was speaking in Slavic. 'You are not the most beautiful. Excuse me, and who is holding me back if I want to leave, for example?' 'You will know that' he said in Italian]. In the same dialogue Francesco and Rozzan, who have been friends for a long time, continue to discuss the dramatic events which are progressively overwhelming Istria and the beginning of the mass exile. By recreating the intimacy of their relationship the narrator underlines Rozzan's need to find a friend to talk to about delicate matters that are usually addressed in the Croatian dialect. Again, the language employed is revealed in the middle of the dialogue by Francesco and leads the reader, who is following the Italian text, to refocus on a dialogue that turns out to have been going on in a different tongue:

'Allora, Franz, pare che anche Milio se ne vada' disse, e la sua voce mi parve quella amichevole di dieci anni prima; come se fossimo sempre rimasti al punto in cui ci eravamo lasciati e adesso fosse venuto il momento di tirare le somme. 'Pare di sì' gli dissi in slavo anch'io. (*M*, p. 46)

['So, Franz, it seems that even Milio is leaving,' he said, and his voice seemed to me that friendly one of ten years earlier; as if we were still at the point where we left each other and now it was time to draw conclusions. 'Apparently yes,' I said in Slavic too.]

There are also more extreme cases in which the narrator does not specify the language and where the reader can only venture a hypothesis. He may be able to deduce the language in use from the context, the descriptions, and other useful details left in the narrative, while, on other occasions, he may only be able to hazard a guess. For example, when Francesco's surname is written in Croatian — 'Kozlović' instead of 'Coslovich' — it suggests that the phone call that follows between Vanja and the judge will most probably be in Croatian: 'C'è qui da me uno dei fratelli Kozlović di Materada' (*M*, p. 87) [I have with me one of the Kozlović brothers from Materada].[33] The hypothesis seems to be confirmed at the end of the conversation, which finishes with 'zdravo'[goodbye]. However, details may also deceive and *Materada* can leave some ambiguous passages where both languages fit.

The device of specifying the language used is evidence that most of the dialogue has been translated. How do these processes affect the narrative and the reader's experience of it? The irruption of a dialect is the first indication to the reader that the situation behind the Italian narrative is not linguistically homogenous. However, just as the reader is getting used to a dialect, he is suddenly shaken by an unexpected change, that is, the introduction of a second dialect being spoken in parallel with the first. In other words, the reader cannot always identify the language and expect it to continue throughout the novel. The reason for employing this technique is to overturn readers' expectations, leaving them with a sense of confusion about languages and identities: the chaotic linguistic undertow, the quick linguistic jumps, and the indeterminacies of the novel inevitably undermine their recognition. As Ballinger suggests: 'Tomizza's protagonist Francesco Koslovic inhabits an impoverished rural world in which distinctions between Italians and Croats (and corresponding cultural spheres) are not at all clear'.[34] The reader is obliged to accept the rather challenging perspective imposed by the text.

This novel made of linguistic layers makes demands on the reader but also on the writer. Among these I will focus on the problems created by employing a language that does not correspond to that of the context in which the work is set. It is in bridging this gap, in adapting and translating his world into a different language where the skill of a writer is displayed. A writer who has faced a similarly demanding set of problems is Verga, whose *Malavoglia* aims to give voice to a Sicilian village and its language. Although the lexical and morphological aspects of the novel are Italian, the author builds the language upon the local dialect. Verga's and Tomizza's aims seem to converge; however, the limit of a comparison between their works can be found in the coming into being of the language of the narratives.

As Verga explains in a letter to Luigi Capuana:

> E il bravo poeta Di Giovanni scrivendo *ccu la parrata girgintana* non si fa capire da nessuno *comu si avissi scrittu turcu*; precisamente voi, io, e tutti quanti scriviamo non facciamo che tradurre mentalmente il pensiero in siciliano, se vogliamo scrivere in dialetto; perché il pensiero nasce in italiano nella nostra mente.[35]

> [And the great poet Di Giovanni, by writing *in the parlance of Agrigento* that is not comprehensible to everyone *as if it was written in Turkish*; specifically you, I, and everyone who writes translates mentally into Sicilian if we want to write in dialect; because the thought is born in Italian in our minds.]

Verga emphasizes that the process he employed was 'translation', as did Tomizza in *Materada*. Nevertheless, Verga is translating from Italian to dialect, while Tomizza does the opposite. Tomizza's Italian is built over a double dialect that, struggling to fit into the Italian narrative, contaminates it. A similar approach seems to be used by Ignazio Silone in *Fontamara*:

> La seconda avvertenza è questa: in che lingua devo adesso raccontare questa storia? A nessuno venga in mente che i Fontamaresi parlino l'italiano. La lingua è per noi una lingua imparata a scuola, come possono essere il latino, il francese, l'esperanto. La lingua italiana è per noi una lingua straniera, una lingua morta, una lingua il cui dizionario, la cui grammatica si sono formati senza alcun rapporto con noi, col nostro modo di agire, col nostro modo di pensare, col nostro modo di esprimerci. [...] Ma basta osservarci per scoprire la nostra goffaggine. La lingua italiana nel ricevere e formulare i vostri pensieri non può fare a meno di storpiarli, di corromperli, di dare ad essi l'apparenza di una traduzione. Ma, per esprimersi direttamente, l'uomo non dovrebbe tradurre. [...] Ma poiché non ho altro mezzo per farmi intendere (ed esprimermi per me adesso è bisogno assoluto), così voglio sforzarmi di tradurre alla meglio, nella lingua imparata, quello che voglio che tutti sappiano: la verità sui fatti di Fontamara.[36]

> [The second caveat is this: In what language do I tell this story now? No one can think that Fontamara speaks Italian. That language is for us a language learned at school like Latin, French, Esperanto. The Italian language is for us a foreign language, a dead language, a language whose dictionary, whose grammar was formed without any relationship to us, to our actions, to our way of thinking, to our way of expressing ourselves. [...] It is enough to observe us to discover our clumsiness. The Italian language in receiving and formulating your thoughts can only distort them, corrupt them, give them the appearance of a translation. But, to express himself directly, man should not translate. [...] But since I have no other way to make myself understood (and to express myself now is an absolute need) I want to force myself to translate as best I can, in the learned language, what I want everyone to know: the truth about the facts of Fontamara.]

Materada's linguistic situation is more complex than that of *Fontamara*. In an area like Istria, where the Central European world meets the Balkans, the role of a 'self-translator' assumes a crucial meaning that relates to multilingualism, and this should now be explored further.

La miglior vita: Towards the Hybridization of the Language

In *Materada*, the hybrid linguistic situation experienced by characters in Istria is filtered through the narrator but it also emerges in fluctuations between dialects, the use of foreign words and translations, and in unpredictable choices. Linguistic complexity is shown and not just implied or even kept hidden. In *La miglior vita* Tomizza experiments with these operations to an even greater extent. Among the most significant cases there is a scene in which one of the priests, Don Kuzma, who prefers Croatian and Slovene, appears from the text to be employing Italian. The narrator specifies that the priest is using his native tongue, Polish, even though the narrative is Italian: '"Digli che l'ho confessata la settimana scorsa", tuonò don Kuzma nella loro lingua polacca' (*MV*, p. 19) ['Tell him that I confessed her last week,' thundered Don Kuzma in his Polish language]. This is not an isolated example: a minor character, Gabriele Pavlovich, is put into the story to mark the existence of a Croatian identity in this context: '"Quest'uomo sta morendo, ostia!" mi comunicò in slavo' (*MV*, p. 106) ['This man is dying!' he announced to me in Slavic].

This passage implies an inextricable relationship existing between language and ethnicity, as suggested by Joshua A. Fishman: 'Although language has rarely been equated with the totality of ethnicity, it has, in certain historical, regional and disciplinary contexts, been accorded priority within that totality'.[37] Fishman formulates the connection between language and ethnicity, or ethnic identity, in three ways: indexically, symbolically, and in a part-whole fashion. He explains that the association of a language with a culture is not an exclusive relationship, but a privileged one: 'no language but the one that has been most historically and intimately associated with a given culture is as well able to express the particular artefacts and concerns of that culture'.[38] This is termed indexical and characterizes the use of language by Don Kuzma and Gabriele Pavlovich, who both employ the most suitable tongue (Polish, but also Croatian and Slovene or the Croatian dialect) to express themselves. Language and ethnicity in this case are connected to a specific culture. In the passages cited above, the two characters find themselves in stressful situations where the connection between language and ethnicity comes to the surface. However, this does not mean that the traditional and historical associations conveyed by a language match exactly with a culture or that a specific language cannot be replaced to express specific purposes. Tomizza's characters show the possibility of overturning indexicality despite maintaining the strong associations existing between language, ethnicity, and culture: a language 'reflects and conveys its culture more felicitously and succinctly than other languages, *while that language-in-culture link remains generally intact*'.[39] This recalls Bourdieu's idea of linguistic habitus, which refers to the dispositions acquired in a certain context, not only regarding language but also including values and social behaviours: 'those features of language, and consequent thoughts, individuals are disposed to have and acquire in the course of their upbringing and trajectories through life, and which come into being in language used in a particular context or field'.[40]

When languages are indexically linked to a culture it means that they are also symbolically related to it: 'they come to stand for or symbolically represent the particular ethnic and/or national collectivities that speak them'.[41] Even though languages are all considered equivalent in linguistic terms, 'the social and political circumstances of those who speak a particular language will have a significant impact on the subsequent symbolic and communicative status attached to that language'.[42] Tomizza takes full advantage of the circumstances that surround his characters to determine their status, identity, personal or political belonging, or aims. Although he would not have been able to define the language on every occasion, he often describes its social and political implications. For instance, when Don Michele Ribari is introduced as a priest who was 'nato in un'isola del Carnaro' (*MV*, p. 28) [born on an island in the Kvarner], this detail does not clarify his linguistic identity. There is no linguistic indication in the episodes in which he talks with parishioners, takes confession, or reads the Gospel, nor is there when Crusich is 'comandato con minacce biascicate' (*MV*, p. 27) [commanded by mumbled threats] by the mother of Don Ribari, who is an angry old lady, or when the priest attacks the sacristan with 'voce alterata' (*MV*, p. 28) [altered voice]. Many other actions, such as the act of reading, confessing, talking, are not linguistically specified. Only at the end of the episode, when Don Ribari is moved to a different parish, does the narrator tell us that several parishioners have complained about his mass: 'Gli si rimproverava di celebrare in italiano' (*MV*, p. 36) [He was reproached for celebrating mass in Italian] — for his 'fedeltà alla "dolce favella"' (*MV*, p. 36) [loyalty to the 'sweet tongue']. This linguistic statement inevitably implies a symbolic (and therefore political) meaning, which contributes to Tomizza's picture of the controversial situation in Istria. The celebration of a mass in a specific language goes beyond its linguistic meaning and points to a symbolic position and context.

The third aspect of Fishman's theory considers the identity of a specific language and culture and is called the 'part-whole link'. In other words, there are social phenomena that become identified with a language. Fishman argues that within the part-whole relationship:

> Child socialization patterns come to be associated with a particular language, that cultural styles of interpersonal relations come to be associated with a particular language, that the ethical principles that undergird everyday life come to be associated with a particular language and that even material culture and aesthetic sensibilities come to be conventionally discussed and evaluated via figures of speech that are merely culturally (i.e. locally) rather than universally applicable.[43]

In Tomizza's case the part-whole link must be related to the political background, which emerges also when language is not specified. The values related to a certain language or ethnicity come out when dialogues turn unpredictable in linguistic terms, such as when the main character Crusich meets a young partisan while he is weeding around the tombs in the graveyard. Here the dialogue begins with the Croatian epithet '*Striče*' [uncle], even though the two seem to be speaking in Italian:

> '*Striče*' mi sentii dare dello zio, quando potevo ormai passare per nonno; 'I tedeschi se ne sono andati?' Mi rivolsi col più paterno dei sorrisi, carico dunque

di preoccupazione. 'No, figliolo. Si sono appena messi nella scuola'. 'Eh,' fece la voce 'torneranno a rastrellare'. (*MV*, p. 165)

['*Striče*' he called me uncle, when I could now pass for grandfather; 'Are the Germans gone?' I turned with the most paternal smile, laiden therefore with concern. 'No, son. They just settled in the school.' 'Eh,' said the voice 'they will come back to mop up'.]

Given that the text often translates foreign terms, in this case one may argue that the dialogue occurs in Croatian, especially because of the initial '*Striče*'. The level of intimacy established by the two characters in the dialogue — they use two familiar terms '*Striče*' and 'figliolo' — sheds light on Crusich's relationship with the Croatian language and culture. The part-whole link component often emerges in conversations between the sacristan, the priests, and secondary characters in relation to more personal subjects such as belief and spirituality, but also from the way in which characters interact.

Delving further into the ambiguity of the language in use in *La miglior vita*, the most remarkable paradox to emerge is that the narrator has to specify when characters talk in Italian, despite the narrative being in Italian. As Damiani observes, this novel should be 'inserito in un contesto bilingue con prevalenza dell'etnia croata (a cominciare dal protagonista, il quale non di rado specifica: "Parlando in italiano")' [inserted in a bilingual environment predominantly of Croat ethnicity (starting with the main character, who often specifies: 'speaking in Italian')].[44] Italian should be considered a foreign language, alien to local characters, who use either Istro-Venetian or Čakavian, but very rarely standard languages. By alternating languages, but above all by letting them flow together, the hybridization of terms and sentences shape new layers of meaning. In his essay 'Uno scrittore tra due dialetti di matrice linguistica diversa', Tomizza discusses some of the dynamics of the Istrian language that are present in his novels. For instance, paradoxically, the words for dog, cat, and horse are from different languages, showing that these fluctuations among languages occurred even in the home. Different functions, bizarre mechanisms of inclusion, which can sometimes be connected to historical motives, shape new words. But above all, three different languages together pattern a new one, which most of the time eliminates the originals:

> Tale ordine mentale viene rispettato per gli animali domestici. Ai cani, che, snelli e sostenuti, accompagnano i cacciatori di città, ci si rivolge generalmente in italiano e l'animale stesso viene chiamato non *pas* bensì *brek*, da bracco; ai gatti si parla in slavo; ai cavalli, poco diffusi da noi e incontrati invece durante il servizio militare nell'esercito austroungarico, si comanda in tedesco: 'oha!' e 'zurik'. (*S*, pp. 188–89)

> [This mental order is respected for domestic animals. Dogs, which, slender and aloof, accompany the hunters of the town, one usually addresses in Italian and the animal itself is not called *pas* but *brek* from bloodhound; to cats one speaks in Slavic; for horses, rarely seen in our place but seen rather during military service in the Austro-Hungarian Empire, the commands are in German: 'oha!' and 'zurik'.]

As in the case of dogs, where *pas* is replaced by the misspelt Italian 'bracco', the linguistic hybridity not only combines different languages, it also fuses them. The word for dog distorts the Italian name of a canine breed, but in more sophisticated examples the same word may overlap in different languages and unintentionally convey several meanings. A similar phenomenon happens in *La miglior vita*, where Crusich gives a plurilingual inventory of Count Ulderico's herbarium, naming herbs which have been written in the hybrid idiom for the first time. As stated by the character: 'L'ho sfogliato con commozione rivedendo, spiaccicate e rinsecchite tante erbe dimenticate che non vedrò più vive; ma soprattutto imbattendomi nei loro nomi uditi e pronunciati mille volte, mai visti scritti nel nostro dialetto' (*MV*, p. 269) [I leafed through it with emotion seeing again, smashed and shrivelled, many forgotten herbs that I will never see alive; but above all finding their names heard and pronounced a thousand times, but never having seen written down in our dialect]. In addition to this list, in order to make it understandable to the reader, the sacristan also adds a concise explanation of what the herbs in question are. Some comments were simply copied from the notes of the count, others added by the sacristan, who enjoyed the procedure: 'Lo doveva divertire il suono e insieme la certezza di essere lui il primo a fermarlo sulla carta' [He enjoyed the sound together with the certainty that he was the first to catch it on paper], but it was more difficult than expected, 'Quanta difficoltà per scrivere questi nomi tanto familiari' [How difficult it is to write these familiar names] (*MV*, p. 269):

> *Tachìs*, perché si attacca alle mani; *pàprut*, felce per pigliare le mosche; *habàt*, sambuco selvatico per fare l'inchiostro; *lèpoh*, per spazzare il forno; *marquarèla*, basilico selvatico; *erba de tajo*, per guarire dalle ferite; *sirca* che invece taglia la mano; *mlìzzak* che contiene un latte; *karìznik*, per impagliar sedie o careghe; *linguadevàca* dalla grande foglia e il fiore come lo spinacio; *rokvèniza*, ravanello selvatico; *muhlîć*, quella tenera per i conigli; *lòquariza*, perché si trova nei lachi; *vilùdola*, vilucchio; *paradaiz salvàdigo*, pomodoro selvatico; *basamàn*, cardo che punge la mano; *koromàz*, finocchio; *metlika*, per far metle ossia scope; *peldemona*, dritto ma scivola sotto la falce; *pirika*, gramigna; rodignazza, loglieto; *graska*, zizzania; *mah*, papavero; *semprevivo*, timo. I radicchi selvatici: *gradonzéa*, *radézka*, *toka*, *konjska broda*, *sùnziza*. (*MV*, p. 269)

> [*Tachìs*, because it sticks to the hands; *pàprut*, fern to get rid of flies; *habàt*, wild elderberries to make ink; *lèpoh*, to sweep the oven; *marquarèla*, wild basil; *erba de tajo*, to heal wounds; *sirca* that, on the other hand, cuts the hand; *mlìzzak* that contains milk; *karìznik*, to stuff chairs or *careghe*; *linguadevàca* with a big leaf and flower like spinach; *rokvèniza*, wild radish; *muhlîć*, that tender stuff for rabbits; *lòquariza*, because it is located in lakes; *vilùdola*, bearbind; *paradaiz salvàdigo*, wild tomato; *basamàn*, thistle that pricks the hand; *koromàz*, fennel; *metlika*, to make *metle*, that is, brooms; *peldemona*, straight but it slips under the sickle; *pirika*, Bermuda grass; couch grass, darnel; *graska*, poison darnel; *mah*, poppy; *semprevivo*, thyme. Wild radicchio: *gradonzéa*, *radézka*, *toka*, *konjska broda*, *sùnziza*.]

The hybrid language can undergo heavy distortions but also overlaps, deforming the language, and so tests the reader's comprehension. This is the case with the word *cuce*, which appears in the description of the landscape of a village:

> Le case di Rupa non si elevavano sui macigni, me le trovai improvvisamente davanti come le *cuce* di pietre a secco dove si ripongono gli arnesi e ci si ripara a malapena in caso di cattivo tempo, altri vi trascorrono le notti calde per far la guardia ai meloni. (*MV*, p. 13)
>
> [The houses of Rupa did not stand on boulders, I suddenly found them in front of me like dry stone *cuce* where you put tools and barely protect yourself in the case of bad weather, or pass warm nights guarding the melons.]

Cuce, which is a combination of the Italian for dog kennel, the Croatian *kuća* ('house') and the Slovene *koča* ('hut'), fuses the three languages, exemplifying the potential of the linguistic hybrid space, which sometimes lets meanings flow together. This new perspective can take words beyond their original attribution, opening out the domain of the writer, who can take advantage of the process of contamination between languages. These new and unpredictable synergies are defined by Tomizza himself: 'contagi cronici risoltisi ormai in simbiosi, gustosissime e significanti' [contaminations formed over time now become a pungent and significant symbiosis] that cannot be conceived in Italian, Croatian, or Slovene (or their dialects) taken singularly.[45] Hybridism tends to 'expand' the language by taking advantage of the wide potential generated by the intersection of two or more codes. As suggested by Olga Anokhina: 'the bilingual creation can choose to respect the two linguistic systems or, on the contrary, to create interferences between them'.[46] The latter is the option which exploits new meanings that can also be generated by translations and the contamination of different languages. Another example concerns the following sentence *'Questa la-la xe poposka jaja'* (*MV*, p. 97) [This is the egg of the priest], which mixes Veneto-Istrian and Čakavian dialects, using the association between eggs and testicles that is common in the Croatian language, to describe the shape of a plant.

The sophisticated structure of *La miglior vita* leads to some final observations, relating to the unique condition of being a writer in between languages. This mediation, the combination of writing and translation, differentiates works such as *Materada* and *La miglior vita*, where languages are able to combine freely, from more linguistically homogeneous ones. The 'deceitful' mechanisms of translation are clearly manifest. This activity becomes an ongoing process, that shapes its linguistic path through writing:

> The interplay between different dimensions of our self has considerable implications for writing. Rather than thinking of texts as simply reflecting a pre-linguistic and pre-defined subjectivity, we must consider how selfhood is constructed in the process of writing. Writing itself is a linguistic activity that shapes the self in complicated ways.[47]

In other words, a process of 'self-translation' takes place in *Materada* and *La miglior vita* as described by Tomizza, who 'transfers' a multilingual background to the narrative:

> Nei romanzi sulle vicende del confine, culminate con l'esodo di quelle popolazioni anche rurali in Italia, mi viene spontaneo di 'tradurre' il nostro particolare dialetto veneto in una lingua italiana quanto più semplice, a costo di

riuscire povera: quella per l'appunto diffusa negli strati popolari, e tenendo a modello l'operazione già compiuta da Verga e Tozzi, da Pavese e Pratolini. Ma avrei potuto forse trascurare i prestiti contratti dalla tradizione popolare con le lingue delle nostre remote origini balcaniche, o quelli avvenuti durante la lunga dominazione austriaca quando i nostri nonni familiarizzavano coi commilitoni stiriani e romeni, boemi e polacchi?[48]

[In novels set on the vicissitudes of the border, culminating in the exodus of those rural populations to Italy, I naturally 'translate' our particular Venetian dialect into the simplest version of the Italian language, at the cost of seeming meagre: this is widespread among ordinary people, and taking as a model the work already accomplished by Verga and Tozzi, by Pavese and Pratolini. But could I have ever neglected borrowings from the folk tradition of languages from our remote Balkan origins, or those that occurred during the long Austrian domination when our grandparents made friends with fellow soldiers who were Styrian and Romanian, Bohemian and Polish?]

The inclusion of translation in the process of writing fulfils the need to adhere to the country of origin and its linguistic background. This means that Tomizza fluctuates within a complex dimension, made up of words from different origins. Bilingual from birth, he is affected by the convergence of languages that he seeks to mediate, as well as by other parallel selves who may surface in the process of writing.

Notes to Chapter 3

1. Guagnini, *Una città d'autore*, p. 27.
2. Tomizza, *Alle spalle di Trieste*, p. 147. For an analysis of Tomizza and Cankar's relationship, see Marianna Deganutti (ed.), 'Lo sguardo a est di Fulvio Tomizza', in *Rileggendo Fulvio Tomizza*, pp. 231–76.
3. Tomizza, *Destino di frontiera*, p. 55.
4. Ivan Cankar, *The Bailiff Yerney and his Rights*, trans. by Sidonie Yeras and H. C. Sewell Grant (London: Rodker, 1930).
5. Tomizza, *Alle spalle di Trieste*, p. 148.
6. Fulvio Tomizza, *Materada* (Milan: Mondadori, 1960), pp. 25–26; hereafter referenced as M.
7. Geno Pampaloni, 'Fulvio Tomizza', *L'Approdo, Radio Rai 2*, 4 February 1961, pp. 16–17.
8. Roberto Damiani, 'Fulvio Tomizza', in *Letteratura italiana: i contemporanei*, ed. by Artal Mazzotti, 6 vols (Milan: Marzorati, 1974), VI, pp. 1959–80 (p. 1962).
9. Tomizza, *Destino di frontiera*, pp. 43–44.
10. Guido Baldi, *L'artificio della regressione: tecnica narrativa e ideologia nel Verga verista* (Naples: Liguori, 1980), p. 81.
11. Ibid.
12. Damiani, 'Fulvio Tomizza', p. 1963.
13. Elvio Guagnini, 'Materada', in *L'eredità di Tomizza e gli scrittori di frontiera*, ed. by Irene Mestrovich (Fiume: Edit, 2001), pp. 11–14 (p. 12).
14. For a detailed analysis of these dynamics, see Marianna Deganutti, 'Il romanzo auto-tradotto: *La miglior vita* di Fulvio Tomizza', *Rivista di letteratura italiana*, 1 (2014), 181–92.
15. Mario Lunetta, 'Tomizza', *Paese sera*, 27 June 1969.
16. Fulvio Tomizza, 'Uno scrittore tra due dialetti di matrice linguistica diversa', in *Alle spalle di Trieste*, pp. 183–94; hereafter referenced as S. The essay was presented by Tomizza at the University of Klagenfurt, which held the conference 'Letteratura e plurilinguismo', organized by Professors Strutz and Zima, in 1990.

17. George Steiner comments on his three native languages as follows: 'I have no recollection whatsoever of a first language. So far as I am aware, I possess equal currency in English, French, and German. [...] But I experience my first three tongues as perfectly equivalent centers of myself. I speak and write them with indistinguishable ease' (*After Babel: Aspects of Language and Translation* (Oxford: Oxford University Press, 1992), p. 120).
18. Tomizza, *Le mie estati letterarie*, p. 155. The verbs *dèlati* and *ráditi* mean 'to work' respectively in Slovene and Croatian; *hiša* and *kuća* stand for 'house' in the two languages; and (Slovene dialect) *das* and *kiša* correspond to 'rain'.
19. Alojz Rebula, *Da Nicea a Trieste: saggi, riflessioni, commenti* (Cinisello Balsamo: San Paolo, 2012).
20. Muysken, *Bilingual Speech*, p. 69.
21. Muysken, *Bilingual Speech*, pp. 8, 3.
22. Jane Miller, 'Writing a Second Language', *Raritan*, 1 (1982), 115–32 (p. 123).
23. Cf. Julien Green, *Le Langage et son double* (Paris: La Différence, 1985), p. 404.
24. Tomizza, *Le mie estati letterarie*, p. 127.
25. Ibid.
26. Elio Vittorini to Fulvio Tomizza, 18 March 1959, typescript (Fondazione Arnoldo e Alberto Mondadori (FAAM), Milan, Archivio storico Arnoldo Mondadori Editore, Arnoldo Mondadori, fasc. Fulvio Tomizza).
27. Fulvio Tomizza to Segretaria, Milan, 6 May 1959, typescript (FAAM, fasc. Fulvio Tomizza).
28. Fulvio Tomizza to Mondadori, Milan, 4 February 1960, typescript (FAAM, fasc. Fulvio Tomizza).
29. Fulvio Tomizza, 'Materada', 28 July 1958, Chapter 2, manuscript 1:1 (Archivio Prezzolini, Lugano, Biblioteca cantonale, Fondo Tomizza).
30. Robert Greenberg, *Language and Identity in the Balkans* (Oxford: Oxford University Press, 2004), p. 9.
31. Fulvio Tomizza, 'Perchè amo vivere e scrivere rintanato nella mia Istria', in *Alle spalle di Trieste*, pp. 175–81 (p. 179).
32. Carlo Sgorlon, 'Amore di terra', *Il Giornale*, 20 March 1983, p. 4.
33. As suggested by Sanja Roić and Ante Brala: 'La distinzione grafica nello scrivere il cognome potrebbe indicare se l'individuo si sente/dichiara italiano o croato' [The graphic distinction in writing the surname might indicate whether the individual feels/declares to be Italian or Croatian] ('Materada oltre i confini linguistici', *Italica belgradensia*, 1 (2013), 70–82 (p. 76)).
34. Ballinger, 'History's "Illegibles"', p. 121.
35. Giovanni Verga, *Lettere a Luigi Capuana* (Florence: Le Monnier, 1975), p. 215.
36. Ignazio Silone, *Romanzi e saggi* (Milan: Mondadori, 2008), pp. 15–16.
37. Joshua A. Fishman (ed.), 'Introduction', in *Handbook of Language and Ethnic Identity* (New York & Oxford: Oxford University Press, 1999), pp. 3–5 (p. 4).
38. Joshua A. Fishman, *Reversing Language Shift: Theoretical and Empirical Foundations of Assistance to Threatened Languages* (Clevedon: Multilingual Matters, 1991), p. 21.
39. Stephen May, *Language and Minority Rights: Ethnicity, Nationalism and the Politics of Language* (New York: Longman, 2001), p. 138.
40. Michael Grenfell and David James (eds.), *Bourdieu and Education: Acts of Practical Theory* (London: Continuum, 2007), p. 74.
41. May, *Language and Minority Rights*, p. 139.
42. Ibid.
43. Fishman, *Reversing Language Shift*, p. 24.
44. Alessandro Damiani, 'Rapsodia istriana', *Panorama*, 7 (1977), 31–37 (p. 34).
45. Tomizza, *Le mie estati letterarie*, p. 127.
46. Cf. Olga Anokhina, *Multilinguisme et créativité littéraire* (Louvain-la-Neuve: Academia Bruylant/Harmattan, 2012), p. 64.
47. Suresh Canagarajah, 'Multilingual Writers and the Struggle for Voice in Academic Discourse', in *Negotiation of Identities in Multilingual Contexts*, ed. by Aneta Pavlenko and Adrian Blackledge (Clevedon: Multilingual Matters, 2004), pp. 266–89 (p. 270).

48. Tomizza, *Alle spalle di Trieste*, p. 179.

CHAPTER 4

The Exilic Rift in
La ragazza di Petrovia and *L'albero dei sogni*

The Fracture of the Exile

The novels *Materada* and *La miglior vita* foreground the dramatic exile that took place in Istria after the Second World War. This event plays a central role in Tomizza's literary production, several of his novels being dedicated to it. He seeks to define the figure of the exile, focusing in detail on the moment at which someone faces the decision to leave their home country, something that very few writers have dealt with. Leaving one's own country (or, in certain cases, remaining in it) represents only the first step towards the state of exile. Tomizza investigates this initial moment to better define the condition. Whatever reasons have caused exile, departure is the moment in which a new geography of emotions fills the mind, marking the break of the self. As Said suggests, exile is 'the unhealable rift forced between a human being and a native place, between the self and its true home'.[1]

Said's definition of exile recalls the idea of trauma, which is the violent rupture between the individual and the world outside, the 'overwhelming experience of sudden or catastrophic events in which the response to the event occurs in the often delayed, uncontrolled repetitive appearance of hallucinations and other intrusive phenomena'.[2] It is, in other words, an event that resurfaces continually and uncontrolledly, tormenting the sufferer. The trauma of exile upsets the spatio-temporal dimension, disrupting the subjects' sense of the linear development of their existence. Radulescu points out that, since the expulsion of Adam and Eve from Paradise, exile has forever been linked with the idea of trauma and related notions: 'the sense of rupture, loss, fragmentation, and nostalgia [...] are generally recognized as common places for the drama of exile'.[3] This sort of exile 'implies related feelings of dissociation, splitting, schizophrenia, a coming apart of the inner soul' that disturbs the identity of the self.[4] Faced with the rupture of exile, the self is doomed to various forms of fragmentation. Indeed:

> While it is true that literature and history contain heroic, romantic, glorious, even triumphant episodes in an exile's life, these are no more than efforts meant to overcome the crippling sorrow of estrangement. The achievements of exile are permanently undermined by the loss of something left behind forever.[5]

Tomizza can identify the initial stage of the exile clearly because Istria offered him a multicultural context that made the decision of whether to let one of one's selves prevail over the other more difficult. Before Yugoslavia annexed the peninsula, the potential exile was free to fluctuate between the two poles of his identity, but at that point he had to choose a definitive option and this in only a short space of time. In comparison to other such experiences, the Istrian experience of exile highlights the loss of one part of the self, which leads to an internal split. A mixed native land that suddenly imposes a univocal identity demands the dismembering of double belongings, increasing still further the displacement suffered.

The etymology of exile (*exilium*) suggests both the act of separation from one's own home country and the state of wandering abroad.[6] Tomizza is inclined to reassess the first of these elements, confirming Brodsky's statement that '*exile* covers, at best, the very moment of departure, of expulsion'.[7] The shock that results from meeting the reality of exile leads to a period of transition from the old to the new country, a phase that will be considered in this chapter in the works *La ragazza di Petrovia* and *L'albero dei sogni*. In Tomizza's novels, exile can be likened to the condition represented by the metaphor of a sinking ship on board which life continues: 'È una situazione in margine, quella del profugo, come quella del passeggero di una nave che affonda, eppure in lui la vita continua. È un aspetto misterioso del mondo moderno, che Fulvio Tomizza ci aiuta forse a comprendere' [It is a marginal situation, that of the refugee, like a passenger on a sinking ship, but in whom life carries on. It is a mysterious aspect of the modern world, that Fulvio Tomizza perhaps helps us to understand].[8] Facing the 'impossible' choice of whether to remain in one's own country or to leave it, the exile is aware that his life may be split and that his future is certainly compromised. As in Hoffman's *Lost in Translation*, the exile knows intimately the degrees and nuances of an absence that will forever mark his life and that becomes manifest in the moment he is forced to choose a life of separation from the country left behind and head towards an uncertain future. As Hoffman writes: 'I come across an enormous, cold blankness — a darkening, an erasure of the imagination, as if a camera eye has snapped shut, or as if a heavy curtain has been pulled over the future'.[9]

Among Tomizza's characters, the experience of Giustina from *La ragazza di Petrovia* epitomizes the rupture of the exile. In this novel, which begins with a terribly difficult choice and ends with the impossibility of return, the close psychological study of the progress of a girl from Istria is the means for an in-depth investigation of the nature of exile. The decision to leave her home country is explored in detail, outlining the innermost dynamics of the process. Giustina experiences two lives simultaneously: her fugitive side drives her towards exile; in opposition, the slower side finds moving an ordeal. The same route towards Italy is taken by what are, it seems, two different girls: a more elusive person, who lives a parallel existence to a real person, who is stuck under the rain and slowly follows until Giustina's death when she attempts to come back to her homeland without permission.

L'albero dei sogni's protagonist, Stefano, expands Giustina's exilic fracture as his doubleness is explored through a sequence of two exiles. The novel is divided into three parts separated by gaps in the narrative. The failure of his first exile to Trieste drives Stefano to consider the other pole of his identity, which is symbolized by the Yugoslav capital Belgrade. Moved by a hidden force, which drives the wandering stranger towards an ideal 'elsewhere', his process of personal 'Balkanization' begins. In the Yugoslav capital, problems with language make it even more difficult for Stefano to come to terms with his situation, and this leads to a collapse of identity. The young man is 'due volte estraneo' (*AS*, p. 159) [twice estranged], because both in Italy and in Yugoslavia he is unable to find the hybrid place he left behind, and he fails to find a home with either of the two communities that, together, made up that hybrid world.

In both works exile is a trauma that weighs heavily upon the character's existence. As pointed out by Jeannie Suk:

> Trauma seems at first to offer a paradoxical model in which a powerfully unusual event is at once inaccessible to the person who 'experiences' it, and yet all too available in nightmare, hallucination, and unwanted repetition... The event evades direct reference and knowledge, and yet provides constant torment.[10]

The traumatic nature of exile affects the way this experience, which is banished from consciousness, may be represented. Given that the fracture might be too difficult to be expressed, characters struggle to portray it, as Judith Herman writes: 'certain violations of the social compact are too terrible to utter aloud: this is the meaning of the word unspeakable'.[11] She also argues that traumatic events lead to overwhelming facts, and that one 'may experience intense emotion but without clear memory of the event, or may remember everything in detail but without emotion'.[12]

Drawing inspiration from Said's 'Reflections in Exile', Freud's *The Uncanny*, Otto Rank's theorization of doubleness, and Lacan's analysis of mirrors, I will investigate exile in the stories of Giustina and Stefano. Thanks to these contributions, exile shows itself to be subject to the paradoxes and inner conflicts of a broken life that will never be pieced back together. The exile's inner break is emphasized further by the question of the border — a new artificial line which is barely recognized by characters — and where a remarkable linguistic displacement takes place. These linguistic troubles unveil the dichotomy existing between the frontier and the border under politically stressful conditions. Once again, language mirrors the innermost aspects of Tomizza's characters' identities and the transitions that they make. In effect, apart from the 'geographical and cultural displacement, exile deterritorializes also because it foregrounds linguistic displacement'.[13]

Fragmented Narratives

While *Materada* and *La miglior vita* should be considered works which explore the plurality of voices of the Istrian community, *La ragazza di Petrovia* and *L'albero dei sogni* investigate the inner vicissitudes of their protagonists coping with the vexed decision as to whether to leave their country. Their internal controversies are mirrored in narratives that do not necessarily follow a coherent sequence of events, but are characterized by fragmentation, omission, and overlapping passages. This, according to Ihab Saloul, constitutes an 'exilic narrativity', that is, a 'particular narrativity through which the stories of exile can be read' and is usually built 'through fragmentation in terms of place, self and other'. This exilic narrativity is present in most narratives of exile and 'is noticeable in the fragmented sequence of storytelling'. Moreover, this fragmentation tends to take the shape of a 'drifting' mode of storytelling: 'This mode of telling introduces "drifting storytelling" as a tool suitable for narrating a mobile event'.[14]

Despite each telling a different story, both *La ragazza di Petrovia* and *L'albero dei sogni* are fragmented narratives of the troubled path of exile. Giustina, who has been made pregnant by a boy who has been moved to a refugee camp in Trieste, seeks to justify to herself her decision as to whether to remain in Istria or to leave the country. On a one-day visit to the refugee camp while she still has both options open to her, she formulates her thoughts in relation to exile. Her whole story revolves around the taking of this decision and the process is presented to us before a backdrop of refugees and displaced people. From her initial reticence — which almost prevents her from acting — to her final choice she unfolds her thoughts. The result is a character whose universe, made up of mixed feelings, silences, and overlapping gestures, constitutes an image of the chaotic experience of exile.

In Giustina's story, the 'new geography of emotion' belonging to exile begins with a state of paralysis. In her native village, where lorries are carrying her countrymen to Italy, she finds herself barely able to walk; she stands in the rain thinking about her departure the following day. This premonition of losing one's country is experienced as a difficulty in moving. The grim reality gnaws at her and her movements slow down — an image that allows the reader to sense the turbulence of her state of mind. Guido Sommavilla underlines the breaks and gestures in this train of thoughts, which is enveloped in a subdued atmosphere: 'Ma essa si muove come un automa, cerca e non cerca, cammina e non cammina, resta e non resta a Petrovia: tutti movimenti che traspaiono imprecisi come dal fondo d'un acquario' [But she moves like a robot, searching and not searching, walking and not walking, staying and not staying in Petrovia: all movements are seen blurred as from the bottom of an aquarium].[15]

Giustina's immobility, which is seen in her difficulty in dealing with these two urges, confirms the strain placed upon her. This is paralleled in the limited number of events of the narrative: the story develops around an almost deserted village, houses that are left empty and boarded up, and the noise of lorries which carry the exiles away. The result is that she wanders between two conditions, which are usually overlapped in a subdued narrative, destroying any temporal reference: 'Il lento tessuto d'immagini e di pensieri vien così, per alterne voci, a ricomporre la immagine del profugo sradicato, in un tempo senza movimento' [The slow fabric of images and thoughts comes, in alternating voices, to recompose the image of the uprooted refugee, in a time without movement].[16] This disruptive state of being pinpoints the universal condition of the exile, as Giorgio Bergamini outlines:

> Plasmandosi in personaggio, ella diventa come l'incarnazione d'una idea

platonica del personaggio, una sorta di proiezione ipostatica di quello 'scisma' avvenuto tra l'universo di 'prima' e la nuova realtà irreale, che non le consente di ritrovare la propria dimensione se non nel sogno-incubo, nel gioco sregolato delle associazioni e dissociazioni della coscienza [...]. Ci si potrebbe ora domandare se questa Giustina (priva quasi di tratti fisici e chiamata per nome non più di tre o quattro volte lungo l'intero arco del romanzo) condensi anche una condizione allegorica, esemplare e rappresentativa, del dramma generale che si svolge intorno a lei.[17]

[By shaping herself into a character, she becomes like the embodiment of a Platonic idea of the character, a kind of hypostatic projection of the 'schism' that has opened up between the universe of 'before' and the new unreal reality, that does not allow her to regain her size if not in the dream-nightmare, in the unregulated game of associations and dissociations of the consciousness [...]. One may now ask whether this Giustina (almost devoid of physical traits and called by name no more than three or four times in the entire arc of the novel) condenses into an allegorical, exemplary, and representative condition of the general drama that unfolds around her.]

Giustina experiences exile through a form of dreamlike adventure, in the puzzling associations and incongruities dictated by the pressing situation.

The fragmented nature of Giustina's thoughts cannot be kept at bay. Her vexed state is defined by Aldo Camerino as an innermost universe that the reader can catch 'nei suoi scompensi e brividi, nelle sue più rarefatte verità, che ci son fatte note per via di languori e tremori e dubbi e difficili comprensioni' [in her imbalances and chills, in her most rarefied truths, which are made known to us by the languor and tremors and doubts and difficult insights].[18] The wandering of the subject away from an anchored position characterizes a narrative that does not support chronological progression or the coherent localization of events; straightforward plot structure is consequently undermined. The reader penetrates this troubled universe, discovering a metaphysical dimension in which subterranean introspection dictates the rhythm, confirming that, as suggested by Said, 'exile [...] is fundamentally a discontinuous state of being'.[19]

In *L'albero dei sogni* discontinuity is used to an even greater extent in the way Stefano's exile is presented: the event takes place in a break of the narrative. The change of setting (and with it the political and linguistic environment) comes unexpectedly to the reader and the logic of the sequence of events is put under strain; Stefano's experiences of unbelonging and exclusion are thus expressed through a narratorial effect. Most importantly it is the omission of important details in the story that characterizes the figure of the exile. As suggested by Maier:

Nell'*Albero dei sogni* il dissidio etnico-politico fra gli italiani e gli slavi passa da una misura, per così dire, esterna, rappresentativa e descrittiva o mnemonico-cronachistica, a una dimensione tutta interiore, ossia viene interamente calato nell'animo di Stefano, e si configura come uno scontro o un incontro tra le due componenti dialettiche della personalità del protagonista. Il quale oscilla fra la nostalgia per un vecchio mondo che sta per crollare (o è di fatto crollato) e la suggestione di un mondo nuovo in via di elaborazione; e subisce in tempi diversi sia il fascino del nazionalismo italiano, sia quello del socialismo jugoslavo, sentendosi variamente attratto dalla concezione patriarcale, ottimistica, euforica della vita, propria di suo padre, e dal senso pratico della madre, e cercando di conciliare in se stesso, non senza fatica e attraverso numerose e per lo più deludenti esperienze, l'influsso paterno e quello materno. Stefano, insomma, si trova sempre di fronte a dei dilemmi, a delle scelte difficili e rischiose; e quasi sempre si mette nella posizione sbagliata, anche se con la più o meno lucida consapevolezza che proprio di errori, di pentimenti, di rimorsi è costellata (e non può non esserlo) la strada tortuosa e ingannevole che porta alla verità.[20]

[In *L'Albero dei sogni* the ethno-political conflict between Italians and Slavs corresponds to a measure, as it were, that is external, representative, and descriptive, or mnemonic-chronicle, to a whole inner dimension, that descends entirely into Stefano's soul, and is set up as a clash or meeting between the two dialectical components of the protagonist's personality. The latter oscillates between nostalgia for an old world that is about to collapse (or has indeed collapsed) and the suggestion of a new world that is under development. At different times he falls under the spell of both Italian nationalism and Yugoslav socialism, feeling variously attracted by the patriarchal optimistic, euphoric view of life, typical of his father, and the practical sense of his mother, and trying to reconcile within himself, not without difficulty and through numerous and mostly disappointing experiences, paternal and maternal influences. In fact Stefano always faces dilemmas, difficult and risky choices; and he almost always puts himself in the wrong position, even though he has a more or less clear self-awareness that mistakes, regrets, and remorse pave (and always will) the winding and deceptive road towards truth.]

Stefano's move from the Istrian countryside to Trieste is one of the most important breaks in the narrative. On frequent occasions, the character's contradictory choices, which remain unexplained by the narrator, bewilder the reader, and there is work to be done to rebuild a coherent sequence of events. This discontinuity marks the surfacing of an 'inexpressible' world that typifies the life of the character in the new city. In the void which surrounds him, the reasons behind the decision to move, the farewell to the lost homeland, as well as the gradual approach to the new country, are expelled from the narrative, leaving space for unsolved questions. As suggested by Mario Lavagetto: 'Lo sconosciuto, lo straniero [...] propone un enigma, lo formula e sollecita una soluzione' [The stranger, the foreigner [...] proposes an enigma, he formulates it and calls for a solution].[21]

The move to Trieste comes unexpectedly to the reader. The previous episode of the novel, where Stefano's father is released, having been imprisoned in Istria for his Italianism, suddenly ends, and the characters' passing into exile is expressed through a quick series of fragmented images. When Stefano's family returns home with the father, the relationships between them have changed due to the lack of communication, but the landscape of Istria appears to have become estranged and inhospitable as well. For instance, the tired face of the father is reflected in the darkness of the night, which hinders the family in their recognition of familiar places:

> Faceva tanto buio che non mi accorsi del bivio Tramòn né delle prime case di Giurizzani. La corriera ci lasciò nel fango ghiacciato di una strada, fra due siepi

secche sopra le quali brulicava una distesa di stelle fitte e lucenti come carta vetrata. (*AS*, p. 105)

[It was so dark that I did not notice the junction Tramòn nor the first houses in Guirizzani. The bus left us in the frozen mud of a road, between two dried hedges over which teemed an expanse of dense and shiny stars like sandpaper.]

The inevitable conclusion is that Stefano's mother begins to prepare bags, under the motionless gaze of her husband. Very little information is given to the reader, who may easily empathize with the father's undeserved imprisonment and the consequent rush after the release, but cannot fully grasp the chaotic movements of Stefano's family.

The concluding scenes of the first part of the novel lead the reader to the expectation of a journey, or to be more exact an escape, though Stefano's mother's suitcase does not give any indication as to the destination of the journey, nor does witnessing this solitary woman pack clarify how many she is packing for. The journey towards Trieste itself is completely omitted from the story, as if it has been hidden away in an obscure pocket, unavailable to the reader. The new setting, which, without any introduction or explanation, introduces the reader to two very specific locations, Piazza dell'Unità and Corso Italia, takes for granted the knowledge that this is now Trieste and that Stefano is living there. Furthermore, the initial presentation of the city under Allied control contradicts the reader's expectations, contrasting with the intimate familiar scene which has just been abandoned.

This lack of information, which can also be described as an empty space, a missing link, or, in Wolfgang Iser's terms, 'a blank', is a vital step in the narrative. It could be defined as a blank because it is an intentional, carefully crafted suspension of connectivity which forces the reader to provide links for what is disconnected. In the space between the knowable and the unknowable, the reader immediately recognizes that something is missing and, above all, now comes face to face with an estranged Stefano. By omitting the description of the journey towards Trieste, the author emphasizes the impact Stefano felt when faced with the new reality, highlighting that something important is missing, or rather cannot be told. The reader, who 'fills in the blank in the text, thereby bringing about a referential field', resigns himself to this discrepancy.[22]

As Mario Petrucciani points out, *L'albero dei sogni*'s narrative is striking as much for its exclusions as for what the author chooses to include: 'Basta notare le interruzioni e le riprese tra un capitolo e l'altro [...] i modi delle pause, degli stacchi tra un brano e l'altro' [Just note the interruptions and resumptions between one chapter and the other [...] the mode of the breaks, of the detachments between one passage and the other].[23] If the text is a ground in which both the author and the reader play their part, the latter should be capable of comprehending the meaning of the new situation, despite not having all the information he or she might have expected to have been given. The lack emphasizes that exile that brings obscurity: 'è un portavoce, un legittimo rappresentante dell'oscurità: non inscrivibile in alcuna anagrafe, costituisce nello stesso tempo una provocazione e una molla narrativa'

[It is a spokesperson, a legitimate representative of darkness: not inscribed in any registry office, it constitutes both a provocation and a narrative impulse].[24]

Stefano's first exile is the result of 'un groviglio inestricabile' [an inextricable tangle] typical of the 'dilemma dell'uomo di confine [...] scelto non senza forti dilacerazioni affettive e ideologiche' [dilemma of a man of the borders [...] chosen not without strong emotional and ideological scars].[25] The Trieste in which Stefano arrives is in political turmoil. The main streets are crowded with people demonstrating against the American and English soldiers who are supervising the city. Stefano observes Italian flags hung on balconies, the fervour which inflames the demonstrators, and the rising agitation that is being kept under control by the Allies. His reactions are far from hesitant; having described the crucial elements of the scene, he immediately declares his impatience. The restlessness of the young man will drive him to his second exile to Belgrade. Far from being a painless choice, Stefano's decision to take the Orient Express to the Yugoslavian capital coincides with the troubled events on the border with Italy. Until the very last moments before his departure, while he is packing, still undecided about his destination, he is tormented by indecision: 'Di corsa andai a fare la valigia non sapendo ancora se mi avrebbe accompagnato oltre il blocco o se l'avrei issata sulla rete dell'Orient Express, quando nella mia camera di disordini irruppero la madre e il fratello' (*AS*, p. 187) [I hurriedly went to pack the suitcase, still without knowing if it would accompany me beyond the block or if I would lift it in to the net of the Orient Express, when my mother and brother broke into my jumbled room].

Stefano's second exile begins with a lie. If the Triestine parenthesis was characterized by a huge omission, aimed at defining the mysterious and troubled condition of the stranger, a series of lies leads Stefano to the decision to move to Belgrade. Once more, the reader is forced to grasp for his intentions and to struggle to work out what is going on despite the unreliability of his claims. Lies and incongruities typify a narrative in which linearity is, for the second time, 'broken'. The behaviours of Tomizza's characters recall Svevo: 'Mente sempre un po' quando dice la verità, è anche vero che dice sempre un po' la verità quando mente' [He lies a bit when he tells the truth, it is also true that he always speaks the truth a bit when he lies].[26]

Both of these works present an exilic 'narrativity' that contains disruptive dynamics correlating with the characters' troubled decision to leave their land. This specific type of 'narrativity' is made out of missing elements, gaps, lies, and other elements that displace a more coherent and linear development of the story. These 'negative' features should not be considered a limit, because as Nicola Gardini points out, a novel is always generated by the necessity to fill a gap, inviting the reader to engage with the text. The work of reconstruction of meaning is the task every text requires from its readers. In Gardini's words: 'quel che si perde si deve recuperare' [What you lose you must retrieve]; therefore 'la sottrazione chiama di necessità il completamento, il danno, il restauro' [subtraction calls of necessity for completion, damage, restoration].[27] These missing elements, that are named 'lacunae' by Gardini, have a particular function within the narrative: 'La lacuna espande il senso, portando la significazione oltre i limiti fisici delle parole scritte.

Il lettore interprete fa agire il testo oltre i limiti della scrittura e, a sua volta, è attraversato dalla voce nascosta del testo' [The gap expands the sense, carrying the meaning beyond the physical limitations of the written word. The interpreting reader makes the text act beyond the limits of writing and, in turn, is crossed by the hidden voice of the text].[28] The exilic text takes full advantage of 'lacunae' to express an experience that is in its essence fragmented and fragmenting.

Doubleness

Exile is an experience the telling of which is difficult to form into a linear narrative, because it is the result of a rupture or trauma. Tomizza takes advantage of the 'machine' of the text to express the uprootedness of his characters and focuses in detail on the moment of fracture. In *La ragazza di Petrovia* exile corresponds to a break in the life of the character, who will progressively be divided into two distinct entities. This condition is typical of exiles, who 'are double, split into a "now" and a "then", a "here" and a "there"'.[29] By analyzing examples of narratives produced by a traumatic event, Roger Lockhurst finds that traumatized figures 'become so disturbed that they split into two or more personae'.[30] When the ego dissociates into two or more people, through 'splitting' or 'identity doubling', two distinct sides, each with its own way of relating to the world and self, begin troubling the oneness of the self. Two entities take control of the behaviour of a person who acts without being connected anymore to a central self, which finally is destroyed. The traumatized person replaces the wholeness of the central self, and this is what happens in Giustina's story.

Facing the unexpected events in Istria that weigh her down under an incessant metaphorical rain, Giustina begins to contemplate two sides within herself: one side anchors her to her homeland, while the other slowly sets out on the path of exile. The vacillation between these two poles is a way of presenting the alternation between, on the one hand, thoughts and memories that stop her in her tracks, and then, on the other, the anticipation of the future that characterizes her freer moments. Signs of this internal division emerge as she walks through her home village. First, I shall consider Giustina's fluctuating position in relation to her trip to Trieste. Her indecision is over whether to remain in Istria (or, rather, return to Istria afterwards) or to stay in Italy for good. The decision is postponed until the very end of the novel, as Giustina's doubleness prevents her from making up her mind. I will now focus in detail on the genesis of Giustina's split and disjointed internal dynamic by looking at the first occasion on which we see her struggle to maintain her wholeness.

The immobility that marks the beginning of the novel, leaving the character in a somewhat peaceful and stable condition, quickly changes. The reader is able to explore Giustina's inner conflicts through the way in which she moves through the already emptying village in the rain. Her movements lack the harmony that comes from the control of a simple, single consciousness. Two opposing forces weigh on her body. The vertical one, which flattens her to the ground limiting her actions, does not allow her to move: 'Se ne sta immobile, come appiattita al suolo' [She rests unmovable as though flattened to the ground].[31] She leans on a wall, looks at her wet shoes but allows herself to be soaked by the rain, incapable of moving. However, an opposing drive pushes her forward. Giustina crosses the village, attracted by disused houses: 'Camminando, passa in rassegna casa per casa. I suoi occhi inquieti si posano di preferenza sulle case più grandi, tutte ormai vuote, sprangate' (*RP*, pp. 69–70) [Walking, she goes house by house. Her restless eyes alight in preference on the larger houses, all empty now, boarded-up]. She walks slowly through puddles; sometimes her slow movements appear to block an urge to walk faster or run.

Moving to a new place or remaining in the current one seems to be the origin of the character's conflicting tensions and indecisions. The border pass that enables her to visit Trieste does not help her come to a quick decision; on the contrary, it gives her the chance to consider several options. Her indecision reveals itself progressively and takes root in her soul as the reality of exile weighs on her. She admits to being unprepared for her journey to Trieste:

> Fuori ha ripreso a piovere e lei non ha molta voglia di affrontare nuovamente la pioggia, né di affrontare la giornata di domani, alzarsi, prendere la corriera, a Trieste è stata solo una volta, che cosa metterà nella valigia? per due o per più giorni?' (*RP*, p. 86)
>
> [Outside it once more started raining and she did not have much desire to brave it once again, nor to face the following day, getting up, taking the bus, she had only been to Trieste once, what to put in the suitcase? for two days or for longer?].

These incompatible trajectories disrupt her existence, leading to the paradoxical situation of a character who combines inactivity and dynamism. The narrator describes this odd contamination as follows: 'Si muove lentamente nella sua pensosa immobilità' (*RP*, p. 62) [She moves slowly in her pensive immobility]. The result is that, although she is walking, she does not feel she is moving forward: 'pur camminando, le pare di star ferma' (*RP*, p. 64) [walking, she seems to stand still]. The situation can be reversed: she is able to walk standing still, but she can also be unaware of moving: 'Quasi senza accorgersene si è messa a camminare' (*RP*, p. 62) [Almost without realizing it she started to walk]. Moving or being stuck in the rain are not two contradictory states, as the former does not exclude the latter and vice versa.

This overlapping, odd situation does not last long. Giustina splits when she can no longer cope with the pressure imposed by her diverging selves. This emerges when she is dripping wet and her heavy clothes swell her form, magnifying the impression of being overwhelmed by reality, and she realizes she cannot move. Here the character breaks apart, the fugitive part of herself can move forward, while the other is held back by her feet that sink into the street. In that specific moment, the disharmony of movements due to the simultaneous coexistence of opposing drives, leads to rupture:

> Muove il piede, fa un passo, raggiunge un'altra pozzanghera o un'altra pietra

provvidenziale che sporge dal selciato, vede i muri grigi delle case che da ambo i
lati si lascia via via alle spalle, eppure sente nel medesimo tempo che i suoi piedi
pesano quintali e non è possibile sollevarli, e le pare che tutto ciò che la rende
sicura del suo vero esistere in quel luogo, in quell'istante, rimanga fermo in un
punto, e solo una parte fuggevole e stravagante di lei la preceda nel cammino.
Ecco infatti che mentre quella si vede giunta davanti alla casa dei Vesnaver [...]
lei in carne e ossa, si trova ancora all'incrocio della strada. Veramente è già sul
selciato ruvido della strada dove non passano macchine, e perciò si accorge,
nonostante l'immobilità in cui è imprigionata, di aver guadagnato un po' di
strada, avendo fatto nel frattempo qualcosa. Di aver superato il breve tratto —
non più di quattro metri — che, attraversando la strada maestra, al tortuoso
sentiero tra le graie immette direttamente nella stradetta formatasi da sé e
diretta al grosso del paese. (*RP*, p. 64)

[She moves her foot, takes a step, reaches another puddle or providential stone
protruding from the pavement, sees the grey walls of the houses on both sides
that she gradually leaves behind, but she feels at the same time that her feet
weigh tons and it is impossible to lift them, it seems that everything that makes
sure of her true existence in that place, at that moment, is suspended in time,
and only a fleeting and extravagant part of her goes ahead on the road. While
that part arrives in front of Vesnaver's house [...] she, in flesh and blood, still
stands at the crossroads. She is effectively already on the rough pavement of the
road where cars do not pass, and therefore realizes, in spite of the immobility
in which she is imprisoned, she has gained a little bit of street having done
something in the meantime. Having navigated this short stretch — of no more
than four metres — which crosses the high street, the winding path between
the *graie* enters directly into the narrow street formed by itself and directly to
the centre of the village.]

Giustina should either still be at the entrance of the village (at the first cross), where there is constant rain, or at the end of it, by Vesnaver's house, following the route taken by the faster self. However, she is in the two places simultaneously, underlining the impossibility of a reconciliation of these two selves. This corresponds to Massimo Fusillo's definition of 'double':

> Si parla di doppio quando, in un contesto spaziotemporale unico, cioè in un
> unico mondo possibile creato dalla finzione letteraria, l'identità di un person-
> aggio si duplica: un uno diventa due; il personaggio ha dunque due incarnazioni:
> due corpi che rispondono alla stessa identità e spesso allo stesso nome.[32]

> [We define the double as when, in a single space-time context, namely in one
> possible world created by literary fiction, the identity of a character is dupli-
> cated: a one becomes two; the character has thus two incarnations: two bodies
> that respond to the same identity and often the same name.]

Giustina's two selves are experienced at the same time, giving rather different impressions, which creates puzzling images, like hallucinations. Doubles may present in different forms, such as the alternation of two different states, the production of a mirroring image, a lookalike, or a metamorphosis. Several definitions can be applied, depending on the interaction and the composition of the two components. Among those that Fusillo lists are: 'specular characters', whose antagonism is so marked as to obtain an effect of unity, as in Robert Louis Stevenson's *Master of Ballantrae*; 'complementary characters', those who, as in Pirandello's *Pari*, integrate harmonically, shaping one identity; and 'apparent doubles' and 'oneiric doubles', like demonic possessions, persecutions, and reincarnations.

The split of Giustina's self immediately assumes unique traits. The scission can be compared to the fluctuation between a more advanced position to one further back: sometimes we are with Giustina's faster self, which explores the path in front, and at other times with the slower part, which stops and even moves backwards. The rhythm of the fluctuation is dictated by the terrible decision that is in the balance: 'E le verrebbe spontaneo di fare un passo indietro fino a raggiungere l'oscura stradetta tortuosa e poi, sempre retrocedendo a passi lenti, raggiungere il "laco" e il cocuzzolo e il bosco' (*RP*, p. 66) [And it would be natural for her to take a step back up to the dark winding narrow road and then, always receding at a slow pace, reaching the 'laco' and the crown and the forest]. Nevertheless, the other part of herself comes on stage moving quickly forward:

> Raggiunge rapida il successivo tronco di gelso non curandosi d'altro, ora, che di sfuggire all'orribile drago che sempre più guadagna terreno facendo sussultare lievemente la groppa alta di masserizie. E quand'è passato, si trova come per incanto incollata a quel gesto [...] in mezzo al paese. (*RP*, p. 69)

> [She rapidly reaches the next mulberry trunk without now taking care of anything else, apart from escaping the horrible dragon that increasingly gains ground, jerking household goods about. And when it is suddenly gone, she finds herself magically glued to that gesture [...] in the middle of the village.]

The redoubling of the girl constitutes a further chance to make a comparison between her previous life and the future she will be forced into. With the doubling, parallel lives are experienced simultaneously, as confirmed by Freud: 'All the unfulfilled but possible futures to which we still like to cling in phantasy, all the strivings of the ego which adverse external circumstances have crushed, and all our suppressed acts of volition which nourish in us the illusion of Free Will'.[33] If doubling allows the character to experience a different life from its own, it also fragments the self.

The girl with the double soul cannot belong to either one place or the other. This discrepancy is destined to make coordination impossible, even when the slower part joins the faster. After the collision of Giustina's drives and the consequent split, she fluctuates along the path of her two selves, which sometimes appear to reassemble them:

> Aguzzando lo sguardo può ora vedere l'incrocio delle strade, laggiù, sgombro d'ogni presenza viva. Anche l'altra parte di lei l'ha dunque raggiunta lentamente, un po' riluttante, in quella specie di riparo dalla pioggia che le procurano le tegole fuoruscenti e sconnesse della stalla degli Stringher. (*RP*, p. 70)

> [By staring, she could now see the intersection of roads down there, emptied of any living presence. Also the other part of herself has thus reached her slowly, a bit reluctantly, in that sort of shelter from the rain made by the protruding and uneven tiles of Stringher's barn.]

The gap between the two dimensions widens and narrows, as one side moves faster than the other. The faster part reaches the crossroads and waits for the other, which has been slowed down by the rain. They are like two instruments, which only at times play the tune together. This art of combining independent melodies (which, although independent, form a coherent texture) is related to exile by Said:

> Most people are principally aware of one culture, one setting, one home; exiles are aware of at least two, and this plurality of vision gives rise to an awareness of simultaneous dimensions, an awareness that — to borrow a phrase from music — is *contrapuntal*.[34]

The twisted process of Giustina's split flows like a piece of contrapuntal music.[35] Although sometimes the self seems to be pieced together, the reconciliation is only temporary, the elusive part immediately moves away from the other, jeopardizing the identity of the self and undermining the complex relationship with its real home. Even though one part cannot be put back into the other and asymmetry prevails, one self is able to talk to the other: 'e dice semplicemente alla parte di sè rimasta a letto con i vestiti umidi indosso: "Guarda: sembra di essere alla fabbrica"' (*RP*, p. 113) [and she simply says to the part of herself that has stayed in bed with wet clothes: 'Look: it seems to be at the factory'].

In another passage the faster side looks for the slower one, which seems to materialize in the figure of a real woman. When Giustina reaches the entrance of the refugee camp following her journey through the Karst plateau, she looks at the floor, waiting for the other part of herself to leave. Once she has crossed the border, she is captured by the eyes of a woman who is staring at her intensely. This magnetism leads her to think that the woman is the other part of herself. Looking into the eyes of the mysterious woman, she argues that the latter might constitute 'l'altra parte di se medesima' (*RP*, p. 115) [the other part of herself]. Giustina immediately realizes her mistake, alerted by the physical difference between her and the woman. This underlines another aspect of Giustina's doubleness, which is embodiment in another person:

> Avverte in qualche modo che lo sdegno e la protesta dell'altra, lungi dall'essere rivolti a lei, sono indirizzati indistintamente a tutti tranne che alla sua persona, per cui distingue subito che ciò che l'ha colpita in fondo a quegli occhi ha da essere qualcosa d'intimamente buono e familiare, che le dà infatti la forza di sostenerne lo sguardo. Ha l'impressione che la donna l'abbia seguita passo per passo alla stazione fino a quell'angolo di strada, o, ancora prima, dalla sera precedente quando aveva vagato a lungo sotto la pioggia; e sarebbe quasi tentata di ravvisare in lei l'altra parte di se medesima, se la ragazza non fosse piuttosto bella e di qualche anno più vecchia, e non avesse dei bei capelli neri come imperlati di rugiada, che spiccano sul pallore del volto, e una fronte alta, come alto è il suo corpo, e le labbra carnose e scure e come gonfie da ripetuti morsi per trattenere il pianto. (*RP*, pp. 114–15)

> [She feels somehow that the indignation and protest of the other, far from being addressed to her, are addressed equally to everyone except her person, so she distinguishes right away what struck her deep in those eyes has to be something good and intimately familiar, that gives her the strength to bear up to the gaze.

She has the impression that the woman has been following her step by step from the station up to that street corner, or even before, from the night before when she wandered for a long time in the rain; and she would almost be tempted to recognize in her the other part of herself, if the girl was not rather beautiful and a few years older, and had nice dark hair as beaded with dew, that stands out against the pallor of her face, and a high forehead, as high is her body, and full and dark lips as if swollen by repeated bites preventing her from crying.]

If the two selves cover the same route at a different speed, they also know that the other can be found at any moment. In their constant chasing of one another, they are easily deceived by similar appearances. Full reconciliation is denied by a progressive break of the self, which cannot be rebuilt. The plot enhances the difference between the two selves: the other side almost becomes a real external presence.

Giustina's doubleness seems to fulfil another aim: being double may be related to self-preservation. By doubling, she will be better able to fit into different contexts, increasing the possibility of adapting to the rules of the changing regime and to the new conditions in the country of destination. As underlined by Freud, doubleness is here the first reaction against the 'extinction' of the self and a defence against the threat of death. Giustina's double self emerges at the moment when her identity is at risk; if Giustina remains in Petrovia, or if she moves to Trieste, her original self would inevitably be distorted. Doubling her self offers a better chance of preserving at least one of them, as remarked by Graziella Berto: 'Il gesto del raddoppiamento, della ripetizione avrebbe dunque avuto un ruolo di conferma, di rafforzamento: ciò che si teme di perdere viene moltiplicato' [The gesture of doubling, repetition would have had a role of confirmation and strengthening: what you fear to lose is multiplied].[36] The actions taken by different parts of the subject lead to overlapping thoughts and impressions, twisting the plot in a continuous alternation. The inner conflicts of the mind caused by the terrible impact of exile and its even more troubling consequences will now be considered in *L'albero dei sogni*.

Mirrors

As a result of the trauma of exile Tomizza's characters undergo an internal splitting that could be viewed as a defence mechanism. Beyond this, exile might cause further fragmentations and multiple identities interacting with others and the environment independently from the central self. The idea of multiple personalities is developed extensively by Tomizza as a way of expressing the experience of exilic displacement.

L'albero dei sogni is the novel in which he works through the trauma of the exile in most depth. Here he employs the device of mirrors that turn the subject into multiple presences annihilating the possibility of cohesive identity. Although appearing to play a minor role, mirrors are found in key moments of the plot, underlining the drift into estrangement of the protagonist, Stefano. He appears to employ them to confirm his identity to himself when he feels it to be under pressure. However, far from providing confirmation, mirrors supply an image that he does not recognize.

This non-dialectical process — Stefano cannot establish a dialogue with mirrors, he is merely subject to their response — is offered by a sequence of mirrors that intensify the sense of not belonging. The final laceration occurs when the mirror returns an image that is the emblem of the otherness embodied by the exile. Let me now focus on the bizarre association of temporal discontinuity and mirrors, before considering the effects of reflections.

Passages in which Stefano's image is reflected onto a variety of surfaces constitute a series of repetitions within the novel. Each time that Stefano faces his image, it links the episode to the previous one, confusing progressive temporal articulation. Mirroring surfaces recall one another in a to and fro of prolepsis and flashback that typifies *L'albero dei sogni*'s disruptive style and narrative. Stefano seems to be attracted to mirrors even before his first significant encounter with one. The root of his estrangement is established when, at his seminary, he looks at a window that reflects his appearance. Alone in the room, he seems to look for confirmation of his facial features, or rather of his identity:

> Ero proprio solo, e all'inizio di ogni ora di studio, ritto in piedi durante la preghiera, fissavo le mie sembianze nel vetro della finestra, socchiudevo gli occhi, buttavo la testa quanto più possibile all'indietro rimanendo un istante immobile a contemplare l'immagine della mia morte. (*AS*, p. 28)
>
> [I was alone, and at the beginning of each hour of study, standing upright during the prayer, I stared at my appearance in the glass of the window, my eyes half closed, my head back as much as possible while remaining a moment to contemplate the image of my death.]

This scene alerts the reader to Stefano's reactions in front of mirrors, given that sight of his own reflection forces him to turn away his gaze. The power of these reflections begins to play an important role in Stefano's life, but at this early stage in the novel he is still able to escape their influence.

The first significant mirror that Stefano meets is when he is leaving his first college and ends up alone with his suitcase with no one to pick him up because his father is in jail. Although he is not yet in exile, the passage underlines the meaning of the mirror in the story and unveils it as a powerful device that will present and analyze Stefano's condition. The episode can be summarized as follows: Stefano looks in the mirror and struggles to recognize his own image. Instead, he is watched by a pair of uncompromising eyes, which judge him. This unexpected inner rupture is directly linked to the change in the external world that drove Stefano to look for confirmation in the mirror.

Two parallel worlds — the inner and the outer — move together towards an inevitable fracture. Stefano's changed appearance (he discovers he is no longer a child) seems to worry and to annihilate him:

> Qualcosa si ruppe dentro di me, qualche cosa doveva essere accaduto nel mondo di fuori. Corsi allo specchio e stentai a riconoscere il mio viso nell'immagine riflessa: i baffi cresciuti, qualche pelo lungo sul mento e soprattutto la presenza ferma e asciutta di due aculei feroci negli occhi sfuggenti che per la prima volta mi giudicavano. [...] La vista si annebbiò di colpo e, sconvolto dalla nausea, feci appena in tempo a piegarmi sul lavabo. (*AS*, pp. 39–40)

> [Something broke inside me, something must have happened in the outside world. I ran to the mirror and hardly recognized my face in the reflected image: the grown moustache, some long hair on the chin and above all the firm and dry presence of two fierce spikes in shifty eyes that for the first time judged me. [...] The vision blurred suddenly and, shocked by nausea, I barely had time to bend over the sink.]

When Stefano looks in the mirror, he finds a strange face reflected there with which he feels he has only a limited resemblance: the image does not correspond to the idea that he has of himself. He begins to realize that he has an 'outside' that is beyond his control. But the stranger reflected in the mirror becomes inseparable from him, recalling Pirandello's Moscarda of *Uno, nessuno e centomila* [One, No One and One Hundred Thousand], who explicitly evokes 'l'estraneo inseparabile da me' [the stranger that is inseparable from me].[37]

The figure of a stranger in the mirror recalls Pirandello's character in several ways. Moscarda becomes aware of the stranger reflected in the mirror who cannot be avoided: 'Ma una maledetta voce mi diceva dentro che era là anche lui, *l'estraneo*, di fronte a me, nello specchio' [But a cursed voice inside me said that he was also there, the *stranger* in front of me, in the mirror].[38] Facing the mirror, the character discovers the impossibility of becoming familiar with the reflected image: 'Come sopportare in me quest'estraneo? quest'estraneo che ero io stesso per me? come non vederlo? come non conoscerlo? come restare per sempre condannato a portarmelo con me, in me, alla vista degli altri e fuori intanto della mia?' [How to bear this stranger in me? The stranger that I was to myself? How not to see it? How not to know it? How to remain forever condemned to take him with me, in me, in the sight of others and out of mine?].[39]

The judgement imposed on Stefano by these uncontrollable eyes is like an accusation against which he cannot defend himself. The mirror's gaze blinds him; his sight becomes dimmed, forcing him to lean over the sink to get closer to the mirror. Stefano believed that the mirror would be able to confirm his identity, to confirm himself to himself, to root him in a decisive form, while in fact he only finds a stranger there. The fluctuation between identity and otherness, which was previously possible, has become a non-negotiable imposition of the image upon the suffering self.

What is significant in Stefano's story, especially for people who do not belong to the country in which they are living, is the link between the mirror and the foreign — the scrutiny imposed on him by the mirror is like that imposed by strangers: 'Con la stessa severa estraneità mi ero sentito fino ad allora guardare da tutte le persone non strettamente del mio luogo' (*AS*, pp. 39–40) [With the same severe estrangement, I felt I had been viewed until then by all people who were not strictly from my place]. Gazes from people from whom he is already alienated alert Stefano to his 'difference', which is thus magnified — it will widen still further through mirrors. The mirror represents, therefore, a disturbing presence that emphasizes the character's displacement. When Stefano checks his image in mirrors, the only confirmation found will be that he is a stranger. The reflecting figure troubles him, creating an antagonism between the self and the mirrored image: 'specchiante e specchiato sono due, nati a uno stesso parto (gemelli) ma separati e nemici uno all'altro' [mirroring and mirrored are two, born in the same birth (twins) but separated and enemies to each other].[40]

The first approach to a mirror is recalled years later, just after he moves to Trieste: 'la mente volata ora spontaneamente allo specchio e al lavabo di G★★★' (*AS*, p. 122) [the mind now spontaneously flown to the mirror and to the sink of G★★★]. Past and present intermingle and the flow of memories combines in rather chaotic associations. The mirror appears again to Stefano, who is again searching for confirmation of his identity, to remind him that he is among strangers. Forever now, the approach to real mirrors is associated for him with a disillusionment that leads to a crisis. What is meant to be a helpful, reassuring tool has assumed a sense of affliction — identification and alienation coincide. This issue is present in the most significant mirror of the novel: the one in which Stefano's face is reflected when he is trying to make the decision whether to move to Italy following his mother and brother, or to Belgrade, taking the Orient Express: 'Solo nella stanza svuotata di quanto mi apparteneva e subito estranea, mi guardai allo specchio. Ero proprio io? Presi la corriera diretta a Sesana, dove il treno Parigi-Istanbul fermava per l'ispezione doganale' (*AS*, p. 189) [Alone in the room emptied of what belonged to me and immediately alien, I looked at the mirror. Was I really myself? I took the direct bus to Sesana, where the Paris-Istanbul train stopped for a customs inspection]. The empty room contains different characters, who present many points of view like actors on a stage. Opposing feelings drive Stefano towards the decision that he will soon have to make. The significance that should be attributed to this passage is primarily due to Stefano's addressing the question about his identity to the mirror. Even though Stefano is aware of the estrangement produced by mirrors, his question implicitly contains the possibility of being someone other than himself. He seems to doubt that the image mirrored may be himself. At another time, Stefano seems to follow the same train of reflections as Moscarda. When Pirandello's character is challenged by mirrors, he challenges the image he sees, raising doubts about the correspondence: 'Chi era? Ero io? Ma poteva anche essere un altro!' [Who was he? Was it I? But it could also be another!].[41]

It might have been another Stefano who was to take that train, as the specular image, which transcends its domain, does not confirm his identity. He goes to the mirror to help him make his decision, but his expectations are frustrated because what he sees is an image created by the mirror's reflection. This is much like what is described by Jacques Lacan in his passage dedicated to the loss of identity in front of mirrors and the new fragmented image:

> In the experience of mirrors, a moment occurs in which the image we think to have is modified. If the specular image that we have in front of us, which is our statue, our face, our pair of eyes, allows to surface the dimension of our gaze, the value of the image begins to change — above all there is a moment in which that gaze which appears in the mirror begins to look no longer at ourselves. *Initium, aura*, the dawn of a feeling of estrangement which opens to anxiety.[42]

Lacan believes that the mirror experience helps build the identity of the subject, which comes out as the result of the difference between the 'I' and what is 'not-I'. To be more specific, Lacan theorized the so-called 'mirror stage', a phase which shapes individual identity in childhood. In this phase, the child can build the image of himself through the image produced by a mirror or the gaze of the others. However, this image tends to include forms of otherness, as the child recognizes himself in his external component, which corresponds to the reflection outside himself:

> Unable as yet to walk, or even to stand up, and held tightly as he is by some support, human or artificial (what, in France, we call a '*trotte-bebe*'), he nevertheless overcomes in a flutter of jubilant activity, the obstructions of his support and, fixing his attitude in a slightly leaning-forward position, in order to hold it in his gaze, brings an instantaneous aspect of the image.
> This jubilant assumption of his specular image by the child at the *infans* stage, still sunk in his motor incapacity and nursling dependence, would seem to exhibit in an exemplary situation the symbolic matrix in which the I is precipitated in a primordial form, before it is objectified in the dialectic of identification with the other, and before language restores it, in the universal, its function as subject.[43]

It follows that the child's contact with the world is related to a form of *méconnaissance*, 'misconstruction', due to the inability of the subject to recognize that the image reflected by the mirror or the gaze of the others is false. It 'situates the agency of the ego, before its social determination, in a fictional direction, which will always remain irreducible for the individual alone, or rather, which will only rejoin the coming-into-being of the subject asymptotically'.[44] The identification of the child with an external other can only give an illusory sense of unity of the subject, prefiguring a sense of alienation later in life. This process of misconstruction of identity leads to the construction of an 'Ideal I', which supports the future alienations of the subject and is further 'subjectivized' by the acquisition of the language. When the child is able to use the pronoun 'I', the latter constitutes also an ideal ego, given that it does have a real continuity in the child's existence. By locating the ego in a fictional dimension, the ego seeks to establish a defensive support against fragmentation. Thus, identity turns into an illusory image provided by the mirror until the subject acknowledges its misrecognition: 'The role of the mirror apparatus [is critical] in the appearance of the double, in which psychical realities, however heterogeneous, are manifested'.[45]

In *L'albero dei sogni* the awareness of the misconstrued mirror image seems to emerge more evidently in Stefano's second exile, when he arrives in Belgrade. Here Stefano's possession of his own image is lost and the identity captured by the mirror's gaze is beyond his control. The gap between the idea of the self and the image of it reflected through the mirror's gaze troubles the young man, who no longer entirely trusts the mirror. Its gaze determines a situation that destroys previously established certainties. If Stefano starts doubting the image reflected in the mirror before moving to Belgrade, 'Ero proprio io?', his identity crisis deepens in his second exile. There the impact with the foreign leaves an impression on his life, leading to a fundamental question: 'In nome di Dio, chi ero?' (*AS*, p. 193) [In the name of God, who was I?]. This key passage is also emphasized by Gaetano De Leo, who identifies it as the question on which the novel itself is based: 'Penso infatti che *L'albero dei sogni* sia stato scritto essenzialmente per rispondere a questa domanda che lo stesso protagonista a un certo punto si pone: "In nome di Dio, chi ero?"' [I think, in fact, that *L'albero dei sogni* was essentially written in answer to the question that the protagonist himself raises at a certain point: "In the name of God, who was I?"].[46]

Lucid moments alternate with rather chaotic ones, leading to doubts. Stefano is not able to recognize himself, being shunted from one pole to the other of his identity. This all leads up to a final mirror scene, which is made up of dozens of mirrors. Under strain in the foreign city, Stefano looks for a café. In its oriental atmosphere, animated by groups of people smoking, Stefano struggles to find the waiter because he is bombarded by the infinite reflections of dozens of mirrors. The reality of Stefano's image is entirely lost to reflections that intermingle in a maze of images, eyes, and gazes, without escape.

> Seduto, incontravo la mia immagine riflessa in decine di specchi a sottolineare l'unico dato reale sul quale avrei potuto sempre contare. Mi spostavo sulla poltrona, la figura seguiva il movimento, e cercando del cameriere, mi imbattevo solo nei miei occhi interroganti. Il gioco di rifrazioni mi restituiva, sardonicamente come non mai, l'inconfessata realtà per cui tutto ciò che avevo finora potuto imporre o pretendere era stato eseguito, a proprio discapito, dalla medesima persona. (*AS*, pp. 194–95)
>
> [Seated, I found my reflected image in dozens of mirrors to underline the only real fact on which I could always count on. I moved to the armchair, the figure followed this movement, and looking for the waiter, I came up only in my questioning eyes. The play of refraction gave back to me, sardonically as never before, the unspoken reality that everything that had so far been able to impose or demand had been made, to its own detriment, by the same person.]

The blinding play of mirrors that reproduces his eyes to infinity, reflects the impalpable weakness of identity: all that Stefano can find is the fragmentation of the reflected image. In other words, he can only rely on the reflected image, which is the emblem of the stranger. Here, the mirror has gathered all its power. An uncanny presence, which cannot correspond to Stefano's identity, the mirror has marked the narrative, challenging the character, whose self is ever more trapped. The comparison with the foreign image makes a deep impression on him. When the mirror is present, whatever the context, the result is always the same: Tomizza's characters will be strangers, confirming that the role the mirror plays is decisive in relation to estrangement and the splitting of the self. As Carmelina Sicari points out, the mirror represents the deepest degree of estrangement: 'Lo specchio è il mito dell'estraniamento [...]. Qui c'è al grado massimo rappresentato il processo di estraneità e l'altro della scissione dell'io' [The mirror is the myth of estrangement [...]. Here is represented to its maximum degree the alienation process and the splitting of the I].[47] The full meaning of Stefano's exilic rift is reflected in the language used by Tomizza in *La ragazza di Petrovia* and *L'albero dei sogni*, and it is to this that I now turn.

The Language of the Border

The fracture of exile is an unusual, sharp break, or trauma, that marks the boundary between the old and the new place. Remarkably, the specific moment of rupture is displayed linguistically by characters such as Giustina and Stefano, who express their displacement while crossing the border. Despite the presence of manifold elements that characterize the fracture of exile, it is the language that makes visible its most subtle paradoxes and consequences. In this unique moment, the frontier and border become two clashing notions, which unveil once more their opposing meanings. By becoming a border, as discussed in Chapter 2, the frontier loses its hybridity. The strip of land characterized by mixed identities, ethnicities, and multilingualisms is transformed into a rigid line requiring a clear belonging.

The encounter and clash of the Italo-Croatian languages, which are present in *La ragazza di Petrovia*, are also used by Tomizza in *L'albero dei sogni*, where Stefano struggles to reach a linguistic reconciliation while crossing the border with his dying father. Though the area where the border takes its place may be seen to be a homogeneous landscape that does not divide two properly different entities, a new political reality emerges around linguistic transitions. This new linguistic divide aims to define clear distinctions, splitting artificially the different languages and related dialects. Although 'national group boundaries can be supported by a variety of objective and subjective "markers" [...] many have seen the linguistic criterion as the most important way of delineating nations'.[48] A specific language itself cannot be conceived as the 'essential requirement for national identity'; however, this does not change 'the fact that it is often seen as *the* pillar of groupness'.[49] The newly arriving Yugoslavian regime, and in parallel that of Italy, aimed to consolidate a national language in border areas where there was contact between languages. The reasons beyond it may be the following:

> The first reason — and the one that is naturally cited by nationalists themselves — is simply that [...] the ancestral group language is necessary for a continuing identity. [...] Other arguments for a strong language-identity linkage include the symbolic power of an ancestral variety as a nationalistic rallying point, the obvious visibility of a language (as opposed, say, to what may be a psychologically real but intangible sense of belonging), the view that different languages imply different conceptions of the world, and the link to history, to tradition, to culture, which continuation of the original language facilitates. It is important to realize that — as with other ethnic markers — an emphasis upon language often follows the development of nationalistic awareness.[50]

Apart from the natural link with language, which contributes to the establishment of national self-awareness, there is also the factor of ethnicity. The significance of this is underlined by Elie Kedourie: 'language was the outward sign of a group's peculiar identity and a significant means of ensuring its continuity. But the nation's language was peculiar to that nation only because such a nation constituted a racial stock distinct from that of the other nations'.[51] However, language itself seems to create '*an aspect of the soul*, a part of the soul', which strongly determines the sense of belonging on which nationalism is built.[52] Language embodies 'the living manifestation of historical growth and the psychological matrix in which man's awareness of his distinctive social heritage is aroused and deepened'.[53] It reflects the polity itself and embodies the spirit of a nation.

Nevertheless, when 'political frontiers separate the members of such a group, these frontiers are arbitrary, unnatural, unique'.[54] Istria is one of those cases where the historical overlapping of different civilizations had led to a hybrid territory, and it is this that the new political regime wanted to eliminate. Linguistic nationalism concerns 'problems of power, status, politics and ideology', all of which are concentrated on the border.[55] The latter became the space where the two entities must be absolutely divided. This creates the impossible situation in which we find Tomizza's characters.

The first time the border appears in *La ragazza di Petrovia* is when Giustina realizes that day has come and that she must take the coach to the refugee camp in Trieste where her fellow countrymen are provisionally located. Tomizza puts the border in an unremarkable setting and Giustina fails to recognize it. Although the reader is aware that an exile is taking place, the passage aims to underline the fact that the border takes place in unremarkable circumstances. The result is that it is perceived as a foreign and displacing presence that brings a feeling of estrangement:

> Per un buon tratto lei si sentì davvero uno dei tanti passeggeri che si recavano a Trieste per far delle compere o incontrarsi col cugino. Ma la sensazione strana di cui è preda soprattutto ora davanti allo sfilare degli identici roveri, aveva cominciato a farsi luce non appena si era trovata a tu per tu con l'ultimo milizionèr, il quale, appoggiato alla sbarra dipinta a tre colori, aveva scherzato parlandole in croato e a lei era parso di trovarsi davanti a Branko. (RP, p. 108)
>
> [For a good stretch she truly felt herself to be one of the many passengers who came to Trieste for shopping or meeting up with a cousin. But the strange feeling that caught up with her now in front of the parade of identical oaks, had begun to appear as soon as she found herself face to face with the last *milizionèr*, who, leaning against the barrier painted in three colours, joked in Croatian and it seemed to her as if she were in front of Branko.]

Giustina is struck by the sudden appearance of the border on her way to Trieste. Once she crosses it, she realizes that the landscape that surrounds her in the new country is the same as the one that she left at home. In addition to the reference to Branko, Giustina's head of department, she also remarks that nature has not changed either (the same oaks are present in both countries). The border irrupts in the life of Giustina: her trip to Trieste turns into an unreal experience. On the one hand, she barely recognizes the tricoloured barrier of the new border, which appears suddenly. On the other, these changes create a new context, where familiar and unfamiliar traits are dangerously mixed, leading her to an awareness of drastic and irretrievable transformations. Together with the sense of displacement, a sense of unreality emerges, due to the absurdity of the situation.

Giustina begins to live in a more accentuated though also apparently suspended dimension once she crosses the border. As suggested by Brodsky, exile is a 'metaphysical condition', an impalpable state.[56] Reality and imagination flow together in Giustina's story: 'attraverso questo sconvolgere, ricomporre e intersecare i piani del reale e dell'immaginato, negli scarti, sviluppi o regressioni [...] prendono valore, quasi una dimensione metafisica, i fatti narrati da Tomizza ne *La ragazza di Petrovia*' [through this upsetting, recomposing and intersecting of the planes of the real and the imagined, in the wastes, developments or regressions [...] are validated, almost in a metaphysical dimension, the facts narrated by Tomizza in *La ragazza di Petrovia*].[57] The border not only splits past and future, it also marks a new awareness; the sense of incredulity quickly leads to an absence of feeling when the bus passes the last village. The journey may be more an itinerary of inner thoughts than a real one:

> Ma se ora guardava oltre, dopo che la corriera, passate le ultime case della città, aveva preso a scalare lentamente l'altipiano, scopriva in se stessa qualche cosa di nuovo, che non era tanto sensazione, quanto assenza piuttosto di ogni sentire. Le pareva che tutto il viaggio compiuto sinora, e quell'ultimo tratto in particolare, fosse immaginazione della mente febbricitante di lei stesa ancora sul letto con gli abiti umidi indosso, costruita nell'attimo in cui si era appisolata e aveva tentato di raffigurarsi il viaggio del giorno dopo, dal confine alla città, della quale non poteva avere che un'immagine superficiale, fino all'ultima località dove doveva arrivare e che, essendo ancora campagna, la sua fantasia non poteva farle apparire se non in una veste familiare, ossia popolata dagli stessi roveri alti e sbandati, le stesse pietre bianche e i cespugli di ginepro, i grebani, i rovi, i pini veduti nell'infanzia quando pascolava le pecore degli Stringher a Vellania e tutto lungo la costiera di Salvore. (*RP*, pp. 110–11)

> [But if she now looked beyond, after the bus, once past the last houses of the city, had begun to slowly climb the plateau, she discovered in herself something new, that was not a feeling, rather the absence of any feeling. It seemed that the whole trip made up to now, and the last stretch in particular, was the imagination of her fevered mind as she lay still on the bed with wet clothes on, constructed at the moment in which she dozed off and tried to picture the journey on the next day, from the border to the city, of which she could have only a superficial image, to the final place where she was to arrive and that, being still countryside, her imagination could only make appear as familiar, namely populated by the same tall and leaning oaks, the same white stone and juniper bushes, the *grebani*, the brambles, the pines seen in childhood when grazing Stringher's sheep in Vellania and all along the coast of Savudrija.]

The 'totale smarrimento' (*RP*, p. 111) [total loss] caused by the impact with the reality of exile leads Giustina to think about the role her imagination might be playing. She doubts her senses, as if she has been dreaming or hallucinating. She cannot believe that this is the new country, so similar is it, made of the same oaks and stone walls, to the Istrian one.

When Giustina decides to return to Istria, she pays no attention to the last woman with whom she comes into contact in the refugee camp, who strongly advises her to renew her border pass. In the grip of an inexplicable haste, Giustina wants to get back as soon as possible and she does not listen to the border guard, who orders her to stop. When she does not stop, he shoots her, killing her. This passage provides a cathartic end to the novel, making clear once more the key role played by the border. The 'irrational' line of the border — 'la irrazionale linea di confine, senza quasi volto per noi' [the irrational borderline, almost without face for us] — which is experienced as an estranged or uncanny element by local people, overwhelms her from the beginning, marking both the boundary between two territories and that between life and death.[58] The dramatic end is foreshadowed the first time she sees the border, when it looks to her like a skull disfigured by an old wound: 'Il colle prima non veduto (o forse quello stesso folto di alberi che la corriera ha poc'anzi fiancheggiato) le si para davanti come un'enorme testa di morto solcata nel mezzo da un'antica terribile ferita' (*RP*, p. 115) [The hill not seen before (or perhaps the same thicket of trees that the bus had just skirted round) appears in front of her as the huge skull engraved in the middle with a terrible ancient wound]. She sees the border only out of the corner of her eye but it leaves its mark. On another occasion, actually on the hill, she is aware of the deathliness of the border, and from there she catches a glimpse of Istria, where the fields are red, dry, and divided by dirt roads:

> Ma com'è giunta sulla cima del poggio e, volgendosi impaurita alla visione del grande colle nudo e tagliato lungo tutta una striscia nel mezzo (la quale se continuasse a correre lungo i poggi più bassi le striscerebbe ora sotto i piedi come la luce di un faro) scopre davanti a sé, giù a valle, più larghe strisce di rosso tagliate nel mezzo da una bianca strada, e campi percorsi da filari di viti scomposte e secche. (*RP*, p. 219)

> [But once she reaches the top of the hill and, turning frightened by the vision of the great bare hill cut along a strip in the middle (which if it continued running along the lower hills would now slither under my feet like the light of a lighthouse) discovers in front of her, down to the valley, wider red strips cut across the middle by a white road, and fields crossed by rows of decomposed and dried vines.]

In proximity, the sense of threat exuded by the border is more acute. The distant image of the skull has come closer and, metaphorically speaking, passed through her body. The border progressively threatens her up to the point where it kills her. If the two previous references to it have built powerful images that are not easily forgotten by the reader (they also constitute the two occasions of analepsis in the story), the final encounter with the physical border seems to take place in a mundane landscape in which the border is not even mentioned. The death of Giustina is described as an enlarging sun that colours the sky with an intense geranium red that finally turns purple:

> Fu infatti un largo sole quello che la acceccò improvvisamente dopo ch'ebbe udito la stessa intimazione a fermarsi — *stòj, stòj* — ripetuta due volte dietro a un lontano cespuglio quasi con la stessa voce gutturale del capo-reparto Branko, e che per lei suonò nell'aria assordata dalle cicale come un caldo invito a proseguire, espresso in una lingua non sua ma ora ancora più familiare della sua. E il sole si allargò smisuratamente fino a comprendere in sé tutta l'aria e a coprire tutto il cielo, che si fece di colpo rosso come un geranio. [...] Ma non fa in tempo a provarne vergogna, perché le gambe vacillano e il cielo diventa viola. (*RP*, pp. 220–21)

> [It was in fact a large sun that suddenly blinded her after she heard the same injunction to stop — *stoj, stoj* — repeated twice behind a far bush almost with

the same throaty voice of the supervisor Branko, and that sounded to her in the air deafened by the cicadas as a warm invitation to continue, expressed in a language not her own, but now even more familiar than hers. And the sun expanded enormously to include all the air within itself and to cover the whole sky, which became suddenly red like a geranium. [...] But she does not have time to be ashamed, because her legs wobble and the sky turns purple.]

Giustina does not stop at the command 'stòj, stòj' [stop]. Crossing the border has been an experience that heightens the disrupted condition of the exile:

> I personaggi del romanzo sono [...] essenzialmente degli individui sradicati: non solo per la condizione materiale di profughi in cui si trovano, quanto piuttosto per una sorta di rottura del loro equilibrio psicologico, in conseguenza di eventi di cui non si rendono conto appieno pur subendoli drammaticamente.[59]

> [The characters in the novel are [...] essentially uprooted people: not only by the material condition of refugees in which they are located, but rather by the kind of rupture of their psychological balance, in consequence of events they are not fully aware of despite suffering them dramatically.]

A crucial discrepancy takes place on the border, where the narrator meshes well known and foreign traits. The Croatian language with which the guard gives the command seems to her more an invitation to cross the border rather than an order to stop. The guard intended to stop her, but having unsuccessfully given his command, kills her. Here, linguistic ambiguity plays a decisive role in the story, and the power borders have to discompose and upset is displayed; Giustina understands Croatian better than her native tongue, but does not stop at the command.[60] A strict linguistic division brings about a fatal event, representing the most evident form of incommutability between people and the harshness of the artificial split of the border. The rules of the border are ignored by the character, who clashes with an unrecognizable command.

The idea of linguistic displacement on the border is reinforced by a parallel episode in *L'albero dei sogni* when Stefano and his father are going to their native village in Istria where the father wants to die. The boundary further emphasizes the lack of comprehension between the two men and the impossibility of reconciliation. It also shows the extent to which the two languages are internal to Tomizza's characters and the inevitability of conflict with an external reality that imposes univocal linguistic identities:

> Giungemmo al confine e l'aria rimaneva fuori a sventagliare le cravatte delle guardie popolari. Il padre boccheggiante non nascondeva il proprio sdegno; diceva 'muoio' e io gridavo 'hitro, presto' nell'inavveduto e risibile tentativo, diventato vizio mentale, di promuovere in extremis l'impossibile riconciliazione. (*AS*, p. 166)

> [We reached the border, the breeze billowing through the ties of the special border guards. The father gasping for breath did not hide his outrage; 'I am dying' he said, and I shouted '*hitro*, soon' in an inadvertent and laughable attempt, verging on madness, to initiate an impossible reconciliation in extremis.]

Father and son use different languages on the border that now separates their homeland from their new country and this leads to a feeling of confusion. These passages represent a key moment of my analysis because they confirm that, from this moment of crossing, Stefano and Tomizza's characters in general will experience a deep sense of estrangement that will never be eased. Tomizza's borders intrude in characters' lives, shaking their worlds, and imposing a division that is felt to be unnatural. A discussion of the life lived in exile and the linguistic troubles Tomizza was to face will complete the analysis of the process of exile.

Notes to Chapter 4

1. Said, 'Reflections on Exile', p. 173.
2. Caruth, *Unclaimed Experience*, p. 11.
3. Domnica Radulescu (ed.), 'Introduction', in *Realms of Exile*, pp. 1–14 (p. 3).
4. Friedrich, 'European and Generic Exile', p. 178.
5. Said, 'Reflections on Exile', p. 173.
6. For a detailed analysis of this aspect, see Robert Edwards, 'Exile, Self and Society', in *Exile in Literature*, ed. by Lagos-Pope, pp. 15–31, and Mireille Courrent, 'Partir d'ici: à propos de l'étymologie latine de l'exil', in *Exils*, ed. by Hyacinthe Carrera (Perpignan: Presses universitaires de Perpignan, 2010), pp. 15–18.
7. Joseph Brodsky, 'The Condition We Call Exile', *Renaissance and Modern Studies*, 34 (1991), 1–8 (p. 7).
8. Alberto Spaini, 'Lo scambio delle popolazioni rimedio peggiore del male', *Il Telegrafo*, 21 June 1963, p. 3.
9. Hoffman, *Lost in Translation*, p. 4.
10. Jeannie Suk, *Postcolonial Paradoxes in French Caribbean Writing: Césaire, Glissant, Condé* (Oxford: Clarendon, 2001), p. 75.
11. Judith Herman, *Trauma and Recovery* (New York: Harper-Collins, 2002), p. 1.
12. Ibid., p. 37.
13. George Gasyna, *Polish, Hybrid and Otherwise: Exilic Discourse in Joseph Conrad and Witold Gombrowicz* (New York: Continuum, 2011), p. 39.
14. Ihab Saloul, ' "Exilic Narrativity": The Invisibility of Home in Palestinian Exile', in *Essays in Migratory Aesthetics: Cultural Practices Between Migration and Art-making* (Amsterdam & New York: Rodopi, 2007), pp. 111–28 (p. 113).
15. Guido Sommavilla, 'Trilogia istriana', *Letture*, 2 (1968), 92–98 (p. 96).
16. Teresa Buongiorno, 'Profughi istriani', *Rotosei*, 3 June 1963, p. 7.
17. Giorgio Bergamini, 'Sotto la cenere cova il primo fuoco', *Il Piccolo*, 12 March 1963, p. 3.
18. Aldo Camerino, 'La ragazza di Tomizza', *Il Gazzettino*, 2 July 1963, p. 3.
19. Said, 'Reflections on Exile', p. 177.
20. Bruno Maier, 'Fulvio Tomizza 1969–1972', *Il Cristallo*, 15 (1973), 1–9 (p. 3).
21. Mario Lavagetto, *Lavorare con piccoli indizi* (Turin: Bollati Boringhieri, 2003), p. 201.
22. Wolfgang Iser, *The Act of Reading: A Theory of Aesthetic Response* (Baltimore, MD: Johns Hopkins University Press, 1978), p. 203.
23. Petrucciani, 'Fulvio Tomizza', p. 124.
24. Lavagetto, *Lavorare con piccoli indizi*, p. 201.
25. Vincenzo De Martinis, 'L'albero dei sogni', *La Civiltà Cattolica*, 19 July 1969, p. 57.
26. Elio Gioanola, *Un killer dolcissimo: indagine psicoanalitica sull'opera di Italo Svevo* (Genoa: Il Melangolo, 1979), p. 81.
27. Nicola Gardini, 'Parole e omissioni: che cosa dicono i grandi romanzi quando tacciono', *La Repubblica*, 29 August 2013, p. 38. See also Nicola Gardini, *Lacuna: saggio sul non detto* (Turin: Einaudi, 2014).
28. Gardini, 'Parole e omissioni', p. 38.

29. Coral Ann Howells, *The Cambridge Companion to Margaret Atwood* (Cambridge: Cambridge University Press, 2006), p. 103.
30. Roger Luckhurst, *The Trauma Question* (London & New York: Routledge, 2008), p. 202.
31. Fulvio Tomizza, *La ragazza di Petrovia* (Milan: Mondadori, 1963), p. 66; hereafter referenced as *RP*.
32. Massimo Fusillo, *L'altro e lo stesso: teoria e storia del doppio* (Florence: La Nuova Italia, 1998), p. 8.
33. Sigmund Freud, 'The Uncanny', in *Writings on Art and Literature*, ed. by James Strachey (Stanford, CA: Stanford University Press, 1997), pp. 193–234 (pp. 211–12).
34. Said, 'Reflections on Exile', p. 186.
35. See Marianna Deganutti, 'The Counterpoint Music of the Exile in Fulvio Tomizza's *La ragazza di Petrovia*', *Romance Studies*, 34:2 (2016), 114–24.
36. Gabriella Berto, *Freud, Heidegger: lo spaesamento* (Milan: Bompiani, 1998), p. 64.
37. Luigi Pirandello, *Uno, nessuno, centomila* (Milan: Mondadori, 1980), p. 20.
38. Ibid., p. 27.
39. Ibid., p. 25.
40. Elio Gioanola, *Pirandello: la follia* (Genoa: Il Melangolo, 1983), p. 109.
41. Pirandello, *Uno, nessuno, centomila*, p. 30.
42. Jacques Lacan, *Le Séminaire de Jacques Lacan: Livre X, L'Angoisse* (Paris: Seuil, 2004), p. 104.
43. Jacques Lacan, 'The Mirror Stage as Formative of the Function of the I as Revealed in Psychoanalytic Experience', in *Ecrits: A Selection*, ed. by Alan Sheridan (New York: Norton, 1977), pp. 1–7 (pp. 1–2).
44. Ibid., p. 2.
45. Ibid., p. 3.
46. Gaetano De Leo, 'La coerenza interna di Fulvio Tomizza', *Messaggero Veneto*, 13 July 1969, p. 3.
47. Carmelina Sicari, *Lo specchio e lo stigma* (Ravenna: Longo, 1979), pp. 40–41.
48. Athena Leoussi, *Encyclopedia of Nationalism* (New Brunswick, NJ: Transaction Publishers at Rutgers University, 2001), p. 171.
49. Ibid.
50. Ibid., p. 172.
51. Elie Kedourie, *Nationalism* (London: Blackwell, 1993), p. 66.
52. Joshua A. Fishman, *Language and Nationalism: Two Integrative Essays* (Rowley, MA: Newbury House, 1973), p. 277.
53. Frederick Barnard, *Herder's Social and Political Thought* (Oxford: Clarendon Press, 1965), p. 57.
54. Kedourie, *Nationalism*, p. 62.
55. Eric Hobsbawm, *Nations and Nationalism since 1780: Programme, Myth, Reality* (Cambridge: Cambridge University Press, 1990), p. 110.
56. Brodsky, 'The Condition We Call Exile', p. 4.
57. Bergamini, 'Sotto la cenere cova il primo fuoco', p. 3.
58. Alberto Bassan, 'La ragazza di Petrovia', *Letture*, 3 (1963), 343–45 (p. 345).
59. Giuseppe Costanzo, 'La ragazza di Petrovia', *Avanti*, 9 June 1963, p. 6.
60. This passage seems to be related to an episode described by Ivo Andrić in the *Bosnian Chronicle*. For an analysis of this see Deganutti, 'Lo sguardo ad est di Fulvio Tomizza', pp. 265–66.

CHAPTER 5

After Exile: The Writer in Translation from *L'amicizia* to *Franziska*

The Writer in the New Language

Scholars of the literature of exile have often investigated the way in which the impact of a new linguistic reality affects writing. Writers themselves, in addressing this question, have contributed with their own perspectives describing a feeling of loss or, on occasion, gain. Norman Manea, the Jewish-Romanian author of novels and essays on the Holocaust and Communism sets out the vexed linguistic dimension of the exilic writer in *The Exiled Language*. Despite his plurilingual background (as a child he heard German, Yiddish, Ukrainian, and Polish), he writes the following: 'In the beginning was the word, the ancients told us. In the beginning for me, the word was Romanian'. The languages he acquired later at school were not able to compete with Romanian: 'In the end, I feel at home in only one language'. Even in exile, this was 'the language of love and friendship and literary apprenticeship, the language my parents and grandparents speak to me even though they are dead'.[1] However, he also suggests that exile should be considered a 'privileged' condition:

> Five years have passed since I felt that burning, and I must confess now I feel not only the curse, but also the privilege, of being an exile. I have finally accepted this honor, doing so in the name of all that is suffering and epiphany, in the name of loneliness and challenge, of all the doubts and never-ending apprenticeship it implies, for its emptiness and richness, for the unfettering of myself and clash within myself. [...] If I have the strength to repeat Dante, '*L'esilio, che m'e dato, onor mi tengo*' (I hold in honor the exile I was given), I am probably in sympathy with our centrifugal century.[2]

In the 'honour' of exile, Manea includes a favourable access to creativity, given that exile provides a profound experience or trauma that, most of the time, must be worked out through writing. Exile may also spur the writer to new linguistic solutions or lead to contaminations that would have been inconceivable in the country of origin.

Scholars have often underlined this double perspective. McClennen suggests that 'discourse studies of exile writing attempt to delimit the use of language to either a positive, transcultural, original, and free use of language; or a negative, nostalgic, and limited use of language'.³ The latter is usually a mutilation, or rather an unnatural break with the native language and its potential, which will never be found in the new language or languages. This perspective has also been pointed out by Nabokov, who exchanged his native Russian for English:

> My private tragedy, which cannot, and indeed should not, be anybody's concern, is that I had to abandon my natural idiom, my untrammelled, rich, and infinitely docile Russian tongue for a second-rate brand of English, devoid of any of those apparatuses — the baffling mirror, the black velvet backdrop, the implied associations and traditions — which the native illusionist, frac-tails flying, can magically use to transcend the heritage in his own way.⁴

In fact, the linguistic switch is often viewed as a loss. As suggested by the Polish exile Horst Bienek:

> The loss of language is probably the most decisive factor in determining exile; it is what makes exile so wretched for the writer. In the process, you lose almost everything: childhood, upbringing, mentality, myth. Even if the exile quickly learns the words of the new language, he still needs a long time to express himself on a literary plane in the new tongue.⁵

Exile, therefore, could be one of the most 'traumatic personal experiences' for a writer or a poet for whom 'language is the most precious possession'.⁶

In her analysis of the relationship between language and self in Stefan Heym (1913–2001) and Jakov Lind (1927–2007), Tamar Steinitz considers a direct confrontation of these opposing, positive and negative, experiences, demonstrating that a model of exile may be built on this dichotomy.⁷ By analyzing the work of two authors who both left their country of origin, Germany and Austria, when the Nazis came to power, she delves into the sophisticated dynamics of translingualism and the shifts of languages caused by exile. The abandonment of one's native tongue and the creation of a new self in English may be felt as a loss, as happens in Lind's case. In his autobiographical work, which is, paradoxically, written in the foreign language, translingualism is associated with alienation, repression, and fragmentation of the self. On the other hand, exile may also be an opportunity to gain a double perspective on the world. Without abandoning his native German, and incorporating English, Heym builds up the identity of a 'man-between', who mediates languages through bilingualism and self-translation.

This dichotomy is conditioned by factors influencing the particular exile: the reasons behind the departure; the distance existing between the culture of departure and destination; the political implications of the exile and the many other considerations I have outlined in Chapter 2. In the case of Tomizza, the choice of Italian is caused by the decision to move to Trieste. There, the writer 'passato per forza di cose da un dialetto semislavo alla lingua italiana' [passed inevitably from a semi-Slavic dialect to the Italian language], where 'per forza di cose' implies the pragmatic necessity to adapt to the new cultural and linguistic situation.⁸ In his essay 'Uno scrittore tra due dialetti di matrice linguistica diversa', he contemplates the difficulty of maintaining his original Italo-Croato-Slovene mixture of languages:

> Se fossi nato poeta lirico, forse le mie immagini, i sentimenti e i pensieri

sarebbero scaturiti direttamente da quella casuale e precaria contaminazione delle tre lingue, col risultato però di riuscire comprensibile a un centinaio di lettori, ma anche con la certezza che qualche mio verso sarebbe stato recepito a Mosca, Praga e più ancora a Varsavia, città nella quale ho sentito ufficializzata la nostra balzana tendenza a trasformare la 'a' in 'o' e dire pertanto come i polacchi mlòd invece di mlàd (giovane), glova in luogo di glàva (testa). (S, p. 191)

[If I was born a lyric poet, maybe my images, feelings, and thoughts would spring directly from the random and precarious contamination of the three languages, with the result of being understandable to a hundred readers, but also with the certainty that some of my verse would be acknowledged in Moscow, Prague, and even more in Warsaw, the city where I heard formalized our bizarre tendency to transform the 'a' into 'o' and say like the Poles *mlád* instead of *mláд* (young), *glova* instead of *glava* (head).]

These considerations led Tomizza to use Italian in his works, which he arrives at through a process of 'self-translation'. The inclusion of 'translation' in the process of writing without the presence of an original text is called 'interior self-translation'. In Tomizza's case he internally mediates a plurilingual background, 'translating' it into an Italian narrative that only from time to time allows 'foreign' words emerge. These are inserted by Tomizza, because he considered them 'untranslatable':

La fragranza di umili piatti accompagnati dalla polenta e consumati nella sola luce del focolare doveva continuare a conservare quel sacrale senso 'domaciò' che in altri luoghi corrisponde a 'casareccio'. Lo stagno all'inizio o alla fine del villaggio in cui si abbeverano le mandrie di ritorno dal pascolo, è passato dal latino al ladino senza alterarsi troppo, ed è divenuto da noi l'irrinunciabile 'laco'. (S, p. 192)

[The fragrance of humble dishes accompanied by polenta and consumed only in the firelight had to continue keeping that sacred 'domacio' sense that in other places corresponded to 'homemade'. The pond at the beginning or end of the village where herds drank when they returned from the pasture, passed from Latin to Ladin without altering too much, has become the indispensable 'laco'.]

As I have described in my consideration of *Materada* and *La miglior vita*, the Italian narrative somehow includes the multilingualism and diglossia of the area. This is more common in the novels belonging to the 'first' Tomizza, such as *La quinta stagione*, where the writer himself admitted there was a wholesale linguistic adherence to his native land:

Con *La quinta stagione*, immergendomi con il candore dell'infanzia nell'ambiente nativo dapprima risparmiato e poi scosso dalla guerra, sono forse riuscito a esprimere la massima adesione alla realtà composita della parrocchia, specialmente nell'evocare gli angoli più amati da noi ragazzi e prescelti per i nostri giochi che parodiavano la guerra: lo spiazzo erboso dietro le case, ossia l'intima *rodìna* dove tra l'altro si trebbiava il frumento (in croato ràditi significa sia nascere sia fruttificare), gli stretti sentieri del campo del Saràjo e quelli più spaziosi della Vèlignìva (grande campo), il pauroso bosco di Vidìa che nascondeva una voragine carsica chiamata fòiba, un campetto ridottissimo per il gioco del calcio, davanti alla misteriosa bottega del fabbro (nelle due lingue slave kovàc) che noi chiamavamo covaztia. Esiste a Bolzano una *schmiderìa* e a Klagenfurt una *kovàhaus*. (S, p. 192)

[With *La quinta stagione*, by immersing myself in the pure childhood of the native environment at first saved and then shaken by the war, I was perhaps able to express the maximum adhesion to the composite reality of the parish, especially in evoking the places dear to us boys and chosen for our games that parodied the war: the grassy area behind the houses, namely the intimate *rodìna* where among other things the wheat was threshed (in Croatian *ràditi* means both to be born and bear fruit), the narrow paths of the Saràjo's field and to the wider Vèlignìva (large field), the scary forest of Vidìa that hid a karst pit called fòiba, a very small pitch for football, before the mysterious blacksmith's shop (in the two languages *kovàc*) that we called *covaztia*. In Bolzen exists a *schmiderìa* and in Klagenfurt a *kovàhaus*.]

Despite choosing Italian, in this first phase the writer was easily able to fluctuate between languages, developing new mixtures, as is pointed out by Cesare De Michelis:

Così non ha mai una sola lingua e nessuna è davvero la sua; per ogni cosa, sentimento, esperienza ci sono parole diverse per dirle e, anche quando si è deciso di scrivere in italiano, i pensieri si esprimono come vogliono loro nella lingua della memoria, che rimescola molti dialetti, lingue diverse, croato, serbo e persino qualche traccia che viene da più lontano.[9]

[So one has never just one language and none is really his own; for everything, feeling, experience, there are different words to say it, and even when it was decided to write in Italian, thoughts express themselves as they want in the language of memory, scrambling many dialects, different languages, Croatian, Serbian and even some traces from further afield.]

The several languages available to a multilingual writer allow him to express himself using the solutions that best suit a particular meaning or condition. The chosen language could contain traces of the others (in terms of sound, meaning, etc.), expanding the position of the writing subject, as noted by Sylvia Molloy:

Multilingual writers can occupy many positions simultaneously depending on which language they choose to use, with whom, on which topic, and depending on the different memories evoked by different codes as well as the different expectations each of these codes raises in their interlocutors or in their readers.[10]

Exile, however, marks a break both in the writer's life and his literary production and this will necessarily affect his writing options. Once the 'first' phase ends, Tomizza's language becomes progressively more 'Italian'. His 'translations' and the 'deceptive' dynamics to which every translation is subject often frustrated him. Tomizza himself considered this challenging perspective as a 'lenta metamorfosi da parte di un immigrato' [slow metamorphosis by an immigrant], a compulsory adaptation to a different cultural, social, and linguistic environment, that, in his case, was also hostile to the one of his origin.[11]

It follows that Tomizza had to limit the linguistic valency of his Istrian background, 'increasing' the translation process. Examples of bilingualism and diglossia are less frequent in the later phases of his production, despite the works often remaining focused on figures characteristic of his homeland:

> Se letterariamente non mi è stato possibile rendere con maggiore immediatezza il corso doppio di una parlata nativa tanto modesta quanto ricca di suggestioni, la presa di coscienza di appartenere a entrambi i gruppi etnici e alle rispettive culture, unitamente al dovere di dare maggiore ascolto alla componente più sacrificata nell'intero arco della storia e meno nota alla letteratura, mi ha guidato nella scelta dei temi, dei personaggi, degli ambienti, fino a sconfinare nell'universo sloveno degli Sposi di via Rossetti, a risalire al sodalizio tra Vergerio e Trubar, a ricostruire il primo difficile amalgama tra abitanti vecchi e nuovi nell'Istria meridionale del '500. Ho assunto in definitiva il punto di vista 'ideale' della mia gente, mettendone in atto la posizione intermediaria da essa mantenuta quasi passivamente nella comunicazione verbale per almeno tre secoli.[12]

> [If literarily I was not able to convey more immediately the double flow of a modest native parlance as modest as full of suggestions, the awareness of belonging to both ethnic groups and their cultures, together with the duty to pay greater attention to the more sacrificed and less known literary component over the entire historical span, guided me in my choice of themes, characters, environments to intrude into the Slovene universe of the Sposi of via Rossetti, to return to the partnership between Vergerius and Trubar, to rebuild the first difficult amalgam of old and new inhabitants of Southern Istria in the sixteenth century. I assumed ultimately the 'ideal' point of view of my people, putting in place the intermediary position they very nearly passively maintained in verbal communication for at least three centuries.]

By considering the switch from a remarkable multilingual approach to a more uniform Italian narrative, I suggest that Tomizza passes from so-called foreignization to domestication, two processes that are at the core of translation. The former is identified by Lawrence Venuti as 'an ethnodeviant pressure on those (cultural) values to register the linguistic and cultural difference of the foreign text, sending the reader abroad'.[13] In this case, the translator emphasizes the break between the two or more languages and cultures, rather than reducing it; there are passages in which the 'foreign' remains and is not adapted to the target culture. Domestication, on the other hand, is defined as 'an ethnocentric reduction of the foreign text to the target-language cultural values, [which] brings the author back home'.[14] This means a minimization of the foreign components in the new text and a deliberate reformulation of the original into a value system that belongs to the target work. Tomizza seeks to accommodate the reader to an ever-greater extent, avoiding any sort of linguistic incomprehension or discomfort. Domestication is not only a linguistic process, but also a cultural-linguistic one. Rita Scotti Jurić underlines this in relation to Tomizza's works:

> Uno scrittore che narra fatti di ambienti culturalmente differenti da quello del lettore modello diventa automaticamente traduttore, mediatore culturale che instaura un'interazione tra le due diverse lingue e culture adeguando dialoghi e parole della lingua di partenza (il croato e lo sloveno) alle esigenze culturali dei lettori nella lingua di arrivo (l'italiano).[15]

[A writer who narrates the facts of environments culturally different from that of the model reader automatically becomes a translator, a cultural mediator who establishes an interaction between two different languages and cultures adapting dialogues and words of the source language (Croatian and Slovene) to the cultural needs of the target language's readers (Italian)].

Writing for Tomizza becomes a form of inner translation, addressed to the target audience. Such is also the case with Milan Kundera, the Czech author who was forced to leave his native country and who adopted the French language: 'Translation did not provide an afterlife for the novels; rather they were written and received as translations'.[16] These works might convey more or less directly a different linguistic underground that flows just below the narrative, contributing a certain instability of meaning, as suggested by Michelle Woods in relation to Kundera's literary production:

> Writing as an act is a form of translation — by making a choice in placing a word in a certain context with a certain meaning, even though it may contain the trace of other meanings and possibilities of future meanings, the writer acts as a mediator of meaning in much the same way as a translator might. This suggests an instability of original meaning in any one language even before transferring that language into another one becomes an issue. That transference, however (the interlingual translation), is a discomfiting process not only because it hints at, or openly shows up, cultural differences but because it exposes the contingency of creating meaning in any language. This instability of meaning in language is a preoccupation of Kundera's work, constantly in tension with his search for precision and constantly exposed by the translation process.[17]

This problem is usually generated by cultural differences embedded in the original, and a lack of correspondence in the target language. In this matter there are limits that cannot be overcome, as suggested by Walter Benjamin:

> The words *Brot* and *pain* 'intend' the same object, but the modes of this intention are not the same. It is owing to these modes that the word *Brot* means something different to a German than the word *pain* to a Frenchman, that these words are not inter-changeable, that, in fact, they strive to exclude each other. As to the intended object, however, the two words mean the very same thing.[18]

Benjamin's consideration is reflected in Roman Jacobson's analysis of the linguistic aspects of translation, an essay in which he considers the English word 'cheese' and its possible translation. Firstly, Jacobson underlines that 'Any representative of a cheese-less culinary culture will understand the English word "cheese" if he is aware that in this language it means "food made of pressed curds" and if he has at least a linguistic acquaintance with "curds"'.[19] Despite being unable to grasp the meaning of mythical words, which have disappeared over time, such as 'ambrosia', 'nectar', or 'gods', 'we understand these words and know in what contexts each of them may be used'.[20] This depends on the linguistic sign that is attributed to introduce an unfamiliar word in order to define a specific object or category. However, the translation of a word into a different linguistic code implies the use of an alternative sign. Thus,

> The English word 'cheese' cannot be completely identified with its standard Russian heteronym 'сыр,' because cottage cheese is a cheese but not a сыр. Russians say: принеси сыру и творогу 'bring cheese and cottage cheese.' In standard Russian, the food made of pressed curds is called сыр only if ferment is used.[21]

Tomizza was aware of the difficulty of transferring his double Istro-Veneto-Čakavian dialect into Italian. As demonstrated in Chapter 3 for words such as *graia* or *druži*, translation risked not conveying the full original meaning. This phenomenon troubled Tomizza to the extent that he was surprised to find a word demonstrating a good correspondence between Italian and Croatian. In treating the *bora*, a particularly strong wind felt from Slovenia to Dalmatia, he noticed that 'Bora, *bura*: una delle poche voci uguali a pieno diritto, che nessuno dell'altra lingua fingerebbe di non capire o si sognerebbe di contestare' [Bora, *bura*: one of the few fully equal voices, that no one of the other language would pretend not to understand, or would dream of challenging].[22]

Being a self-translator, he had better control of the languages at his disposal than a more traditional translator, he did not have to be 'faithful' to any original text and audience and so could modify words and expressions, explaining them further if necessary and so find the right linguistic balance. He could modify the linguistic features and identities of his characters according to their sense of belonging and above all could have full control of the translation issue within the narrative, that is, whether to draw attention to it or to leave it below the surface.

In this chapter, my aim is to review the strategies used by Tomizza to depict plurilingual cultures in a narrative in which Italian is dominant. For instance, in the novel *L'amicizia*, he regulates the use of direct and indirect speech to allow different languages (or at least the idea of them) to surface in the narrative. In the novel that bears her name he reproduces the broken Italian of Franziska, an immigrant in Trieste at the time of the First World War. This is done with the purpose of both representing the harsh political conditions to which she is subject and her emotional response. *Franziska* also gives us a better understanding of Tomizza's linguistic development. The result of Tomizza's literary operation — his 'translated' Italian — has been also defined as 'un-literary', a notion that will be explained in the last part of the chapter. This term was coined to attack Tomizza for a supposed inability to write literary or beautiful Italian, but once fully developed the concept indirectly points to the expressive potential of Tomizza's interior self-translation.

Direct Versus Indirect Speech

Like *Materada* and *La miglior vita*, *L'amicizia* is the result of a process of self-translation that transfers a complex linguistic situation into an Italian narrative. Subterranean plurilingual mechanisms emerge, revealing the linguistic richness of the 'land beyond Trieste', which in this case is the Karst plateau inhabited by the Slovene minority. Using the processes I have been discussing in previous chapters, Tomizza is able to present the bilingual background, rich in contaminations, interferences, and contrasts. However, in comparison to the 'first' Tomizza, the Italian narrative 'covers' more extensively the plurilingual background. Despite taking advantage of direct speech, which allows him to state directly the languages or dialects used by characters, the main tool remains indirect speech. This gives him the opportunity to 'translate' his background into a narrative which becomes ever more Italian.

To start with I shall focus on direct speech, which allows the narrator to highlight the linguistic shifts of his characters and to display two contrasting languages. I will consider this in relation to Giorgio Pressburger's *Il sussurro della grande voce* [The Whisper of the Big Voice]. By drawing a parallel between the two works, it will be possible to see Tomizza's process more clearly. *L'amicizia* is the story of friendship between two very different young men: Marco, who comes from the Istrian countryside and who has a similar complex ethnic background to Tomizza, and Alessandro, his friend from the city, who, according to Ragusa, recalls the ineptitude of Alfondo Nitti, the protagonist of Svevo's *Una vita* [A Life].[23] While the first part of the novel is set in Trieste, the second switches to the Karst. The linguistic and cultural gap between these two settings becomes evident. In the Karst, Marco finds a place that is not too dissimilar to his native peninsula:

> Marco si accosta alla gente che vive sul Carso, si rispecchia nell'umanità insediata in un piccolo paese dove si parla una lingua a lui nota, dove una minoranza etnica non vuole lasciarsi cancellare, e si è perciò organizzata anche politicamente. Nel Carso, i cui aspetti gli richiamano qua e là il paesaggio istriano, Marco ritrova le sue stesse origini o almeno una civiltà contadina molto simile a quella delle sue radici. La riscoperta del Carso, sottolineata dal recupero della sua parlata slovena che viene ad arricchire in senso mistilingue il romanzo, costituisce di esso la parte migliore.[24]

> [Marco approaches the people living on the Karst, finds himself reflected in the humanity settled in a small town where people speak a language known to him, where an ethnic minority does not wish to be erased, and is therefore also politically organized. On the Karst, whose aspects recall the Istrian landscape, Marco finds his own origins, or at least a peasant culture very similar to that of his roots. The rediscovery of the Karst, underlined by the recovery of his Slovene language, that enriches the mixed-language of the novel, constitutes the best part of it.]

Direct and indirect speech offer the possibility of putting language in the foreground. Direct speech helps the author express the language employed by characters, and so to convey the real linguistic background of the story, without any mediation:

> In un tipo di narrazione in cui ciò che dice la gente, i vari gruppi e le varie persone della comunità, è la prevalente materia del racconto, il discorso indiretto libero è lo strumento espressivo di gran lunga prevalente, sapientemente alternato con il discorso diretto, ed utilizzato con un'ampia gamma di manifestazioni e sfumature, più o meno vicine al discorso diretto.[25]

> [In a type of narration in which what people say, the various groups and people of the community, is the dominant material of the story, free indirect speech is by far the most prevalent expressive instrument, skilfully alternated with direct speech, and used with a wide range of expressions and shades, more or less close to the direct speech.]

Let us consider direct speech more closely. Following Genette's approach, that is, that direct speech should be considered 'mimetic' or realistic, Isabelle Simoes Marques argues that it 'shows less distance, because the narrator leaves room to characters to express themselves'.[26] She adds that 'It gives the illusion of objectivity and releases information neutrally. It is probably the most authentic reproduction of the word of the other'.[27] In the context of plurilingualism, direct speech allows characters to use their own tongue directly.

The friendship between Marco and Alessandro often leaves room for secondary characters, who together form a varied linguistic texture. The novel is characterized by a sequence of events, usually corresponding to the appearance of these secondary characters: 'Gli accadimenti si riducono a passeggiate, soste in un bar, appuntamenti, visite, gite sul vicino Carso' [The events are reduced to walks, stops at bars, meetings, visits, and trips to the nearby Karst].[28] At the same time Tomizza sets out the linguistic situation of Karst, employing dialogue to clarify the characters' interactions. This may be introduced either by the narrator or by the main characters. An example of direct speech comes from Marco, when the character interacts with siora Gigia, the owner of San Giovanni's *osteria* [inn]:

> La porta si aprì, siora Gigia sportasi per vuotare un catino mi riconobbe sotto il lampione dell'insegna. 'Cossa la fa qua che tuti zo i la speta? E la signorina Cinzia no la xe con lei? La xe vignuda e subito sparida. I ga pensà che i do colombi i xe andai per le sue, e xe nato bacan. No i voi 'ndar vanti co la comedia'.
> 'Come sparida?'
> 'La lo dovessi saver meio de mi. La gaveva visto che no la iera e via ela'.
> 'Torno subito' mentii. 'Ma lei no la stia dir de gaverme visto' e me ne tornai a casa cercando di soffocare dentro spasimi di commozione e di felicità.[29]
>
> [The door opened, siora Gigia leaning out to empty a basin recognized me under the streetlight of the sign. 'What are you doing here that are all waiting for you downstairs! And Miss Cinzia is not with you? She came and immediately left. And thought that the two lovebirds went their way, and a mess happened. You do not want to carry on the comedy'.
> 'How she disappeared?'
> 'You should know it better than me. She saw that you were not and left'.
> 'Back soon' I lied. 'But do not tell her that you saw me' and I came back home trying to repress the spasms of emotion and happiness.]

In this dialogue, Tomizza lets siora Gigia and Marco use dialect so the Italian narrative is 'broken' by a remarkable example of code-switching. What is significant here is that, through direct speech, the narrator can change languages easily.

Direct speech is also needed to provide the reader with a better overview of the circumstances in which the dialogue takes place and the type of interactions going on between characters. The use of a specific language already conveys a context that goes beyond the meaning of the words — in effect, it is a sort of 'style'. The German language employed by the characters represents a remarkable example of the irruption of a foreign language in the story. It has a particular expressive purpose:

> Tra le poche cose in comune avevate il tedesco, da entrambi scelto quale lingua straniera al ginnasio-liceo e che tu possedevi meglio. 'Mein lieber', ti scompigliava lievemente i capelli 'verzeih mir'. 'Es macht doch nichts' le rispondesti fingendoti rappacificato, quasi in omaggio alla parlata. Questi assaggi e le inevitabili correzioni, i bisticci di parole, chissà che non avessero giocato una parte non trascurabile nella vostra relazione, colmando vuoti, rompendo indugi, forse suggerendo un comportamento, uno stile, che tale lingua impone da sé in una città qual è la nostra. (*A*, p. 43)

> [Among the few things in common you had the German, chosen by both as a foreign language at the Gymnasium-Lyceum and that you mastered better. 'Mein lieber' he gently ruffled your hair 'verzeih mir'. 'Es macht doch nichts' you answered pretending to be pacified, as a tribute to the language. These samples and the inevitable corrections, the squabbling words, who knows whether they played a significant part in your relationship, filling voids, breaking hesitations, perhaps suggesting a behaviour, a style, that that language imposes itself in a city like ours.]

Direct speech allows Tomizza to show interactions between characters more authentically, and so display the political situation. In this sense, the intentional mistakes made by characters in the following passage play a significant role in portraying vexed political relationships:

> Iniziando con linguaggio aulico perché il contrasto si facesse più stridente, mi rivelasti quasi una seconda natura, la quale, bisogna riconoscerlo, ti rendeva più sciolto se non addirittura più simpatico: 'Ella non mi dirà che grato suona ai suoi orecchi il loro coscia xe di tanto mal per ciamar scvasi subito dotor?' e ne ridesti discretamente appagato. Sorrisi anch'io, poi obiettai calmo: 'Vede, li trascinate in un'emulazione da loro mai richiesta soltanto per vederli perdenti. Si rende o non si rende conto che si sforzano, come possono, di parlare la nostra lingua? Andrebbero piuttosto premiati considerando che hanno una loro lingua!'.
> 'E che lingva!' sbruffasti in modo un po' sgangherato.
> 'Non è certo quella del Dolce stil nuovo'.
> 'Slatko stil novo' gorgogliavi un po' preso dal vino, la testa ricciuta tra le braccia posate sul tavolo. (*A*, p. 23)

> [Starting with courtly language in order to make a jarring contrast, you disclosed almost a second nature, which, we have to admit, made you freer if not more pleasant: 'You will not tell me that it sounds good to your ears their "what is wrong to call them slav doctor?"' and he laughed quietly satisfied. I smiled too, then I objected calmly: 'You see, you drag them into an emulation never asked for by them only to see them losers. Do not you realize that they struggle, as best they can, to speak our language? They should be rewarded considering they have their own language!'
> 'And what language!' You grumbled in an unhinged way.
> 'It is certainly not that of the Dolce stil nuovo'.
> 'Slatko stil novo' he gurgled a bit affected by the wine, his curly head between his arms placed on the table.]

Language is the barometer of these characters' exchanges: through nuances, mistakes, and distortions it signals discomfort and even the giving of offence. Scotti

Jurić analyzes the above passage in these terms:

> Ma di colpo viene freddato dall'ironica battuta del suo interlocutore: 'E che lingva!' nella quale l'italofono imita la pronuncia slavofona che riproduce il nesso 'gu' o 'ku' come 'gv' o 'kv'. 'Non certo quella del Dolce stil nuovo', incalzerà Tomizza in difesa dei suoi compaesani, ma la spinta burlesca del compagno italiano non sembra placarsi: 'Slatko stil novo'.[30]

> [But suddenly he is chilled by the ironic joke of his interlocutor: 'And what langvage!' in which the Italophone imitates the Slavophone pronunciation that reproduces the link 'gu' or 'ku' like 'gv' or 'kv'. 'Certainly not that of the Dolce stil nuovo', pursued Tomizza in defence of his countrymen, but the jesting push of the Italian partner does not seem to subside: 'Slatko stil novo'].

The use of a specific language or dialect leads characters to interact differently. This phenomenon appears in passages where the language plays a significant role itself:

> Decisi di accorciare lo svantaggio col domandarle nella sua lingua a che ora chiudevano, e se fosse stanca. Mi ero espresso a voce bassa, la mia poteva riuscire una proposta ben chiara, ma in sloveno ebbe un suono diverso. Fu come mi fossi appoggiato su un interruttore nascosto dietro una tenda facendo scattare una seconda luce che ne illuminò il volto di un'allegria giocosa, addirittura infantile. 'Lei parla la nostra lingua, e piuttosto bene! Dove l'ha imparata?' (*A*, p. 159)

> [I decided to reduce the disadvantage by asking in her tongue when they closed, and if she was tired. I expressed myself in a low voice, my own could result in a very clear proposal, but in Slovene had a different sound. It was as if I leaned on a switch hidden behind a curtain snapping on a second light that illuminated the face of playful, even infantile cheerfulness. 'You speak our language, and quite well! Where did you learn it?'.]

With indirect speech, as with direct speech, the narrator can also detail the linguistic pluralism present. However, the happy directness of letting the characters speak for themselves is often lost in the process of translation effected by the narrator who takes control of the characters' interactions. Many pieces of dialogue in *L'amicizia* are mediated by the narrator, who specifies the language in use. For instance, the scene of a lunch at the trattoria Pri Lipi in the Karst village of Prosecco:

> Nonostante la fragilità addirittura fanciullesca, quello che aspettava le nostre ordinazioni era un volto freddamente attento. Ci elencò le specialità e i piatti comuni in buon dialetto triestino, appena pronunciato alla slovena. La lieve diversità si accentuava proprio sulle labbra che facendo sibilare qualche 's', addolcire troppo la 'e' e aspirare qualche 'g', apparivano molli, di una volubilità infantile e di una disinvoltura superiore all'età. (*A*, p. 152)

> [Despite the even childish fragility, the one who was waiting for our orders was a coldly attentive face. She listed the specialities and the common dishes in a good Triestine dialect, slightly spoken in Slovene. The difference was accentuated on the lips that by hissing some 's's, softening too much the 'e' and aspirating some 'g's appeared soft, with childish fickleness and an ease superior to their age.]

A similar phenomenon appears in Pressburger's *Il sussurro della grande voce*, where the main character, Andreas, leaves Hungary, crossing a dangerous border, to arrive in Italy.[31] The initial setting is the 'viuzze del Settimo Distretto' [alleys of the Seventh District], the centre of Budapest, where the young character describes life in his family, his passion for theatre, and his encounter with an actress a few days before the Hungarian Revolution.[32] From the beginning, it is evident that language will play a crucial role in a novel characterized by linguistic shifts, indirect speech, and translations, but also by an indeterminacy that stops the reader from easily grasping the language actually being spoken by characters. The reader realizes that the main character does not know Italian but the narrator mediates all the dialogue, translating it into Italian. It is stated that Andreas understands very few words, that people try to talk to him slowly in order to facilitate his comprehension, and that he is barely able to express himself: 'Egli comprendeva poche parole — padre, madre, giudice (nel pronunciare quest'ultima rovesciò la testa indicando il ritratto) — anche se la signora cercava di parlare — o parlava sempre — molto lentamente' [He understood a few words — father, mother, judge (by pronouncing the latter he threw his head towards the portrait) — also the lady was trying to talk — or always spoke — very slowly].[33] He uses the words 'Non lo so' [I do not know] to communicate and to protect himself: 'Andreas rispondeva con l'unica frase che sapeva dire con piena coscienza del significato: "Non lo so!"' [Andreas responded with the only phrase he could say with full awareness of meaning: 'I don't know!'].[34]

In *L'amicizia*, Marco is able to speak Slovene and Italian as well as the Triestine dialect and may be considered plurilingual. In contrast, at home Andreas has only acquired his mother tongue, and this is progressively replaced in his acquisition of Italian. Therefore, as Andreas struggles to learn Italian right up until the end of the novel, dialogue is necessarily translated, or rather mediated, by the narrator and the use of indirect speech creates a distance that makes this possible. On many occasions, the narrator of *Il sussurro della grande voce* focuses on Andreas's process of learning a language:

> Le parole italiane annotate e tradotte vi si moltiplicano in modo impressionante: a un certo punto i caratteri diventano minuscoli e la scrittura pare prendere d'assalto la pagina e la mente del ragazzo. Dapprima si incontrano termini un po' astratti, che riguardano lo spazio, come 'profondità' 'altezza' 'indietro' 'destra' 'sinistra'. Probabilmente Andreas aveva bisogno di quelle nozioni così elementari ma tanto più significative, per poter ricostruire dentro di sé il Mondo, a cominciare dalle fondamenta. Poi seguono alcune coppie di parole, come 'luce-oscurità' 'pesante-leggero' 'piccolo-grande', insieme a nomi di animali e di parti del corpo umano. Le traduzioni di quelle parole sono semplici, come se Andreas non mirasse a raggiungere la precisione, ma soltanto una possibilità ancora vaga di conoscenza. Soltanto l'espressione 'ci sono' è tradotta con perifrasi e spiegazioni, sia perché non esiste l'equivalente nella lingua di Andreas, sia perché quelle tre sillabe per avere un significato richiedono una certa cognizione dell'universo e di se stessi. Oltre al vocabolario c'è una serie di brevi annotazioni [...]. Ma le parole recitate nella sua lingua cominciarono ad avere un suono estraneo, per lui, in quel luogo. La Dottoressa venne verso di lui emergendo quasi dal nulla. Quando furono vicini, si fermò e si dondolò lievemente, guardandolo. 'Come va?' domandò e Andreas non seppe

> come rispondere. Conosceva le parole 'bene' e 'male' ma non poteva rispondere né con l'una né con l'altra. [...] Cercava di non dare alcun significato ai suoni che udiva.³⁵

> [The translated and annotated Italian words multiply dramatically: at one point the characters become tiny and writing seems to assault the page and the boy's mind. Initially they meet in abstract terms, related to space, such as 'depth' 'height' 'behind' 'right' 'left'. Probably Andreas needed those basic but meaningful notions, in order to rebuild the World within himself, starting from the ground. Then some pairs of words, such as 'light-dark', 'heavy-light', 'small-great', together with names of animals and parts of the human body. The translations of those words are simple, as if Andreas did not aim to achieve precision, but only a vague possibility of knowledge. Only the expression 'there are' is translated with circumlocutions and explanations, both because there is no equivalent in the language of Andreas, and because those three syllables to be meaningful require a certain knowledge of the universe and of oneself. In addition to the vocabulary there is a series of short notes [...]. But the words recited in his language began to have an estranged sound, for him, in that place. The Doctor came toward him emerging from almost nothing. When they were close to each other, he stopped and wobbled slightly, looking at him. 'How are you?' he asked, and Andreas did not know how to respond. He knew the words 'good' and 'bad' but could not answer either with one nor the other. [...] He tried not to give any meaning to the sounds he heard.]

This extract is a clear example of the translation of a different linguistic background. Even though his notebook is full of new Italian words, his thoughts are translated from Hungarian while the transition from one language to the other is already expressed in the new language.

To draw a further parallel with *L'amicizia* and its languages, I shall recall the beginning of *Il sussurro della grande voce*. Pressburger's novel presents a varied linguistic context that filters into the narrative from time to time. When Andreas is still in Hungary, his words are clearly translated into Italian, but Pressburger also employs indirect speech to a considerable extent, as can be seen during Andreas's first encounter with the actress:

> Poi prese coraggio, disse il proprio nome e descrisse la circostanza in cui era venuto in possesso di quel numero. [...] Parlarono ancora per qualche minuto. Le guance del ragazzo bruciavano. Attraverso la finestra si vedevano le colline e l'azzurro un po' opaco del cielo. Parlarono della scuola, Andreas accennò anche ai suoi primi versi e all'abbozzo di una tragedia modellata, con un adattamento circa l'epoca dell'azione, sulla storia di Tristano e Isotta.³⁶

> [And he took courage, said his name and described the circumstance in which he came to possess that number. [...] They talked for a few minutes. The cheeks of the boy were burning. Through the window one could see the hills and the dull blue sky. They spoke of school, Andreas also mentioned his first verses and the sketch of a tragedy modelled, with a change to the period of the action, on the story of Tristan and Isolde.]

Due to the use of indirect speech, the series of actions that imply a dialogue between characters is translated, indeed, to such an extent that the language in use is forgotten. When Andreas goes into exile the linguistic situation changes. Hungarian cannot be taken for granted anymore, as Andreas is overwhelmed by new, alien tongues. The rather chaotic experience outside his homeland — his life as a fugitive struggling to find money for food and housing — is immediately characterized by difficult encounters that reveal the linguistic underground of the novel, as in the encounter with a priest:

> Il vecchio che mescolava le parole di varie lingue e le pronunciava con difficoltà, ora gli ribattè con noncurante arroganza: 'Non domandare mai cosa c'era prima, cosa verrà dopo, cosa c'è davanti e cosa c'è dietro di te. Hai capito?'. Parlava in modo quasi incomprensibile, ma nel suo discorso c'erano vecchi vocaboli che Andreas aveva creduto di esclusivo uso della sua famiglia. A queste isole si aggrappò nel tentativo di afferrare ciò che il frate stava dicendo.[37]
>
> [The old man who shuffled words of various languages and pronounced them with difficulty, now replied with careless arrogance: 'Never ask what was there before, what comes next, what is ahead and what is behind you. Do you understand?'. He almost spoke in an incomprehensible way, but in his speech there were old words that Andreas believed to be used exclusively by his family. He grabbed on to these islands in his attempt to grasp what the friar was saying.]

Paradoxically, Andreas does not understand the old priest, even though the narrator mediates the scene in Italian. The reader becomes aware of Andreas's linguistic displacement, but the effect it produces is more of a noise rather than a mixture of languages, which later on will be explained as follows: 'Anche il Vecchio olivastro, come il frate della sera prima, parlava una lingua appena comprensibile fatta di parole tedesche, spagnole, ungheresi, ebraiche' [Even the olive-skinned old man, as the friar of the evening before, spoke a barely understandable language composed of German, Spanish, Hungarian, Jewish words].[38]

There is another phenomenon which goes hand in hand with the appearance of a multilingual underground in the story. The words that Andreas is master of in his native tongue lose their power abroad, being transformed into sounds and later into silence: 'Tutto scompare. Restano soltanto i suoni. Spero che non scompaiano anche quelli' [Everything disappears. Only sounds remain. I hope that those will not disappear too].[39] The familiar linguistic background disappears from the narrative, leaving space for thoughts that express the new multi-linguistic condition. Once the border is crossed and the character begins his troubled exile, the words of other fugitives turn into alien sounds: 'un centinaio di fuggiaschi parlottavano tra loro, le loro parole, con suo sgomento, cominciarono a suonargli un po' strane' [a hundred fugitives were whispering to each other, their words, to his dismay, began to sound a bit strange to him].[40] From this moment on, Andreas starts a process of translation that parallels the ambiguity generated by the clash of languages.

In *L'amicizia*, the narrator plays a crucial role for readers who might otherwise be unaware of linguistic changes. However, Tomizza's annotations are usually detailed, especially when he refers to specific linguistic changes or makes extra references. By using indirect speech, he points out the use of a specific language also to express political controversies or feelings. For instance, when Marco interacts with the daughter of the host, because of the troubled relations between Italians and Slovenes her mother is concerned about their use of Slovene: 'La madre trasecolò nell'udirla sciolta nella parlata di casa, spostò lo sguardo sospeso su di me, pronta a correggere lo scatto della figlia ma anche riservandomi un principio di diffidenza' (*A*, p. 159) [The mother was stunned hearing her fluent in the language spoken at home, moved her gaze suspended on me, ready to fix the jerk of her daughter but also reserving for me a principle of distrust]. Marco's position — an Istrian able to talk Slovene — is explained further: 'Non potevo fingere d'ignorare come nell'idioma imposto e doppiamente disprezzato si traducesse casa, orto, mano, scuola, che con suono pressoché identico ricorrevano nel dialetto paesano' (*A*, p. 160) [I could not pretend to ignore how the imposed and doubly despised idiom would translate home, garden, hand, school, with a sound almost identical to that which occurred in the peasant dialect]. Further explanations are usually provided through indirect speech or expansions that give the writer more space to portray the context.

Another similarity between the works is that in *Il sussurro della grande voce* the mixture of languages is described through the mediation of the narrator. The native tongue of the main character is progressively 'polluted' by the acquired one: 'Ebbe la spiacevole impressione che la lingua appresa da sua madre improvvisamente si fosse contaminata' [He had the unpleasant impression that the language learned from his mother was suddenly contaminated], but the Italian language that carries the narrative is not subject to any such degeneration.[41] From the beginning to the end, despite the linguistic observations of Andreas and the narrator, the Italian remains consistent. In *L'amicizia*, as well as in many others of Tomizza's works, the hybrid linguistic background of Karst is filtered through the narrator and experienced internally by characters, emerging strongly but also indirectly in the switch from one language and dialect to another through the mediation of foreign words, translations, unpredictable changes, and choices. Both direct and indirect speech constitute useful devices to express the complex linguistic background of the Karst area. However, indirect speech tends to prevail in this phase of Tomizza's literary production, corresponding to a form of translation from a multilingual world experienced by characters into the Italian language of the novel.

Franziska's Mistakes

The abandoning of his double dialect was not an easy process for Tomizza. Beaujour, who analyzes in depth the relationship between language and exile, writes that 'the bilingual writer, especially in exile, may feel traitorous, amputated, and divided, not so much the bearer of a *bi-destin*, a "double destiny," as Triolet and Roman Jacobson put it, but of a *mi-destin* a "half-destiny"'.[42] What Beaujour suggests here is that a 'half-destiny' is the most common situation among exilic writers as they carry 'the sense of a profound, irreducible psychic split' that is the result of the abandonment of the mother tongue. Both writers who remain faithful to their first language and those who change language after their exile '*do* feel mortally split and even in danger of psychic disintegration, at least during the period immediately following their apostasy'.[43]

The loss of a language for an exile may be, as the comparison with Giorgio Pressburger also demonstrated, 'devastating, depriving the subject of access to the living word', to cite Nochlin once again. Meanwhile, the new language — the one that will establish the 'half-destiny' of the exile — progressively takes more space. Tomizza's transition is not a total abandonment of his native tongue but rather the loss of his double dialect in favour of a standard language. He does not fully investigate this passage in his essays but he does capture the struggle of acquiring a 'new' language in the novel *Franziska*. As Blagoni wrote, the situation can be summarized in these terms: 'La questione dell'identità nazionale diventa, così una questione di sangue, o più precisamente, una guerra. Quello che doveva essere appartenenza etnico-culturale è degenerato in un'appartenenza esclusivamente nazionale sociopatica' [The national identity issue becomes a matter of blood, or more precisely, a war. What was supposed to be ethno-cultural affiliation has degenerated into a solely national sociopathic belonging].[44]

This work should neither be considered autobiographical nor its female protagonist an alter ego or projection of the writer. Nevertheless, *Franziska*'s linguistic and political struggles do have some sort of parallel with Tomizza's linguistic 'purification', which also was a fight against adverse political conditions. *Franziska* is the story of a young Slovene girl, born on the first day of the twentieth century and named after Emperor Franz Joseph, whose empire was fated to collapse after the First World War. When she was born a stable coexistence among different peoples still prevailed in the area: 'Sotto la luminaria cittadina la gente danzava e si abbracciava offrendosi la bottiglia, greci con turchi, italiani con sloveni, serbi con croati, tedeschi con ebrei' [Under the street lights, people danced and hugged offering the bottle, Greeks with Turks, Italians and Slovenes, Serbs and Croats, Germans and Jews].[45] However, the war brings Nino Ferrari, an Italian officer from Cremona, to the Soča/Isonzo front, and he soon begins a relationship with Franziska. Ferrari presumes himself superior to Franziska and treats her with contempt. The end of their relationship, which demolishes the girl's hopes, does not come unexpectedly:

> L'innamorato, ricco, colto, più anziano di lei, desidera sposarla, ne ammira la bellezza e la sincerità ma ne avverte anche la profonda diversità umana ed etnica, il differente atteggiamento nei confronti della realtà e finisce per allontanarsene senza una parola di addio.[46]
>
> [The rich, educated, older lover wanted to marry her, admired her beauty and sincerity but also feels the deep human and ethnic diversity, the different attitude to reality and eventually leaves her without a word of goodbye].

From the very beginning, Tomizza marks the contrast existing between the Slovene and Italian cultures and above all the sense of superiority affirmed by Ferrari. As observed by Marta Moretto, even the name of the female character is Italianized in the story (at that time and in the interwar period Slovene names and surnames were widely mistaken and Italianized): 'Il vero nome della protagonista è Franciška, pronunciato nella zona Franziska in omaggio al grande padrino Nino, italiano, la chiamerà Francesca' [The real name of the protagonist is Franciška, pronounced in the area Franziska in honour of the great godfather Nino, Italian, who will call her

Francesca].[47] The character herself immediately realizes what her Slovene identity meant to the Italians: 'Franziska si rese conto che l'identità slovena era un attributo il quale sottostava a tanti altri: alla condizione sociale, all'educazione ricevuta in famiglia, all'essere nati in città o l'avervi messo piede di recente' (F, p. 83) [Franziska realized that the Slovene identity was an attribute which underlaid many others: the social condition, the education received in the family, being born in the city or having set foot there recently]. In this atmosphere, Italians would often use the offensive term 'slave' to indicate a Slav: 'Quando transitavano in gruppo verso il centro venivano accolti con urla, fischi, insulto scandito di "S'cia-vi! S'cia-vi!", perfino dai ragazzi delle elementari' (F, p. 83) [When they transited in a group towards the centre they were greeted with screams, whistles, the articulated insult 'S'cia-vi! S'cia-vi!', even by children from elementary school].

As with Tomizza himself, Franziska's home language was probably characterized by the use of a dialect, mixtures, and contaminations, which could hardly be improved in Trieste, where she was surrounded by people who rarely spoke standard Italian. This is the reason for the character's silence:

> Lei continuava a parlare il meno possibile, si limitava a replicare alle domande sforzandosi di adoperare la lingua italiana, non il dialetto poiché esso era il banco di prova che attestava se uno era del centro o della periferia, della città o del contrado slavo' (F, p. 83)
>
> [She continued to talk as little as possible, she merely replied to questions by forcing herself to use the Italian language, not the dialect because it was the test-bed of whether one was from the centre or the outskirts, from the city or the Slav quarter].

Tomizza, when pointing out the difficulties of learning a new language given the constant interferences created by the other tongues, seems to draw a parallel between his condition and that of Franziska:

> Il suo impedimento ad apprendere bene la nuova lingua ufficiale deriva dalla padronanza dello sloveno e del tedesco, che vicendevolmente le guidavano la mano nel trascrivere certi suoni italiani, i quali richiedevano un accoppiamento piuttosto estroso di consonanti, la *gl* (i), la *gn* (i), la *sc* (i), e si complicavano con l'uso capriccioso delle maledette doppie. Interferiva inoltre il dialetto locale che lei masticava parecchio, risultandole più accessibile della lingua pura, per cui imparava molto di più dai compagni d'ufficio, come preparati a quelle piccole insidie. (F, p. 122)
>
> [The impediment to learning well the new official language derives from mastering the Slovene and German, that together guided her hand in transcribing certain Italian sounds, which required a rather fanciful pairing of consonants, the *gl* (i), *gn* (i), *sc* (i), and were complicated by the capricious use of the damned doubles. It also interfered with the local dialect that she knew quite well, making it more accessible than the pure language, so that she learned a lot more from her office mates, as they were prepared for those little incongruities.]

This passage recalls Nabokov's impressions of the American language described in *Speak, Memory*, his autobiographical memoir. He describes the American sounds, even dividing the letters of the alphabet into the colours that were generated by the sound they produced. For instance, in the:

> Blue group, there is steely x, thundercloud z, and huckleberry k. Since a subtle interaction exists between sound and shape, I see q as browner than k, while s is not the light blue of c, but a curious mixture of azure and mother-of-pearl.[48]

Without formulating anything like Nabokov's grapheme-colour system, Tomizza recounts the impressions generated by the Italian language to a non-native speaker.

The acquisition of a new language is a long and frustrating process that troubles Franziska throughout the novel especially because it is bound up with her romantic relationship with the officer. Far from being only a problem of language, Franziska's struggle is determined by an antagonistic political environment that often emerges in the dialogue between the two lovers. The Italian officer abruptly points out the mistakes made by the girl, without even the minimum of empathy or understanding of her situation:

> Non afferrava in pieno come l'appartenere a un altro popolo, il parlare una diversa lingua, poteva costruire un problema, e per giunta continuo, peggio che in Guerra dove non si stava sempre a badare alla propria pellaccia.
> Estrasse di tasca il fazzoletto e glielo porse dicendo 'Ora asciugati gli occhi e pianta anche tu!'.
> Franziska lo guardò sorpresa per il modo brusco e l'improvviso tu. Aderendovi e un po' pungendolo si accertò: 'è neto?'.
> 'Non è uscito adesso adesso dal bucato, ma è pulito'. Subito quest'aggettivo gli riassunse quanto di più esplicito emanava dalla personcina che aveva di fronte: un che di pulito.
> 'Già' aggiunse lei soffiandosi il naso. 'Si dice pulitto'.
> 'Ma lo fai apposta?' ridacchiò il giovanotto. 'Si dice è giusto, pulitto no. Come fa in sloveno pulito?'
> 'Čist. Ma tacato con fazzoleto è čisto'.
> 'É neto da dove ti viene?'
> La ragazza sbarrò gli occhi. 'Tutti qui si dice neto, è dialeto?' (F, p. 104)

> [He did not fully grasp how belonging to another population, speaking a different language, could constitute a problem, and in addition continual, worse than in war where one was not always looking to save one's skin.
> He pulled out his handkerchief and handed it to her saying 'Now dry your eyes and stop it!'.
> Franziska looked at him surprised at his abrupt manner and sudden *tu*. Coming closer and prodding him, she checked: 'Is it *neto*?'.
> 'It hasn't right now come from the laundry, but it is clean'. This adjective immediately summed up what the little person in front of him emanated: something clean.
> 'Indeed' she added, blowing her nose. 'You say cleean'.
> 'Are you doing it on purpose' sniggered the young man. 'You should say it right, cleean no. How do you say clean in Slovene?'
> 'Čist. But related to the tissue is čisto'.
> 'Where does neto come from?'
> She opened her eyes wide. 'Everyone here says neto, is it dialect?']

To fully understand the meaning of Franziska's mistakes, I will draw a parallel with Nabokov's *Pnin*, a work in which there is a remarkable 'deficiency in English'.[49] The story of Timofey Pavlovich Pnin, a Russian assistant professor in exile in the United States where he teaches his native tongue at the fictional Waindell College, touches upon the difficult relationship between the maternal and the acquired language. Pnin faces the most common linguistic challenges encountered by Russian émigrés. His relationship with the two languages is summarized by the following passage: 'If his Russian was music, his English was murder. He had enormous difficulty ('dzeefeecooltsee' in Pninian English) with depalletisation, never managing to remove the extra Russian moisture from t's and d's before the vowels he so quaintly softened'.[50] There are many other ways in which Pnin's linguistic troubles are treated by the narrator. The accent of the immigrant speaker is usually caught, as well as some mistakes of grammar: '"I haf nofing!", as opposed to "I have lost everything!" or some other properly unhappy version of the statement?'.[51] But also 'Pnin's utterances often constitute a literal translation of Russian grammar and vocabulary' such as '"to make a long story short" (a variant on "to cut"...)'.[52] The narrator mediates Pnin's unspoken intentions: '"Quittance?" queried Pnin, Englishing the Russian for "receipt" (kvitantsiya)'.[53]

We find, in parallel with *Franziska*, mistakes made by the character and then the correcting mediation of the writer, who feels the need to explain. However, Tomizza's plurilingual background is more complex. Franziska's Slovene is mediated by the Triestine dialect (as well as being inflected by her knowledge of German) before reaching Italian; some of her mistakes derive, as the character herself seems to suggest, from the interaction of this local form of the language. Tomizza's mediation presents a slightly different form: he gives a lot of space to dialogue to make the contrast between his characters more evident. The dialogue cited above between Franziska and the officer lets them interact directly and a vivid impression results. The reader can easily sense the indifference of the officer to the girl's language and culture, and this emerges also from her reaction:

'Tu venuto e sempre arabiato con me a Štanjel'.
Si trovavano alla scala che divideva i loro due uffici. 'Dove hai detto?'
Franziska lasciò passare un impiegato del reparto contabilità. Poi disse: 'Mio paese è Štanjel'.
'Non ricordo nessun Stanel' negò col paio il suo interlocutore.
'Štanjel, no Stanel. Š come scioco. Vedi che nianche tu sei pulito in mia lingua? Come io in tua, e così pari, zero al zero'. (F, p. 104)

['You come and always upset at me in Štanjel'.
They were on the staircase that divided their two offices. 'Where did you say?'
Franziska let an office worker from to the accounting department pass. Then she said: 'My village is Štanjel'.
'I do not remember any Stanel' denied her interlocutor.
'Štanjel, not Stanel. Š as sh. See, not even you are clean in my language? As I in yours, and so equal, zero to zero'.]

Despite the result of the dialogue seeming to be a draw (she makes many mistakes in Italian, he could not pronounce the name of the girl's home town), Franziska is the one speaking in the 'other' language, while there is no effort at all on the part of the officer. From his perspective, the girl should conform to the Italian language and culture and not the other way around, as he demands of her:

> 'Se questo è il nostro proposito, dovremmo lavorare ancora, sistemare le cose, mettere tutto a posto. Io non sono ricco, ricordatelo. Potrei esserlo, ma non m'importano le ricchezze, voglio crescere con le mie fatiche. Tu dovrai aspettare che prepari il mio ambiente, il quale si è sempre aspettato gran cose da me. E dovrai studiare, perché come ti farai capire a Cremona se parli come adesso?'
> Lei fu pronta a informare: 'Io sono comperata gramatica e vocaleva... no, vocabolario'.
> 'Lascia perdere il vocabolario e di' piuttosto: "Io ho comperato la grammatica e il dizionario italiano"'.
> 'Sloveno-italiano, prego'. (*F*, p. 118)

> ['If this is our purpose, we should still work, fix things, put everything in place. I am not rich, remember that. I could be, but I do not care for riches, I want to grow with my efforts. You will have to wait while I prepare my environment, which has always expected great things from me. And you will have to study, because how will you be understood if you speak in Cremona like you do now?'
> She was ready to let him know: 'I bought gramar and vocalav... no, vocabulary'.
> 'Forget the vocabulary and say rather: "I have bought a grammar and an Italian dictionary"'.
> 'Slovene-Italian, please'.]

The effect produced by errors in *Franziska* contrasts with the one created by *Pnin*, which are comic. Pnin aims to be ironic, as observed by Besemeres, given that behind his words 'the immigrant idiom [is] made so irresistibly funny'.[54] Among many examples, there is the 'comically urgent, "But where to check properly?" [which] reproduces Russian syntax, "No gde proverit?"'.[55] On many occasions the character's accent or his bizarre associations and mistakes make the reader laugh. Despite being potentially funny — the Triestine dialect is a picturesque one — Franziska's mistakes do not produce an ironic effect. The hostile behaviour of the officer may leave the reader disappointed.

Both novels (more or less directly) depict Nabokov's and Tomizza's delicate plurilingual issues. The two writers use language as a tool to recreate a very specific context that can be conveyed only through linguistic insecurity, errors, wrong associations, and accents. The characters' change of language is a privileged angle of observation with which to approach the complex situation of the exile. Nabokov knew that this device could offer him the chance to shorten the distance between him and his reader: 'Obviously, Nabokov wants to be loyal to the accent he has been transcribing so carefully all along, but the accent's appearance with peculiar strength at this moment is evidence that Nabokov is almost testing our level of empathy'.[56] More than anywhere else, in the case of Franziska Tomizza managed to use her use of language to convey all her frustration and her whole emotional world. The following comment on Pnin is valid for Franziska as well: 'we realize that the linguistic mistakes that Pnin makes affect not merely our judgment of language but also our judgement of Pnin's emotional state'.[57] Through the broken use of language, Tomizza manages to portray a hostile situation that reflects his own struggles.

'Un-literariness'

As we have seen in the novels presented in this analysis, Tomizza's chosen narrative language has to cope with the presence, both in his subject matter and in his own memory and imagination, of a non-simple linguistic situation and this affects its linearity and 'correctness'. This presence could be viewed in psychoanalytical terms as the pressure of an unruly repressed that troubles the dominant narrative language. The potential and the limits of Tomizza's language can be seen in the term 'anti-letterarietà', a phrase that has often been used to attack Triestine writers. The word is explained by Claudio Magris as follows: 'L'antiletterarietà viene invece per lo più intesa, non senza nebulose ambiguità, come rifiuto del dettato adorno, delle "false" convenzioni formali, dell'eleganza stilistica priva di impegno umano. Un'esigenza di cose e di sentimenti, di verità, contrapposta dunque all'esigenza di parole' [Un-literariness is instead mostly intended, not without vague ambiguity, as the refusal of the adorned dictation, the 'false' formal conventions, stylish elegance without human effort. A need for things and feelings, of truth, opposed therefore to the need for words].[58] Magris's definition recalls an essay written by the most famous Triestine poet Umberto Saba, 'Quello che resta da fare ai poeti', in which he stresses the need to adhere to so-called 'onestà letteraria' [literary honesty]: 'non sforzare mai l'ispirazione, poi non tentare, per meschini motivi di ambizione o di successo, di farla parere più vasta e trascendente di quanto per avventura essa sia' [never strain the inspiration, then do not attempt, for wretched reasons of ambition or success, to make it more comprehensive and transcendent than what it is].[59]

'Anti-letterarietà' as a term used in hostile criticism implies the inability to write good Italian. Writing in Trieste and the surrounding areas meant coping with linguistic contaminations and this made Italian difficult to master. Italian in these places had to deal with the presence of the Triestine dialect, spoken widely by the population, as well as other languages such as Slovene, Croatian, and German, which affected its lexicon and syntax. Therefore, the Italian language in Trieste was something to be aimed for rather than a familiar tongue employed by all. For this reason, many authors decided to move to Florence to improve their Italian:

> A 'sciacquare i panni in Arno' si sarebbero avviati sulle orme del Manzoni e ormai a distanza di quasi un secolo la maggior parte degli scrittori giuliani, che, divisi tra tedesco e dialetto triestino, avvertivano più a rischio la propria italofonia: Scipio Slataper, i due Stuparich, Carlo Michelstaedter, Biagio Marin, Umberto Saba, Guido Devescovi, Alberto Spaini.[60]
>
> [To 'rinse clothes in the Arno' they would have proceeded in the footsteps of Manzoni and now after almost a century most of the Giuliani writers, who, divided between German and Triestine dialect, felt their Italophony was more

at risk: Scipio Slataper, the two Stuparich, Carlo Michelstaedter, Biagio Marin, Umberto Saba, Guido Devescovi, Alberto Spaini.]

The most famous exponent of 'un-literariness' is probably Italo Svevo, who was many times accused of writing badly. Apart from using the Triestine dialect in everyday life, Svevo studied in Germany. In his novels, his Italian is the result of a complex process, that was summarized by Serge Vanvolsen as follows: 'il vettore linguistico tedesco, l'elemento dialettale triestino, un'ammirazione per il toscano letterario che risultò in una lingua piuttosto arcaica e ricercata, qualche francesismo e naturalmente l'influsso del linguaggio bancario e commerciale usato per giorni interi nel lavoro' [The German language vector, the Triestine dialect element, an admiration for the literary Tuscan language which resulted in a rather archaic and sophisticated language, some Gallicism and of course the influence of the banking and commercial language used for days at work].[61] Such a mixture struggled to be appreciated by the Italian public and critics who at the beginning described it as hopeless. Bruno Maier summarized the prevailing opinion on Svevo's language:

> Il barbaro triestino, lo scrittore italo-tedesco che sin nello pseudonimo adattato tradiva la sua ibrida origine, con quel suo gergo ingrato e rozzo, pieno di calchi germani e di residui dialettali, irto di sgrammaticature e d'improprietà lessicali e sintattiche, non poteva essere accolto nel nobile castello della tradizione letteraria italiana.[62]

> [The barbarian Triestine, the Italo-German writer that even in the adapted pseudonym betrayed his hybrid origin, with his ungrateful and rude jargon, full of Germanic calques and dialect residues, fraught with errors of grammar and lexical and syntactic inaccuracies, could not be accepted in the noble castle of the Italian literary tradition.]

Tomizza, who is constantly afflicted both by the impossibility of fully displaying his linguistic subject matter and by the awareness of being confused by multiple linguistic presences that undermine the fluidity of his Italian, discusses the same linguistic insecurity that emerges in the above characterization of Svevo:

> La cosa che più mi angustiava, e tuttora non mi rende sempre quieto, era l'insicurezza linguistica, destinata a emergere soprattutto nella narrazione analitica che richiede l'impiego di una lingua maggiormente articolata. E qui si erge una questione che non mi riguarda solamente quale scrittore e individuo singolo, bensì investe l'intera area storico-geografica in cui sono nato e cresciuto. [...] Anche i degustatori di poesia dialettale (per non parlare degli estimatori di prose pirotecniche) i quali si deliziano di risonanze remote, affluite sia pure dalle regioni contermini o perchennó dai paesi neolatini, come reagirebbero di fronte a una pagina infarcita di etimi tedeschi e di desinenze croate?[63]

> [The thing that distressed me, and still now does not make me calmer, was the language insecurity, destined to emerge especially in the analytical narrative that requires the use of a more articulate language. And here lies a question that does not only concern me as a writer and individual, but involves the whole historical and geographic area in which I was born and grown up. [...] Also the tasters of dialect poetry (not to forget the admirers of pyrotechnic

prose) who are delighted by remote resonances, which had flowed either from neighbouring regions or from Latin countries, how would they react in front of a page filled with German etymologies and Croatian endings?]

From the very beginning the reaction of critics to Tomizza's language was polarized: on the one hand, the presence of words and expressions not considered suitable for a literary text was often pointed out and his Italian was accused of being sometimes obscure and not without mistakes. On the other hand, by quoting two reviews, Tomizza himself points out the contrasting reactions he experienced:

> Del resto, che devo pensare io stesso della mia lingua se, all'uscita di *L'albero dei sogni,* quasi nello stesso giorno mi è capitato di registrare commenti alquanto discordi?
>
> È una lingua rozza, ibrida, irta di solecismi, è l'italiano bastardo e approssimativo (s'immagina), di un ragazzo istriano, o di un molto incerto 'io narratore' che, volendo rievocare una sua storia, non riesce che a comunicarcene i fatti, e anche questo confusamente. (Paolo Milano)
>
> L'italiano di Tomizza è una lingua eterna, dalla perfezione cristallina e un po' tediosa dei manuali di bello scrivere, con movimenti eleganti e solenni e toni dolci e teneri sempre uguali a se stessi, all'interno del cui codice la vitale maleducazione dell'imprevisto è contraddizione che non trova ospitalità. (Mario Lunetta).[64]

> [After all what I have to think myself of my tongue if, at the appearance of *L'albero dei sogni*, almost on the same day I happened to record very discordant comments?
>
> It is a coarse, hybrid tongue, bristling with solecisms, it is the bastard and rough Italian (one imagines) of an Istrian guy, or a very uncertain 'I narrator' who, by wanting to recall a story, can only communicate the facts, and confusingly at that. (Paolo Milano)
>
> The Italian of Tomizza is an eternal language of crystalline perfection and a bit tedious from the manual of good writing, with elegant and solemn movements and sweet and tender tones always equal to themselves, inside which the lively unexpected rudeness is a contradiction that does not find a welcome. (Mario Lunetta).]

Even Lunetta's positive remarks cannot be taken as a compliment to the fluidity of Tomizza's Italian. The language of the 'manuali di bello scrivere' seems to suggest the presence of so-called 'ipercorrettismi', which was something already said of Svevo. According to Domenico Cernecca, such words can be defined as follows:

> Se vi sono termini dialettali facilmente individuabili [...] altri ve ne sono i quali, pur essendo comuni alla lingua, tradiscono la loro natura, sia per l'impegno che se ne fa, sia per la frequenza con la quale ricorrono, là dove l'italiano userebbe vocaboli diversi.[65]

> [If there are easily identifiable terms in dialect [...] there are others that, despite being common to the language, betray their nature, both for how they are used, and for the frequency with which they occur, where the Italian would use different words].

The fear of writing bad Italian led both Svevo and Tomizza to use words that might be termed 'hypercorrect' and that would register as odd to the ear of the ordinary Italian speaker.

As described in Chapter 3, Tomizza's Italian needed a process of accurate revision; Vittorini's letters show the most common mistakes. The versions of Italian he creates, versions that might be characterized as linguistically hybrid, are a challenge to the reader. Apart from transferring multiple languages into his works, Tomizza faced the issue of transferring an oral plurilingual tradition into the Italian written text which resulted in the 'polluting' of both languages, Italian and Croatian:

> Le reazioni più negative da parte del pubblico furono di sentirmi accusare a Trieste di aver sporcato la lingua italiana, a Zagabria di avere svilito la lingua croata. Ma resta il fatto incontrovertibile, e sul quale sono disposto a puntare tutto il mio onore di uomo, che ogniqualvolta mi è accaduto di scoprire la radice slava di un vocabolo ritenuto italiano, e viceversa, ho riportato quella voce alla sua matrice originaria con identica soddisfazione. Com'è anche vero che leggendo le traduzioni croate di alcuni miei romanzi, certi passi mi sono riusciti superiori al testo originale: li scorrevo muovendo le labbra come per seguire un canto del quale conoscevo la melodia ma ignoravo le parole.[66]

> [The most negative reactions from the public were to be accused in Trieste of making the Italian language dirty, in Zagreb to have demeaned the Croatian language. But the incontrovertible fact, on which I am prepared to wager all my honour as a man, remains that whenever I happened to discover the Slavic root of a word considered Italian, and vice versa, I reported that entry to its original form with identical satisfaction. As it is also true that reading the Croatian translations of some of my novels, certain passages exceeded the original text: I went through them moving my lips as to follow a song of which I knew the melody, but did not know the words.]

In relation to the 'transfer' of an oral tradition into a written language, Farah demolishes the limits imposed by 'beautiful' writing, by suggesting that the linguistic barrier can be easily overcome:

> I seem to represent a total minority, I was born in the oral tradition. The move from an oral tradition to a written tradition is itself one form of exile. A second point: English — the language in which I write — is my fourth language. Is it language that is so important, or the ideas contained therein? The important thing in the writer is the fire, the flame of his ideas. An editor can clean up a stylistically flawed book, making it a better book than one written by someone who is extremely articulate but basically void of ideas.[67]

Tomizza's 'anti-letterarietà' offered the perspective of a linguistic world in which the language not only reflects the encounter or collision of two or more backgrounds, it also further develops linguistic creativity. Therefore, 'un-literariness' should not be conceived as the impoverishment of the language: 'il travaglio linguistico, la presunta "anti-letterarietà" (che per me è piuttosto altra aspirazione frustrata, quella di poter fare fine letteratura), erano ulteriori prove che mi trovavo nel giusto, e sia pure un giusto faticoso e patetico' [the linguistic labour, the presumed 'un-literariness' (that for me is rather another frustrated aspiration, to be able to make fine literature), were further proofs that I was right, even if tiresomely and pathetically right].⁶⁸ Tomizza overturns the idea of 'un-literariness', arguing that his novels are not the result of 'bad' Italian, but rather a project of linguistic research. This sort of writing, 'self-translating', should be viewed as an opportunity for the reader to get past the barrier usually present in monolingual works and gain access to the linguistic process behind the novel.

Anokhina in her work *Multilinguisme et créativité littéraire* observes that the bilingual creation 'can choose to respect both linguistic systems or, on the contrary, create interferences between the two'.⁶⁹ If plurilingual creativity respects different codes, the two different linguistic systems may flow parallel to one another, combine, or even collide. Anokhina continues: 'If the use of an original foreign lexicon can answer multiple needs of writing, one of these functions is to compensate for the gaps of the national lexicon and, in this perspective, be assimilated to a form of occasional lexicon'.⁷⁰ Far from being a negative phenomenon leading to bad Italian, the creativity generated by plurilingualism may expand the linguistic potential of a text. Where there is interference between two codes the writer shapes an intermediate linguistic space within which he is able to set up new rules.

Despite the language used by the later Tomizza being Italian, the imagination of the writer is widely influenced by a plurilingual background that struggles to come to the surface of the narrative. It is not, however, only direct linguistic interferences that thus emerge; sometimes it is new ideas or sources of inspiration for new stories. Among such examples there is the section 'Il letto della Pizia' included in *Rapporti colpevoli* where, in the form of a diary, many unconnected dreams (often related to the family of the author) follow one after the other. Rita Ferreri explains these dreams as follows: 'Taken together, the chapters form a sort of autobiography made up of erotic dreams, childhood memories, and the acquisition of new self-awareness. The writer's consciousness is built on a reviewing of his land of origin and of his adventures, trips, and encounters as an adult'.⁷¹ On 7 January 1990, the first-person narrator recounts a dream in which he is attending the wrong funeral. In the unreal atmosphere, the narrator recognizes Croatian intellectuals, among whom is Zvane Črnja: 'Ai funerali partecipavano perlopiù letterati, anche croati tra i quali l'amico Zvane Črnja. "Zvane, *moj dragi* Zvane..." lo rincorsi' [At the funeral there were mostly men of letters, also Croats including the friend Zvane Črnja. 'Zvane, *moj dragi* Zvane...' I chased him].⁷² However, the narrator immediately realizes his mistake and apologizes to the widow whom he realizes that he did not know at all. In this dream, the story revolves around a pun: the similarity between the Croatian words for killing and hoeing the ground generates the idea of killing by being struck with the hoe:

> Per di più mi esprimevo malissimo in croato, non mi veniva il termine funerale, conclusi col dire che un'altra persona attendeva di essere sepolta, usando il febbrile verbo all'infinito pokopati che associa lo slavo dialettale kopat (zappare) al verbo copar (ammazzare) e mi dà dunque l'immagine dell'uccidere a colpi di zappa.⁷³
>
> [Furthermore I expressed myself badly in Croatian, I could not find the word funeral, I concluded by saying that another person was waiting to be buried, using the feverish verb in the infinitive form *pokopati* that links the Slavic

dialect *kopat* (hoe) to the verb *copar* (murder) and thus gives me the image of killing by blows from a hoe.]

Puns or new associations of ideas that would otherwise be unthinkable come from linguistic contaminations such as the above mentioned 'pokopati'. A similar example can be found in *Ieri, un secolo fa*, where the word *ureni*, which is used to pinpoint the specific moment in which birds are ready to fly, can be only explained in Italian with a long periphrasis:

> Per poter contare su un proprio uccello di richiamo, Tin aspettava che i cardellini del nido fossero, secondo il nostro gergo semi-slavo, *ureni* ossia giusto pronti a spiccare il volo. Bisognava infatti intervenire al momento esatto; un giorno prima o un giorno dopo sarebbero stati ugualmente fatali: o avremmo avuto in gabbia dei piccoli incapaci di nutrirsi e che la madre immancabilmente lasciava al loro destino, oppure avremmo trovato il nido vuoto e loro a saltellare liberi dal noce al susino.[74]

> [To be able to count on his own decoy, Tin expected that the finches were in the nest, in our semi-Slavic lingo, *ureni* namely just ready to take flight. One had indeed to intervene at the exact time; a day before or a day after would be equally fatal: otherwise we would have had small animals incapable of feeding themselves and that the mother invariably left to their fate, or we would find their empty nest and them free to jump from the walnut to the plum.]

This process can be grasped only in comparison with a contrasting example, the case of Boris Pahor, who did not accept the challenge of translating himself into Italian. This Slovene author, born in Trieste discusses the troubles he would have had if he had tried to transfer an idea generated in one language to another. He details the problem of transferring Slovene verbs into the Italian narrative. There is a parallel with Tomizza's need to explain the meaning of *ureni*:

> I miei libri nascono in sloveno, non si possono tradurre, bisogna riscriverli, allora tanto vale. Non è che sia contrario all'autotraduzione in sé, semplicemente non ne sento l'esigenza e mi riesce difficile, dato che la lingua slovena opera per lo più con i verbi: noi con un verbo combiniamo dieci proposizioni diverse. Come si fa a tradurre, per esempio, 'potovati' (andare in qualche posto), 'dopotovati' vuol dire 'quando si finisce di viaggiare', 'prepotovati' significa 'fare tanti viaggi differenti, viaggiare attraverso tanti posti'? Quando lei deve tradurre questi verbi deve cambiare completamente la frase, come faccio a tradurli in modo che si combinino con quanto io volevo dire pensando in sloveno?[75]

> [My books are born in Slovene, you cannot translate them, you have to rewrite them, then you might as well. It is not that I am against self-translation itself, simply I do not feel the need and I find it difficult, as the Slovene language works mostly with verbs: we combine with a verb ten different propositions. How do you translate, for example, 'potovati' (go somewhere), 'dopotovati' means 'when you finish travelling', 'prepotovati' means 'to make many different trips, to travel through many places'? When you have to translate these verbs you must completely change the sentence, how do I translate them so as to combine them with what I wanted to say thinking in Slovene?]

From ideas generated in different tongues it is possible to investigate the relationship between language and thought. The issue has been formulated many times by scholars and writers, such as Julien Green, who explicitly asked: 'Does one think in the same way in both languages and in terms, which are, so to speak, interchangeable?'.[76] Green seems to suggest that different languages shape different thoughts, as 'new trains of thought were started in mind, new associations of ideas were formed'.[77] The same hypothesis is suggested also by Wilhelm von Humboldt: 'Each language draws a circle around the people to whom it adheres which it is possible for the individual to escape only by stepping into a different one'.[78] He states also that a new language 'means the gaining of a new standpoint toward one's world-view, and it does this in fact to a considerable degree, because each language contains the entire conceptual web and mental images of a part of humanity'.[79] Not even the process of interior self-translation used by Tomizza could limit the inevitable differences between two codes.

In *L'albero dei sogni*, Tomizza underlines the difference between the languages at his disposal. When the main character Stefano considers the similarities existing between the language (but also the mentality and way of thinking) of the actor he saw in Belgrade and his Croatian compatriots, at the same time he affirms the difficulty the Italian language has in conveying the same meaning:

> Chiusi gli occhi e la parlata scandita dall'attore mi filtrava nel sangue come farmaco e insieme veleno. Chi avrebbe potuto condividere l'acuta sensazione al di fuori del Silvano e del Celso e dell'Alfredo che appioppavano rozzi, incomprensibili nomignoli a insegnanti e condiscepoli? O dell'altra gente di Materada per la quale il fuscio delle frasche nel bosco si racchiudeva in uno *sciuskati*, lo scoppiare e sfrigolare del fuoco in un *puhati*, il silenzio notturno nel prolungato *tihooo* sperdentesi sulla campagna? (*AS*, p. 214–15)

> [I closed my eyes and the parlance articulated by the actor filtered into my blood like a medication and poison together. Who could have shared the acute feeling apart from Silvano and Celso and Alfredo who gave rough, incomprehensible nicknames to teachers and fellow students? Or the other people from Materada for whom the rustle of branches in the forest is contained in a *sciuskati*, the burst and sizzle of the fire in a *puhati*, the night silence in the extended *tihooo* dispersing across the countryside?]

In this passage, where Tomizza doubles three Italian expressions by adding their corresponding ones in Croatian, he indirectly points out the possibility of expanding the text through a different language. The onomatopoeic Croatian expressions enrich the text with new nuances and references, highlighting the impossibility of one code to encapsulate fully the linguistic and cultural domain in the possession of a plurilingual writer. The translation provided, which is not needed by the Italian reader to understand the story, aims to further emphasize the limits imposed by the use of a single language.

On many other occasions Tomizza stressed the distance between Italian and Croatian codes and cultures, such when in *L'amicizia* he details the colours of the wine (red wine in Italian corresponds to black wine in Croatian):

> 'Ci porti mezzo litro di bianco' [...]. Il marito ci faceva cenno di raggiungerlo in cantina. [...] 'Perché non provare il nero?' si sforzò di canzonarci. 'Io lo so:

> perché non ha color' quasi canterellò seguendo suono e cadenze di un'altra lingua. Per questa stessa ragione, come la moglie, come tutti loro del carso, gesticolava con eccesso o in tempo sbagliato.
> 'Sono per assaggiare il nero' mi feci avanti.
> 'Bravo' e accese la luce [...]. L'uomo spillò dall'ultima botticella un vino rosato, lo alzò verso la luce e me lo porse. [...] 'é di viti giovani' dissi. 'Non può aver colore'.
> 'Ecco chi se ne intende' s'illuminò incredulo il carsolino. 'Ma è sempre terrano'.
>
> ['Bring us half a litre of white' [...]. The husband beckoned us to join him in the cellar. [...] 'Why don't you try the black?' he forced himself to tease us. 'I know: because it has no colour' he almost hummed following the sound and cadence of another language. For this same reason, like his wife, like all of them on the Karst, gesturing excessively or at the wrong time.
> 'I'm for tasting the black' I came forward.
> 'Bravo' and he turned on the light [...]. The man drew from the last barrel of rose wine, he raised it toward the light and gave it to me. [...] 'It is from young vines' I said. 'It can't have colour'.
> 'Here is one who understands' the man from the Karst lit up in disbelief. 'But it is always *terrano*'.]

Linguistic relativity, or the Sapir-Whorf hypothesis, is the concept that best defines this situation. According to this definition, the structure of a language tends to influence the speakers' world view. A specific language determines the thoughts of the speakers through linguistic categories and use. Scotti Jurić, who applied linguistic relativity to this passage, observed that:

> C'è poi la distinzione tra vino nero/vino bianco, e vino rosso/vino bianco che fa parte di quella teoria del relativismo culturale avanzata da Sapir e Whorf definibile in questi termini: gli uomini sezionano la natura secondo linee tracciate dalla propria lingua madre; le categorie e i tipi che isoliamo dal mondo dei fenomeni non sono evidenti e individuabili a tutti gli osservatori in quanto il mondo si presenta come un flusso caleidoscopico di impressioni che devono essere organizzate dal sistema linguistico della nostra mente. Nello specifico coloro che vedono il terrano di color nero (e più è scuro più è di qualità) estendono questa caratteristica a tutti i vini non bianchi.[80]
>
> [Then there is the distinction between black/white wine, and red/white wine that is part of the theory of cultural relativism advanced by Sapir and Whorf definable in these terms: men dissect nature along lines drawn by their mother tongue; the categories and types that we isolate from the world of phenomena are not obvious and identifiable to all observers as the world looks like a kaleidoscopic flux of impressions to be organized by the linguistic system of our mind. Specifically, those who see *terrano* as black (and the darker the better the quality) extend this characteristic to all non-white wines.]

Exile is for Tomizza a traumatic event that comes out in the language he uses in his later novels. These works do not show the remarkable plurilingualism displayed in *Materada* or *La miglior vita*, rather they point out the loss involved in the translation into Italian. Complete equivalence between languages is not possible, as Susan Bassnett writes: 'sameness cannot exist between two languages'.[81] As self-translator

Tomizza has the chance to bypass technically untranslatable words or expressions by using creative transpositions and explanations, such as those mentioned above. The risk of this operation is falling into 'un-literariness' and lack of correctness or fluidity. However, these parameters should be revisited in the light of a better understanding of the creative and expressive potential of self-translation and associated multilingual processes.

In conclusion, the transition to the Italian language should not be considered simply as a loss for a writer like Tomizza. Loss is certainly the most obvious effect of his 'Italianization': it is evident in the untranslatability of certain passages, the lack of correspondence of several words, and the wide use of indirect speech. However, a more developed employment of self-translation and a reduction of the plurilingual contribution in his later work also means new linguistic challenges and effects, which are typical of the condition of exile.

Notes to Chapter 5

1. Norman Manea, *The Fifth Impossibility: Essays on Exile and Language* (New Haven, CT, & London: Yale University Press, 2012), pp. 253, 254, 260.
2. Ibid., p. 22.
3. McClennen, *The Dialectics of Exile*, p. 122.
4. Vladimir Nabokov, *Lolita* (New York: Putnam, 1955), p. 318.
5. Horst Bienek, 'Exile is Rebellion', in *Literature in Exile*, ed. by Glad, pp. 41–48 (p. 41).
6. Matthew McGowan, *Ovid in Exile: Power and Poetic Redress in the Tristia and Epistulae ex Ponto* (Leiden: Brill, 2009), p. 149.
7. Tamar Steinitz, *Translingual Identities: Language and the Self in Stefan Heym and Jakov Lind* (Rochester, NY: Camden House, 2013).
8. Fulvio Tomizza, *Adriatico e altre rotte: viaggi e reportages* (Reggio Emilia: Diabasis, 2007), p. 238.
9. Cesare De Michelis, 'Introduzione', in Fulvio Tomizza, *Le mie estati letterarie*, pp. 11–14 (p. 13).
10. Sylvia Molloy, 'Bilingualism, Writing, and the Feeling of Not Quite Being There' in *Lives in Translation. Bilingual Writers on Identity and Creativity*, ed. by Isabelle de Courtivron (New York: Palgrave Macmillan, 2003), pp. 69–78 (p. 20).
11. Tomizza, *Alle spalle di Trieste*, p. 193.
12. Ibid.
13. Lawrence Venuti, *The Translator's Invisibility: A History of Translation* (London & New York: Routledge, 1995), p. 20.
14. Ibid.
15. Rita Scotti Jurić, 'Fulvio Tomizza: le sfide della comunicazione interculturale', in *Rileggendo Fulvio Tomizza*, ed. by Deganutti, pp. 275–304 (pp. 283–84).
16. Michelle Woods, *Translating Milan Kundera* (Clevedon: Multilingual Matters, 2006), p. 9.
17. Ibid.
18. Walter Benjamin, 'The Task of the Translator', in *The Translation Studies Reader*, ed. by Lawrence Venuti (London: Routledge, 2000), pp. 15–22 (p. 18).
19. Roman Jacobson, 'On Linguistic Aspects of Translation', in *The Translation Studies Reader*, ed. by Venuti, pp. 113–18 (p. 113).
20. Ibid.
21. Ibid., p. 114.
22. Tomizza, *Alle spalle di Trieste*, p. 204.
23. Olga Ragusa, 'L'amicizia', *World Literature Today*, 55:1 (Winter 1981), 82.
24. Antonio de Lorenzi, 'Amicizia come categoria dell'anima', *Messaggero Veneto*, 27 April 1980, p. 30.
25. Giovanni Pirodda, *L'eclissi dell'autore: tecnica ed esperimenti verghiani* (Cagliari: Editrice democratica sarda, 1976), p. 92.

26. Isabelle Simoes Marques, 'Autour de la question du plurilinguisme littéraire: la textualisation des langues dans les écritures francophones', *Les Cahiers du Grelcef*, 2 (2011), 227–43 (p. 228).
27. Ibid.
28. De Lorenzi, 'Amicizia come categoria dell'anima', p. 30.
29. Fulvio Tomizza, *L'amicizia* (Milan: Rizzoli, 1980), p. 80; hereafter referenced as *A*.
30. Scotti Jurić, 'Fulvio Tomizza', p. 280.
31. *Il sussurro della grande voce* is the story of Andreas, a young Hungarian man who decides to escape from his country during the Hungarian Revolution. Andreas's destination is Italy, where he struggles to settle in, mainly because he does not know the language well. The story is therefore also an investigation of the difficult process of acquiring a foreign language.
32. Giorgio Pressburger, *Il sussurro della grande voce* (Milan: Rizzoli, 1990), p. 11.
33. Ibid., p. 98.
34. Ibid., p. 99.
35. Ibid., pp. 88–89.
36. Ibid., pp. 17–18.
37. Ibid., p. 63.
38. Ibid., p. 69.
39. Ibid., p. 37.
40. Ibid., p. 61.
41. Pressburger, *Il sussurro della grande voce*, p. 92.
42. Beaujour, *Alien Tongues*, p. 43.
43. Ibid.
44. Robert Blagoni, 'La Franziska di Tomizza', *La Battana*, 128 (April-June 1998), 13–16 (p. 15).
45. Fulvio Tomizza, *Franziska* (Milan: Mondadori, 1999), p. 14; hereafter referenced as *F*.
46. Irena Visintini, 'Franziska, il più recente romanzo di Fulvio Tomizza', *La Voce Giuliana*, 1 November 1997, p. 127.
47. Marta Moretto, '"Il bene e il male quando vengono piovono": paradossi, antinomie e ossimori nella narrativa di Fulvio Tomizza (1935–1999)' (unpublished doctoral thesis, University of Trieste, 2008–09, p. 100).
48. Vladimir Nabokov, *Speak, Memory: An Autobiography Revisited* (New York: Putnam, 1989), pp. 34–35.
49. Evelyn Nien-Ming Ch'ien, *Weird English* (Cambridge, MA: Harvard University Press, 2004), p. 74.
50. Vladimir Nabokov, *Pnin* (New York: Avon Books, 1969), p. 66.
51. Nien-Ming Ch'ien, *Weird English*, p. 73.
52. Mary Besemeres, 'Self-translation in Vladimir Nabokov's Pnin', *The Russian Review*, 59:3 (July 2000), 390–407 (p. 92).
53. Nabokov, *Pnin*, p. 18.
54. Besemeres, 'Self-translation in Vladimir Nabokov's Pnin', p. 396.
55. Ibid., p. 397.
56. Nien-Ming Ch'ien, *Weird English*, p. 73.
57. Ibid., p. 74.
58. Claudio Magris, 'Equivoci e compiacimenti sull'"antiletterarietà" triestina', *Trieste*, 87 (1969), 3–11 (p. 10).
59. Umberto Saba, *Quello che resta da fare ai poeti* (Milan: Henry Beyle, 2012), p. 31.
60. Franco Brevini, *La letteratura degli italiani: perché molti la celebrano e pochi la amano* (Milan: Feltrinelli, 2010), p. 55.
61. Serge Vanvolsen, 'La lingua e il problema della lingua in Svevo: una polimorfia che non piacque', in *Italo Svevo scrittore europeo: atti del convegno internazionale, Perugia, 18–21 marzo 1992*, ed. by N. Cacciaglia and L. Fava Guzzetta (Florence: Olschki, 1994), pp. 429–45 (p. 433).
62. Bruno Maier, 'Introduzione allo studio di Italo Svevo', in Italo Svevo, *Opere* (Milan: Dall'Oglio, 1954), pp. 1–123 (pp. 22–23).
63. Tomizza, *Le mie estati letterarie*, p. 127.
64. Ibid., p. 128.

65. Domenico Cernecca, 'Dialetto, lingua e processo creativo in Italo Svevo', *La Battana*, 18:63–64 (1982), 99–106 (p. 104).
66. Tomizza, *Alle spalle di Trieste*, p. 110.
67. Farah, 'In Praise of Exile', p. 63.
68. Fulvio Tomizza, 'Uno scrittore di confine', *Le Conferenze dell'Associazione culturale italiana*, 25 (1969–70), 30–42 (p. 34).
69. Cf. Anokhina, *Multilinguisme et créativité littéraire*, p. 64.
70. Cf. Ibid., p. 83.
71. Rita Ferreri, 'I rapporti colpevoli', *World Literature Today*, 67:4 (1993), 802.
72. Tomizza, *I rapporti colpevoli*, pp. 283–84.
73. Ibid..
74. Fulvio Tomizza, *Ieri un secolo fa* (Milan: Rizzoli, 1985), p. 22.
75. Anna Bogaro, *Letterature nascoste: storia della scrittura e degli autori in lingua minoritaria in Italia* (Bologna: Carocci, 2011), p. 57.
76. Julien Green, *The Apprentice Writer* (New York-London: Marion Boyars, 1993), p. 83.
77. Ibid., p. 62.
78. Wilhelm von Humboldt, *Wilhelm von Humboldts Werke, Berlin 1903–1936*, cited in English in Aneta Pavlenko, *The Bilingual Mind: And What it Tells Us about Language and Thought* (Cambridge: Cambridge University Press, 2014), p. 2.
79. Ibid.
80. Scotti Jurić, 'Fulvio Tomizza', p. 283.
81. Susan Bassnett, *Translation Studies* (New York & London: Routledge, 2014), p. 38.

CONCLUSION

An experience of exile is fundamentally determinant in the career of a writer: it conditions in depth the act of writing. In fact, the primary issue when considering such a writer usually concerns the influence exile has played on the narrative voice. This process is undoubtedly bidirectional, as suggested by Roger Whitehouse: 'If exile shapes writing, providing it with subjects and themes, writing also shapes exile'.[1] But in what forms does exile make its presence felt in the works of Fulvio Tomizza and how is it expressed in the text? To answer these questions it is first necessary to outline how he composed his works; such an investigation may uncover the hidden dynamics that lie behind the author's trauma. I will then go on to consider that trauma itself.

Tomizza was aware of the influence his homeland of Istria had on him: 'Ciò che mi ha condizionato e forse definito per sempre è il luogo, secondo me particolarissimo, nel quale sono nato' [What has affected me and maybe forever defined me is the place, very special to me, where I was born].[2] This also emerges in studying the detailed account he provides of the composition of his works. What immediately becomes clear is that exile strongly influenced Tomizza's decision to begin the draft of his first novel *Materada*. The pressing situation in Istria spurred him to draw parallels between stories and mould them into a novel:

> Al termine ritornai puntuale alla mia estate di *Materada*, che trovai sconvolta dalla difficile scelta aperta dall'intesa londinese tra i due paesi, se restare definitivamente nella terra degli avi sottoposta a un comunismo sciovinista o invece optare per l'Italia poco conosciuta ma compresa nell'emisfero occidentale. Successe che in quei tre mesi, in cui i paesani di solito si ammazzavano di fatica, ogni attività rimanesse paralizzata per lasciar posto a febbrili interrogativi e severi bilanci sul decennio trascorso, i quali nella maggior parte dei casi si risolsero con l'abbandono delle cose più care e sicure. Forse il solo a lavorare, quasi di nascosto, fui io, che presto presi a registrare quanto avveniva sotto i miei occhi. Penso con autocompatimento e un pizzico di franco rimpianto a quel mio disinvolto spreco di fogli di carta protocollo, riempiti da una scrittura spavalda e frettolosa. Elaborai una serie di bozzetti sulle vicissitudini presenti e passate di un gruppo di famiglie che avevano mostrato un differente atteggiamento verso il regime e si erano ugualmente decise alla partenza.[3]

> [When I returned to my regular summer in *Materada*, that I found shocked by the stark choice opened up by the London agreement between the two countries, whether to stay permanently in the land of the ancestors subject to a chauvinistic Communism or instead to opt for Italy which was little known but part of the Western hemisphere. It happened that during those three months, in which countrymen usually toiled, every activity remained paralyzed to

allow room for feverish questions and tight balances of the past decade, which in most cases were resolved with the abandonment of the dearest and safest things. Perhaps the only one working, almost in secret, was I, who soon started recording what was happening before my eyes. I think with self-pity and a bit of frank regret at my casual waste of foolscap sheets, filled with a bold and hurried writing. I worked out a series of sketches on the vicissitudes of the past and present group of families who had shown a different attitude toward the regime and also decided to depart.]

Tomizza experiences first-hand the troubles to which his village is subjected. Like the families he describes in *Materada*, he lives through these dramatic conditions himself, participating in the story that he begins to write. However, his personal troubles do not surface in the novel and Francesco, the main character, cannot be considered his alter ego. Rather he is a voice borrowed from the chorus:

> I miei primi due romanzi non sono affatto autobiografici come qualcuno, legittimamente, era stato indotto a sottolineare. Posso anzi dire che non è lasciato uno spiraglio in essi non solo alla vita privata dell'autore, ma anche a quelli che sono i suoi problemi, le finalità che più gli stanno a cuore.[4]
>
> [My first two novels are not autobiographical as someone legitimately was determined to emphasize. I can even say that there is not a chink left in them onto the private life of the author, nor onto his problems, the goals that are closest to his heart.]

Materada's genesis argues against its consideration as an autobiographical novel because Tomizza's aim is to give voice to the troubled story of his home village, drawing sketches of some of the families without stressing his own experience. At the same time, *Materada* takes advantage of its writer's involvement in the exile. The speed that characterizes the writing evokes a pressing necessity. As soon as he settles in Trieste, Tomizza reviews his notes and transforms them into a novel. The impulse to compose his first work, and his 'improvisation' in becoming a writer ('m'improvvisai scrittore') [I improvised myself as writer], reinforces the idea of the creative power of the exile.[5]

On the other hand, *L'albero dei sogni* transforms a collective story putting autobiography at the centre: 'è seguito un altro momento della mia narrativa, nel quale mi rivedo più autobiografico' [another moment of my narrative followed, in which I see myself more as an autobiographer].[6] Tomizza is here aware of a closer relationship between his personal identity and his writing. He feels that the effect of exile and the troubles of a frontier land should be experienced on the page in the first person:

> Sino a quel momento, era stata per me una specie di prova o prestito di voce, un assaggio delle mie possibilità e insieme il sondaggio di una materia, in attesa che dentro si sciogliessero i nodi di una vicenda vissuta con incredulità e spasimo fino all'ultima goccia. Perché, infatti, dopo aver prestato la voce agli altri e dibattendomi ancora in quei problemi, ignorare un'esperienza di vita che nelle ore di maggior sconforto aveva valutato per la prima volta il soccorso di un foglio bianco e di una penna? perché non tentare di tracciare nella sua intierezza la condizione di essere uomo e scrittore di confine?[7]

[Until then, it had been for me a kind of test or borrowing of voice, a sample of my ability and together a survey of a subject, waiting until inside it the knots of a story lived in disbelief and anguish at last unravelled. Why, in effect, after having lent my voice to others still debating those problems, ignore an experience of life that in the hours of greatest despair could benefit for the first time from the help of a blank sheet of paper and a pen? Why not try to track in its entirety the condition of being a man and border writer?]

The autobiographical nature of Tomizza's novel results in a twisted narrative that reflects the complex dynamic of the main character: 'La scrittura che mi necessitava per questo itinerario tutto interiore era da conquistare riga per riga' [The writing that I needed for this completely interior route was to be conquered line by line].[8] In writing *L'albero dei sogni* Tomizza begins to write his autobiography, he starts to locate his self on paper and give an account of his life; from this point on, the exploration of the inner maze proceeds step by step. The self does not pre-exist the novel, it is a work in progress, continually shaped by the process of writing. As Adriana Cavarero underlines, to be a 'narratable self' the self needs to meet the page, accepting the challenge of being externalized and developed. In order to tell its story it requires the act of turning into someone else: 'the strange pretence of a self which makes himself an other in order to be able to tell his own story'.[9] In the novel, the self is transformed into another, due to its desire to be narrated: 'I will tell you my story in order to make you capable of telling it to me. The narratable self's desire for narration manifests itself in autobiographical exercises'.[10]

The reader may be struck by the image of a writer who expresses his need to tell the story: 'Ed eccomi solo, davanti alla nuda tavola e un foglio bianco. Non vi sono ricorso per confessarmi vergogne brucianti, ma stando come stanno le cose lo avrei fatto anche se non mi fossi mai mosso da Mat., usando magari una foglia di granoturco' (*AS*, p. 261) [And here I am alone, in front of the naked table and a white sheet of paper. I did not turn to it to confess a burning shame, but as things stand I would have done it even if I had never moved from Mat., perhaps using a maize leaf]. If he had not become a writer, he would still have had this urgent need to express himself in some way. A maize leaf would have helped him to turn his self into a 'narratable self', becoming the 'other' that allows the self to give his account. A few lines later, he reaffirms that he is seeking to tell his story: 'Proviamo a raccontare' (*AS*, p. 261) [Let us try to tell]. The process of writing an autobiographical novel comes from the drive to transform the self into a 'narratable self'. Tomizza talks about an intense and pressing desire, that cannot be contained: 'Chi aveva mai pensato di scrivere qualcosa di me, per me, un giorno? È così che si diventa scrittori: una cosa non la si tiene più dentro?' (*AS*, p. 261) [Who had ever thought of writing something about me, for me, one day? Is it like this that one becomes writer: you cannot hold one thing inside anymore?].

When Tomizza describes how and where he started to write his first novel, he also discusses the forces that guided him to approach the blank page. On reaching Trieste he gathered together his notes and started writing *Materada*. He describes this in a story in *La casa del mandorlo*, where he reconstructs his initial years:

> Istintivamente afferravo un foglio, svitavo la penna stilografica, mi mettevo a tracciare figure geometriche e a ricalcarle, dando così ordine alla folla di pensieri e sentimenti che mi premevano da ogni lato. In quella stanzetta, di cui mi sono rimasti nella memoria il colore verde tenero di certi interni di moschea e un vago odore di mele cotte, forse si compì il mio destino. Incominciai a scrivere, ossia a cercare di colmare l'improvviso vuoto prodottosi tra me e quanto viveva fuori.[11]
>
> [Instinctively I grabbed a sheet, unscrewed the fountain pen, began to draw geometric figures and traced them, thus giving order to the multitude of thoughts and feelings that pressed in from each side. In that little room, that has left in my memory the soft green colour of certain mosque interiors and a faint smell of baked apples, my destiny was maybe fulfilled. I began to write, that is, to try to fill the sudden vacuum generated between me and what lived outside.]

Tomizza says that he is overcome by chaotic feelings and thoughts and his attempt to write helps him to get some control over them. The main impetus to begin *Materada* was the need to compensate for the impossibility of fitting into any context. Although he had previously developed a passion for writing, these events compelled him to write:

> Non saprei dire quanto veramente entrasse in me il proposito di scrivere; ma certo esisteva in me un latente desiderio, già sui banchi del Liceo, di narrare della mia Matterada,[12] così umile, così disadorna e stramba e quasi nascosta alla vista degli altri. E questa mia esigenza, coincidendo con la stagione dell'esodo, andò lentamente prendendo corpo.[13]
>
> [I wouldn't be able to say how much exactly the intention of writing entered into me; but there was certainly in me a latent desire, already at the secondary school desks, to recount the story of my Matterada, so humble, so unadorned and weird and almost hidden from the view of others. And this need, coinciding with the season of the exodus, slowly took shape.]

Exile spurs Tomizza to write the experiences that are ever-present in his works, but, at the same time, transcend them. Although in *Materada* he gives a voice to a village without making himself a character, the story he tells is generated by the situation that he shares with his countrymen. If Francesco is not a proxy for the author and so the novel cannot be considered autobiographical, Tomizza nonetheless stresses that he identifies with the character, or even with the characters of the chorus:

> Per esempio ho cominciato a scrivere *Materada* a ventitré anni e mi calavo nella mentalità di un contadino molto più vecchio di me, che deve decidere se andare o restare. Naturalmente non si trattava di me, però portavo con me tutta l'ottica di quel mondo, le tradizioni di quel mondo, il modo di parlare, i problemi via via vissuti anche da me.[14]
>
> [For example, I started writing *Materada* at twenty-three and I identified myself in the mindset of a farmer much older than me, who has to decide whether to go or stay. Of course it was not about me, but I carried with me the whole viewpoint of that world, the traditions of that world, the way of speaking, the problems bit by bit experienced also by me.]

Tomizza does not draw on his troubles to create a character who embodies his self; rather, he realizes a character who belongs to his (Tomizza's) land and in so doing interprets it and its inhabitants. The novel in which he most clearly indicates that he is only the observer of events without being the main character still shows the involvement of the writer in the story. In this sense, exile, as well as being an obstacle, is a source of creative power for him.

Writing allows the author to digest exile, to externalize and work through his story: 'Da cronista o cantastorie disinteressato, mi spoglio man mano di questo canto ed entro nell'animo dei miei personaggi, entro nell'animo mio, e comincia per me una nuova possibilità' [From reporter or disinterested storyteller, I progressively remove this song from myself and enter the soul of my characters, I enter my soul, and so begins a new opportunity for me].[15] New stories are also opportunities for Tomizza to extend and to develop his experience, building up new situations, opportunities to live multiple and parallel existences, new episodes and accounts, living exile in different ways. In his essay *Reading and Writing: A Personal Account*, V. S. Naipaul confirms that the condition of a writer in exile is unique. Being abroad means undergoing an experience that marks him profoundly: 'Nearly all my adult life had been spent in countries where I was a stranger. I couldn't as a writer go beyond that experience. To be true to that experience I had to write about people in that kind of position'.[16] The person who physically writes the novel cannot get rid of the person who left his country, and he carries the inevitable fracture within himself. Naipaul intertwines the two figures and says that his specific condition had leaked into the narrative: 'The experience I had had was particular to me. To do a novel about it, it would have been necessary to create someone like me [...] it would have been necessary more or less to duplicate the original experience and it would have added nothing'.[17]

Tomizza's working through of exile in the process of writing questions the idea explored in Chapter 2 that it may not be possible for trauma to be told at all. LaCapra and many others believe that trauma is not fully representable: 'It calls for discursive and affective responses that are never adequate to [it]'.[18] The fact of a traumatic event being told inevitably implies an absence or, as Lacan argues, 'a missed encounter with the Real'.[19] Also Caruth claims that it is impossible to fully grasp trauma:

> Central to the very immediacy of this experience... is a gap that carries the force of the event and does so precisely at the expense of simple knowledge and memory. The force of this experience would appear to arise precisely, in other words, in the collapse of its understanding.[20]

Trauma is a particular form of memory that, in contrast to common memories, struggles to be completely understood.

However, LaCapra allows for the possibility of expressing at least what the subject can represent with the support of language, that 'provides some measure of conscious control, critical distance, and perspective'.[21] This requires two complementary processes: acting out and working through the trauma. Acting out is the condition:

> In which one is haunted or possessed by the past and performatively caught up in the compulsive repetition of traumatic scenes — scenes in which the past returns and the future is blocked or fatalistically caught up in a melancholic feedback loop. In acting out, tenses implode, and it is as if one were back there in the past reliving the traumatic scene.[22]

Acting out should support the process of working through the trauma:

> Working through is an articulatory practice: to the extent one works through trauma (as well as transferential relations in general), one is able to distinguish between past and present and to recall in memory that something happened to one (or one's people) back then while realizing that one is living here and now with openings to the future'.[23]

These two processes could help the traumatized subject to cope with his past. LaCapra also stresses the importance of the device of narrative, which might facilitate retelling:

> Narrative at best helps one not to change the past through a dubious rewriting of history but to work through posttraumatic symptoms in the present in a manner that opens possible futures. It also enables one to recount events and perhaps to evoke experience, typically through nonlinear movements that allow trauma to register in language and its hesitations, indirections, pauses, and silences. And, particularly by bearing witness and giving testimony, narrative may help performatively to create openings in existence that did not exist before.[24]

The 'nonlinear movements' mentioned by LaCapra are widely employed by Tomizza in his more introspective works, such as *La ragazza di Petrovia* and *L'albero dei sogni*. Fiction, with its space for creativity and the devices and tools at its disposal, can go beyond the limits of linearity imposed by other narratives.[25]

The 'ambivalence and doubts about successful retelling' develop further in relation to the language used by the writer and this is the core of this analysis.[26] Understanding Tomizza's linguistic mechanisms means being able to support the possibility of processing his trauma through writing. In theoretical terms, we must first consider the following question: does the language in which the trauma happened and that of the narrative have to be the same? If not, the transformation of trauma into a narrative written in a foreign language might be conceived as an act of transformation and therefore development. Shoshana Felman explains this phenomenon by suggesting that the occurrence of a traumatic event can happen in a different language and 'the significance of the occurrence can only be articulated in a language foreign to the language(s) of the occurrence'.[27] Felman seems to suggest that an act of translation is required for the assimilation of the trauma in that it involves an interpretation that may be a sort of working through.

Tatjana Aleksić, on the other hand, suggests that trauma can only be worked out in one's native language, which few exilic writers decide to keep once abroad. In her analysis, the narrator of David Albahari's *Bait*, a self-exile living in Canada since the collapse of Yugoslavia, seeks to 'verbalize his history-induced trauma but his refusal to do so in his mother tongue takes him on a tortuous path from utter silence to a novel written in a foreign language'. The result is that the narrator fails to deal with his trauma, leaving the reader 'no less confused and alienated from his being than the beginning of his search'.[28] Aleksić concludes that 'By decisively rejecting his mother tongue, the narrator never really makes peace with his memory and never fully works through the historic/personal trauma'.[29]

In between these two positions Radulescu argues that both languages (the native and the acquired) prevent the working through of the exilic trauma:

> The use of a foreign language to express both joyous and horrible experiences of the past is in itself traumatic precisely because of this double bind of 'remembering and obscuring memory.' As the past is being remembered in a foreign language, the very memory of it is being obscured as it is being translated, while that same language is incapable of entirely erasing or creating oblivion of a painful past.[30]

The translation necessitated by the foreign language is not part of the working through of the trauma anymore, but rather a deviation from it. Neither language lets the inexpressible nature of trauma transform into an event that can potentially, at least in part, be dealt with through writing.

Tomizza offers an innovative approach to this question. As I have demonstrated in my analysis, there are several original traits that emerge from an analysis of Tomizza's novels related to exile. For instance, simple ethnic identity and monolingualism had already been called into question by the multi-ethnic and multi-linguistic situation in Istria before the exile. Identity in Istria was a choice: a way of feeling one nationality more than the other, rather than a univocal attribution. In many cases, identity cannot be established once and for all and undergoes constant shifts. But also exile, which is usually considered the destruction of all that is familiar, acquires in Tomizza a different meaning. Above all, it is his rich linguistic background, put under pressure by exile, that offers an opportunity to advance trauma studies in relation to language. Tomizza's case does not correspond to the three options developed by Felman, Aleksić, and Radulescu. The Italian he chooses is both native and foreign to him and may include from time to time Sloveno-Croatian elements. This complicated linguistic starting point allows him to work through the trauma of exile in his writing, or at least what can be told about it, because it is both a translation (which means transposition and development) and at the same time a native language — Venetian-Istrian's matrix is Italian. Here both distance and proximity, the conditions that are required to work through trauma, seem to be satisfied.

Finally, exile motivated Tomizza to begin writing novels in which he aimed to examine the most difficult and vexed aspects of a hybrid homeland shaken by an unexpected change of regime. In the end, Tomizza accepted the challenge formulated by Andrić, who insisted that a life spent in a frontier land put under pressure by unexpected events cannot be truly understood by people who have not experienced these conditions. In his works, Tomizza has tried to open a passage into this hidden universe.

Notes to the Conclusion

1. Roger Whitehouse (ed.), 'Introduction', in *Literary Expressions of Exile: A Collection of Essays* (Lewiston, NY, & Lampeter: Edwin Mellen Press, 2000), pp. 1–9 (p. 3).
2. Tomizza, 'Autoritratto', p. 224.
3. Tomizza, *Le mie estati letterarie*, p. 121.
4. Fulvio Tomizza as quoted by Bruno De Marchi, 'La letteratura ha bisogno di uomini', *Relazioni sociali*, 17–18 (1965), 10–15 (p. 14).
5. Tomizza, 'Autoritratto', p. 227.
6. Fulvio Tomizza, 'Incontro', in *Annali del Circolo culturale Istro-Veneto Istria* (2001), 44–48 (p. 44).
7. Claudio Toscani, 'Incontro con Fulvio Tomizza', *Il Ragguaglio librario*, 41 (1974), 12–20 (p. 13).
8. Tomizza, *Le mie estati letterarie*, p. 134.
9. Adriana Cavarero, *Relating Narratives: Storytelling and Selfhood* (London: Routledge, 2000), p. 84.
10. Ibid., p. 114.
11. Tomizza, *La casa col mandorlo*, pp. 11–12.
12. Here Tomizza uses the Italian version of the village's name.
13. Tomizza, 'Intervista', p. 3.
14. Ibid., p. 71.
15. Ibid., p. 13.
16. V. S. Naipaul, *Reading and Writing: A Personal Account* (New York: New York Review, 2000), pp. 28–29.
17. Ibid., p. 50.
18. LaCapra, *Writing History, Writing Trauma*, p. 92.
19. Jacques Lacan, 'The Unconscious and Repetition', in *The Four Fundamental Concepts of Psychoanalysis*, trans. by Alan Sheridan (New York: Norton, 1981), pp. 17–65 (p. 50).
20. Caruth, *Unclaimed Experience*, p. 7.
21. LaCapra, *Writing History, Writing Trauma*, p. 91.
22. Ibid., p. 21.
23. Ibid., pp. 21–22.
24. Dominick LaCapra, 'Trauma Studies: Its Critics and Vicissitudes', in *History in Transit: Experience, Identity, Critical Theory* (Ithaca, NY: Cornell University Press, 2004), pp. 106–43 (pp. 121–22).
25. See Anne Whitehead, *Trauma Fiction* (Edinburgh: Edinburgh University Press, 2004), p. 83.
26. LaCapra, *Writing History. Writing Trauma*, p. 92.
27. Emily Sun, Eyal Peretz, and Ulrich Baer (eds), *The Claims of Literature: A Shoshana Felman Reader* (New York: Fordham University Press, 2007), p. 303.
28. Tatjana Aleksić, 'Grief Can Only be Written in One's Mother Tongue: Exile and Identity in the Work of David Albahari', in *Literature in Exile of East and Central Europe*, ed. by Agnieszka Gutthy (New York: Peter Lang, 2009), pp. 155–73 (p. 155).
29. Ibid., p. 171.
30. Domnica Radulescu (ed.), 'Theorizing Exile', in *Realms of Exile*, pp. 185–204 (p. 196).

BIBLIOGRAPHY

Works by Fulvio Tomizza

Novels

Materada (Milan: Mondadori, 1960)
La ragazza di Petrovia (Milan: Mondadori, 1963)
La quinta stagione (Milan: Mondadori, 1965)
Il bosco di acacie (Milan: Mondadori, 1966)
L'albero dei sogni (Milan: Mondadori, 1969)
La torre capovolta (Milan: Mondadori, 1971)
La città di Miriam (Milan: Mondadori, 1972)
Dove tornare (Milan: Mondadori, 1974)
La miglior vita (Milan: Rizzoli, 1977)
L'amicizia (Milan: Rizzoli, 1980)
La finzione di Maria (Milan: Rizzoli, 1981)
Il male viene dal nord: il romanzo del vescovo Vergerio (Milan: Mondadori, 1984)
Ieri un secolo fa (Milan: Rizzoli, 1985)
Gli sposi di via Rossetti (Milan: Mondadori, 1986)
Quando Dio uscì di chiesa (Milan: Mondadori, 1986)
Poi venne Cernobyl (Venice: Marsilio, 1989)
L'ereditiera veneziana (Milan: Bompiani, 1989)
Fughe incrociate (Milan: Bompiani, 1990)
I rapporti colpevoli (Milan: Bompiani, 1992)
L'abate Roys e il fatto innominabile (Milan: Bompiani, 1994)
Dal luogo del sequestro (Milan: Mondadori, 1996)
Franziska (Milan: Mondadori, 1999)
Nel chiaro della notte (Milan: Mondadori, 1999)
La casa col mandorlo (Milan: Mondadori, 2000)
La visitatrice (Milan: Mondadori, 2001)
Il sogno dalmata (Milan: Mondadori, 2001)

Essays and Interviews

'Intervista', *Radio Trieste*, 28 September 1960, p. 1
'Fulvio Tomizza spiega se stesso', *Il Gazzettino*, 6 May 1969, p. 3
'Uno scrittore di confine', *Le Conferenze dell'Associazione culturale italiana*, 25 (1969–70), 30–42
'Autoritratto', *L'Approdo letterario*, 77–78 (1977), 221–30
'Autoritratto: uomo e scrittore di frontiera', *Novecento* (1984), 140–43
Destino di frontiera: dialogo con Riccardo Ferrante (Genoa: Marietti, 1992)
Alle spalle di Trieste: scritti 1969–1994 (Milan: Bompiani, 1995)
'Intervista', *Annali del Liceo scientifico Albert Einstein Rimini*, 17 February 1998, pp. 68–89

'Incontro', *Annali del Circolo culturale Istro-Veneto Istria* (2001), 44–48
Adriatico e altre rotte: viaggi e reportages (Reggio Emilia: Diabasis, 2007)
Le mie estati letterarie (Venice: Marsilio, 2009)

Archive Material

Archivio Prezzolini, Lugano, Biblioteca cantonale, Fondo Tomizza
Fulvio Tomizza, 'Materada', 28 July 1958, Chapter 2, manuscript 1:1
Fondazione Arnoldo e Alberto Mondadori, Milan, Archivio storico Arnoldo Mondadori Editore, Arnoldo Mondadori, fasc. Fulvio Tomizza
Elio Vittorini to Fulvio Tomizza, 18 March 1959, typescript
Fulvio Tomizza to Segretaria, Milan, 6 May 1959, typescript
Fulvio Tomizza to Mondadori, Milan, 4 February 1960, typescript

Selected Critical Works on Fulvio Tomizza

ALIBERTI, CARMELO, *Fulvio Tomizza e la frontiera dell'anima* (Foggia: Bastogi, 2001)
BASSAN, ALBERTO, 'La ragazza di Petrovia', *Letture*, 3 (1963), 343–45
BELLUCCI, MARIA CLAUDIA, *L'itinerario narrativo di Fulvio Tomizza* (Brescia: Tesi, 1973)
BERGAMINI, GIORGIO, 'Sotto la cenere cova il primo fuoco', *Il Piccolo*, 12 March 1963, p. 3
BLAGONI, ROBERT, 'La Franziska di Tomizza', *La Battana*, 128 (April–June 1998), 13–16
BUONGIORNO, TERESA, 'Profughi istriani', *Rotosei*, 3 June 1963, p. 7
CAMERINO, ALDO, 'La ragazza di Tomizza', *Il Gazzettino*, 2 July 1963, p. 3
CASAGRANDE, MARCO, 'Un narratore tra narrazione e modernità', *La Battana*, 135:3–8 (2000), 3–20
CASOLI, CLAUDIO, 'L'albero dei sogni di Fulvio Tomizza', *Città Nuova*, 10 September 1969, p. 35
CASTELLI, SILVANA, 'L'eterno straniero di Tomizza', *Avanti*, 2 August 1969, p. 3
COSTANZO, GIUSEPPE, 'La ragazza di Petrovia', *Avanti*, 9 June 1963, p. 6
DAMIANI, ALESSANDRO, 'Rapsodia istriana', *Panorama*, 7 (1977), 31–37
DAMIANI, ROBERTO, 'Fulvio Tomizza', in *Letteratura italiana: i contemporanei*, ed. by Artal Mazzotti, 6 vols (Milan: Marzorati, 1974), VI, 1959–80
DE LORENZI, ANTONIO, 'Amicizia come categoria dell'anima', *Messaggero Veneto*, 27 April 1980, p. 30
DEGANUTTI, MARIANNA, 'Fulvio Tomizza: un autore da ripensare', *Cartevive*, 50 (2013), 4–33
—— 'Fulvio Tomizza's "eènza": Hybridity as Origin', in *Shifting and Shaping a National Identity: Migration Literature Today*, ed. by Grace Russo Bullaro and Elena Benelli (Leicester: Troubador, 2014), pp. 87–106
—— 'Il romanzo auto-tradotto: *La miglior vita* di Fulvio Tomizza', *Rivista di letteratura italiana*, 1 (2014), 181–92
—— 'Lo sguardo a est di Fulvio Tomizza', in *Rileggendo Fulvio Tomizza*, ed. by Marianna Deganutti (Rome: Aracne, 2014), pp. 231–76
—— 'The Counterpoint Music of the Exile in Fulvio Tomizza's *La ragazza di Petrovia*', *Romance Studies*, 34:2 (2016), 114–24
—— 'Il dialetto mistilingue di Levi e Tomizza', *Letteratura e dialetti*, 8 (2016), 75–85
DE LEO, GAETANO, 'La coerenza interna di Fulvio Tomizza', *Messaggero Veneto*, 13 July 1969, p. 3
DE MARCHI, BRUNO, 'La letteratura ha bisogno di uomini', *Relazioni sociali*, 17–18 (1965), 10–15

DE MARTINIS, VINCENZO, 'L'albero dei sogni', *La Civiltà Cattolica*, 19 July 1969, p. 57
DE MICHELIS, CESARE, 'Introduzione', in Fulvio Tomizza, *Le mie estati letterarie* (Venice: Marsilio, 2009), pp. 11–14
DI BENEDETTI, ANTONIO, 'Fulvio Tomizza', *Corriere della Sera*, 7 July 1977, p. 3
FERRERI, RITA, 'I rapporti colpevoli', *World Literature Today*, 67:4 (1993), 802
GUAGNINI, ELVIO, 'Con quelle storie riusciva a polverizzare i confini', *Il Piccolo*, 16 May 2000, p. 49
—— 'Materada', in *L'eredità di Tomizza e gli scrittori di frontiera*, ed. by Irene Mestrovich (Fiume: Edit, 2001), pp. 11–14
GUAGNINI, ELVIO, GIANNI CIMADOR, and MARTA MORETTO, *Fulvio Tomizza: destino di frontiera* (Trieste: Comune, 2009)
LIVI, GRAZIA, 'Intervista', *Epoca*, 3 August 1969, p. 93
LUNETTA, MARIO, 'Tomizza', *Paese Sera*, 27 June 1969, p. 99
MAGRIS, CLAUDIO, 'Ritorno all'epica della frontiera', *Corriere della Sera*, 10 April 1977, p. 19
MAIER, BRUNO, 'Introduzione allo studio di Italo Svevo', in Italo Svevo, *Opere* (Milan: Dall'Oglio, 1954), pp. 1–123
—— 'Fulvio Tomizza 1969–1972', *Il Cristallo*, 15 (1973), 1–9
MARIN, BIAGIO, 'Materada', *Voce Giuliana*, 16 February 1961, p. 4
MILANO, PAOLO, 'Un lungo addio a Materada', *L'Espresso*, 15 January1961, p. 17
MODENA, ANNA, 'L'esilio ininterrotto di Fulvio Tomizza', in *Rileggendo Fulvio Tomizza*, ed. by Marianna Deganutti (Rome: Aracne, 2014), 115–44
MORETTO, MARTA, '"Il bene e il male quando vengono piovono": paradossi, antinomie e ossimori nella narrativa di Fulvio Tomizza (1935–1999)' (unpublished doctoral thesis, University of Trieste, 2008–09)
NEIROTTI, MARCO, *Invito alla lettura di Fulvio Tomizza* (Milan: Mursia, 1979)
PAMPALONI, GENO, 'Fulvio Tomizza', *L'Approdo, Radio Rai 2*, 4 February 1961, pp. 16–17
PASOLINI, PIER PAOLO, *Il Caos* (Rome: Editori riuniti, 1999)
PETRUCCIANI, MARIO, 'Fulvio Tomizza: la ragione e i sogni', *Rassegna di cultura e vita scolastica*, 1 (1970), 118–30
QUIGLY, ISABEL, 'On the Borderline', *The Times Literary Supplement*, 15 October 1971, p. 1291
RAGUSA, OLGA, 'L'amicizia', *World Literature Today*, 55:1 (Winter 1981), 82
ROIĆ, SANJA, and ANTE BRALA, 'Materada oltre i confini linguistici', *Italica belgradensia*, 1 (2013), 70–82
SCHUTTE JACOBSON, ANNE, 'Tradurre Tomizza', in *Rileggendo Fulvio Tomizza*, ed. by Marianna Deganutti (Rome: Aracne, 2014), pp. 313–20
SCOTTI JURIĆ, RITA, 'Fulvio Tomizza: le sfide della comunicazione interculturale', in *Rileggendo Fulvio Tomizza*, ed. by Marianna Deganutti (Rome: Aracne, 2014), pp. 275–304
SGORLON, CARLO, 'La torre capovolta', *I quaderni della FACE*, 39 (1971), 20–25
—— 'Amore di terra', *Il Giornale*, 20 March 1983, p. 4
SICILIANO, ENZO, 'Una ladra racconta', *Il Mondo*, 12 May 1972, p. 21
SOMMAVILLA, GUIDO, 'Trilogia istriana', *Letture*, 2 (1968), 92–98
SPAINI, ALBERTO, 'Lo scambio delle popolazioni rimedio peggiore del male', *Il Telegrafo*, 21 June 1963, p. 3
SPINAZZOLA, VITTORIO, 'Lo scrittore? Diventa biografo', *L'Unità*, 9 June 1984, p. 13
TOSCANI, CLAUDIO, 'Incontro con Fulvio Tomizza', *Il Ragguaglio Librario*, 41 (1974), 12–20
VISINTINI, IRENA, 'Franziska, il più recente romanzo di Fulvio Tomizza', *La Voce Giuliana*, 1 November 1997, p. 127

Other Works

ACIMAN, ANDRÉ, *Letters of Transit: Reflections on Exile, Identity, Language, and Loss* (New York: New Press, 2000)

ALEKSIĆ, TATJANA, 'Grief Can Only be Written in One's Mother Tongue: Exile and Identity in the Work of David Albahari', in *Literature in Exile of East and Central Europe*, ed. by Agnieszka Gutthy (New York: Peter Lang, 2009), pp. 155–73

ANDERSON, BENEDICT, *Imagined Communities: Reflections on the Origin and Spread of Nationalism* (London: Verso, 1983)

ANDRIĆ, IVO, *Bosnian Chronicle* (London: Harvill, 1996)

ANOKHINA, OLGA, *Multilinguisme et créativité littéraire* (Louvain-la-Neuve: Academia Bruylant/Harmattan, 2012)

ANSELMI, SIMONA, *On Self-translation: An Exploration in Self-translators' Teloi and Strategies* (Milan: LED, 2012)

ANTZE, PAUL, and MICHAEL LAMBEK, *Tense Past: Cultural Essays in Trauma and Memory* (New York & London: Routledge, 1996)

ANZALDÙA, GLORIA, *Borderlands/La Frontera: The New Mestiza* (San Francisco: Aunt Lute Books, 2012)

ARA, ANGELO, and CLAUDIO MAGRIS, *Trieste: un'identità di frontiera* (Turin: Einaudi, 2007)

AROSIO, SANDRA, *Scrittori di frontiera: Scipio Slataper, Giani e Carlo Stuparich* (Milan: Guerini scientifica, 1996)

ASSENZA, SILVIA, *Il confine nella letteratura: la Sicilia e Trieste* (Acireale & Rome: Bonanno, 2012)

AVERIS, KATE, *Exile and Nomadism in French and Hispanic Women's Writing* (Oxford: Legenda, 2014)

BAKHTIN, MIKHAIL, *The Dialogic Imagination: Four Essays*, trans. by Caryl Emerson and Michael Holquist (Austin, TX: Austin University Press, 1981)

BALAEV, MICHELLE, *Contemporary Approaches in Literary Trauma Theory* (Basingstoke: Palgrave Macmillan, 2014)

BALDI, GUIDO, *L'artificio della regressione: tecnica narrativa e ideologia nel Verga verista* (Naples: Liguori, 1980)

BALIBAR, ÉTIENNE, 'World Borders, Political Borders', trans. by Erin M. Williams, *PMLA*, 117:1 (2002), 71–78

BALLINGER, PAMELA, *History in Exile: Memory and Identity at the Borders of the Balkans* (Princeton, NJ: Princeton University Press, 2002)

—— 'History's "Illegibles": National Indeterminacy in Istria', *Austrian History Yearbook*, 43 (April 2012), 116–37

BARNARD, FREDERICK, *Herder's Social and Political Thought* (Oxford: Clarendon Press, 1965)

BARROTTA, PIERLUIGI, and LAURA LEPSCHY, *Freud and Italian Culture* (Bern & Oxford: Peter Lang, 2008)

BASSNETT, SUSAN, 'The Self-translator as Rewriter', in *Self-translation: Brokering Originality in Hybrid Culture*, ed. by Anthony Cordingley (London: Continuum, 2013), pp. 13–26

—— *Translation Studies* (New York & London: Routledge, 2014)

BEAUJOUR, ELIZABETH KLOSTY, *Alien Tongues: Bilingual Russian Writers of the 'First' Emigration* (Ithaca, NY: Cornell University Press, 1989)

BENJAMIN, WALTER, 'The Task of the Translator', in *The Translation Studies Reader*, ed. by Lawrence Venuti (London: Routledge, 2000), pp. 15–22

BERG, NANCY, *Exile from Exile: Israeli Writers from Iraq* (Albany: University of New York Press, 1996)

BERRUTO, GAETANO, 'Situazioni di plurilinguismo, commutazione di codice e mescolanza di sistemi', *Babylonia*, 6:1 (1998), 16–21

BERTO, GABRIELLA, *Freud, Heidegger: lo spaesamento* (Milan: Bompiani, 1998)
BERTONE, GIORGIO, *Il confine del paesaggio: lettura di Francesco Biamonti* (Novara: Interlinea, 2006)
BESEMERES, MARY, 'Self-translation in Vladimir Nabokov's Pnin', *The Russian Review*, 59:3 (July 2000), 390–407
—— *Translating One's Self: Language and Selfhood in Cross-cultural Autobiography* (Oxford: Peter Lang, 2002)
BHABHA, HOMI, *Nation and Narration* (New York: Routledge, 1990)
—— *The Location of Culture* (New York: Routledge, 1994)
BIENEK, HORST, 'Exile is Rebellion', in *Literature in Exile: Conference Transcripts and Papers*, ed. by John Glad (Durham, NC, & London: Duke University Press, 1990), pp. 41–48
BINNI, WALTER, *Storia letteraria delle regioni d'Italia* (Florence: Sadea-Sansoni, 1968)
BISANTI, TATIANA, *L'opera plurilingue di Amelia Rosselli: un distorto, inesperto, espertissimo linguaggio* (Pisa: Edizioni ETS, 2007)
BOGARO, ANNA, *Letterature nascoste: storia della scrittura e degli autori in lingua minoritaria in Italia* (Bologna: Carocci, 2011)
BOSETTI, GILBERT, 'La letteratura triestina: modello di cultura di frontiera', *Rivista di letteratura italiana*, 2–3 (2000), 159–90
BREVINI, FRANCO, *La letteratura degli italiani: perché molti la celebrano e pochi la amano* (Milan: Feltrinelli, 2010)
BRISON, SUSAN, *Aftermath: Violence and the Remaking of a Self* (Princeton, NJ: Princeton University Press, 2002)
BRODSKY, JOSEPH, 'The Condition We Call Exile', *Renaissance and Modern Studies*, 34 (1991), 1–8
BROOKE-ROSE, CHRISTINE, 'Exsul', in *Exile and Creativity: Signposts, Travelers, Outsiders, Backward Glances*, ed. by Susan Rubin Suleiman (Durham, NC: Duke University Press, 1998), pp. 9–24
BRUBAKER, ROGERS, *Ethnicity Without Groups* (Cambridge, MA: Harvard University Press, 2006)
BRUGNOLO, FURIO, *Plurilinguismo e lirica medievale: da Raimbaut de Vaqueiras a Dante* (Rome: Bulzoni, 1983)
BUDICK, SANFORD, and WOLFGANG ISER (eds), *Languages of the Unsayable: The Play of Negativity in Literature and Literary Theory* (New York: Columbia University Press, 1989)
CANAGARAJAH, SURESH, 'Multilingual Writers and the Struggle for Voice in Academic Discourse', in *Negotiation of Identities in Multilingual Contexts*, ed. by Aneta Pavlenko and Adrian Blackledge (Clevedon: Multilingual Matters, 2004), pp. 266–89
CANETTI, ELIAS, *The Tongue Set Free: Remembrance of a European Childhood* (London: Granta, 2011)
CANKAR, IVAN, *The Bailiff Yerney and His Rights*, trans. by Sidonie Years and H. C. Sewell Grant (London: Rodker, 1930)
—— *Kačur Martin: The Biography of an Idealist*, trans. by John K. Cox (Budapest & New York: Central European University Press, 2009)
CARUTH, CATHY, *Unclaimed Experience: Trauma, Narrative and History* (Baltimore, MD: Johns Hopkins University Press, 1996)
CAVARERO, ADRIANA, *Relating Narratives: Storytelling and Selfhood* (London: Routledge, 2000)
CERNECCA, DOMENICO, 'Dialetto, lingua e processo creativo in Italo Svevo', *La Battana*, 18:63–64 (1982), 99–106
CERVIGNI, DINO, 'Exile Literature', *Annali di italianistica*, 20 (2001), 11–14
CHAMBERS, IAIN, *Migrancy, Culture, Identity* (New York: Routledge, 1994)

CICCARELLI, ANDREA, 'Frontier, Exile, and Migration in the Contemporary Italian Novel', in *The Cambridge Companion to the Italian Novel*, ed. by Peter Bondanella and Andrea Ciccarelli (Cambridge: Cambridge University Press, 2003), pp. 197–213
CONTE, FRANCIS, *The Slavs* (Boulder, CO: East European Monographs, 1995)
CORDINGLEY, ANTHONY (ed.), *Self-translation: Brokering Originality in Hybrid Culture* (London: Continuum, 2013)
CORNI, GUSTAV, 'The Exodus of Italians from Istria and Dalmatia, 1945–56', in *The Disentanglement of Populations: Migration, Expulsion and Displacement in Postwar Europe 1944–1949*, ed. by Jessica Reinisch and Elizabeth White (Basingstoke: Palgrave, 2011), pp. 71–90
COURRENT, MIREILLE, 'Partir d'ici: à propos de l'étymologie latine de l'exil', in *Exils*, ed. by Hyacinthe Carrera (Perpignan: Presses universitaires de Perpignan, 2010), pp. 15–18
CRAINZ, GUIDO, *Il dolore e l'esilio: l'Istria e le memorie divise d'Europa* (Rome: Donzelli, 2005)
CRAINZ, GUIDO, RAOUL PUPO, and SILVIA SALVATICI, *Naufraghi della pace: il 1945, i profughi e le memorie divise d'Europa* (Rome: Donzelli, 2008)
DE MICHELIS, CESARE, *Dizionario critico della letteratura italiana* (Turin: UTET, 1987)
DERRIDA, JACQUES, *Monolingualism of the Other, or, The Prosthesis of Origin*, trans. by Patrick Mensah (Stanford, CA: Stanford University Press, 1998)
EBNER, MICHAEL, *Ordinary Violence in Mussolini's Italy* (New York: Syracuse University, 2010)
ECO, UMBERTO, *Il nome della rosa* (Milan: Bompiani, 1980)
EDWARDS, JOHN, 'Foundations of Bilingualism', in *The Handbook of Bilingualism*, ed. by Tej K. Bhatia and William C. Ritchie (Malden, MA: Blackwell, 2006), pp. 7–31
EDWARDS, ROBERT, 'Exile, Self and Society', in *Exile in Literature*, ed. by María-Inés Lagos-Pope (Lehigh, PA: Bucknell University Press, 1988), pp. 15–31
ELWERT, THEODOR, 'Das zweisprachige Individuum und andere Aufsätze zur romanischen und allgemeinen Sprachwissenschaft', in *Studien zu den Romanischen Sprachen und Literaturen*, 8 vols (Wiesbaden: Franz Steiner, 1967–79), VI
ENGLUND, AXEL, and ANDERS OLSSON (eds), *Languages of Exile: Migration and Multilingualism in Twentieth-century Literature* (Bern: Peter Lang, 2013)
EVANS, ROBERT JOHN WESTON, 'Essay and Reflections: Frontiers and National Identities in Central Europe', *The International History Review*, 14:3 (August 1992), 480–502
FARAH, NURRUDIN, 'In Praise of Exile', in *Literature in Exile: Conference Transcripts and Papers*, ed. by John Glad (Durham, NC, & London: Duke University Press, 1990), pp. 64–77
FENOGLIO, BEPPE, *Il partigiano Johnny* (Turin: Einaudi, 1994)
—— *La malora* (Turin: Einaudi, 2014)
FERGUSON, CHARLES, 'Diglossia', *Word*, 15 (1959), 325–40
FERRONI, GIULIO, *Profilo storico della letteratura italiana* (Turin: Einaudi, 1991)
FISHMAN, JOSHUA A., *Language and Nationalism: Two Integrative Essays* (Rowley, MA: Newbury House, 1973)
—— *Reversing Language Shift: Theoretical and Empirical Foundations of Assistance to Threatened Languages* (Clevedon: Multilingual Matters, 1991)
FISHMAN, JOSHUA A. (ed.), *Handbook of Language and Ethnic Identity* (New York & Oxford: Oxford University Press, 1999)
FOOT, JOHN, *Italy's Divided Memory* (New York: Palgrave Macmillan, 2009)
FORLENZA, ROSARIO, 'Sacrificial Memory and Political Legitimacy in Postwar Italy: Reliving and Remembering World War II', *History and Memory*, 24:2 (2012), 73–116
FREUD, SIGMUND, 'The Uncanny', in *Writings on Art and Literature*, ed. by James Strachey (Stanford, CA: Stanford University Press, 1997), pp. 193–234

FRIEDRICH, PAUL, 'European and Generic Exile', in *Realms of Exile: Nomadism, Diasporas and Eastern European Voices*, ed. by Domnica Radulescu (Lanham, MD: Lexington Books, 2002), pp. 159–83

FUČIĆ, BRANKO, *Croatian Glagolitic Epigraphy* (London: Stephen Osborne, 1999)

FUSILLO, MASSIMO, *L'altro e lo stesso: teoria e storia del doppio* (Florence: La Nuova Italia, 1998)

GALLI, LINA, *Il volto dell'Istria attraverso i secoli* (Trieste: Cappelli, 1959)

GANTEAU, JEAN-MICHEL, and SUSANA ONEGA JAÉN, *Contemporary Trauma Narratives: Liminality and the Ethics of Form* (New York: Routledge, 2014)

GARDINI, NICOLA, 'Parole e omissioni: che cosa dicono i grandi romanzi quando tacciono', *La Repubblica*, 29 Augusut 2013, p. 38

—— *Lacuna: saggio sul non detto* (Turin: Einaudi, 2014)

GARTON ASH, TIMOTHY, 'Does Central Europe Exist?', *The New York Review of Books*, 9 October 1986, pp. 51–80

—— *The Uses of Adversity: Essays on the Fate of Central Europe* (London: Penguin, 1999)

GILMORE, LEIGH, *The Limits of Autobiography: Trauma and Testimony* (Ithaca, NY, & London: Cornell University Press, 2001)

GINZBURG, CARLO, *Il formaggio e i vermi: il cosmo di un mugnaio del '500* (Turin: Einaudi 1999)

GINZBURG, NATALIA, *La famiglia Manzoni* (Turin: Einaudi, 1983)

—— *Lessico famigliare* (Turin: Einaudi, 2010)

GIOANOLA, ELIO, *Un killer dolcissimo: indagine psicanalitica sull'opera di Italo Svevo* (Genoa: Il Melangolo, 1979)

—— *Pirandello: la follia* (Genoa: Il Melangolo, 1983)

GLAD, JOHN (ed.), *Literature in Exile: Conference Transcripts and Papers* (Durham, NC, & London: Duke University Press, 1990)

GOLDSWORTHY, VESNA, *Inventing Ruritania: The Imperialism of the Imagination* (New Haven, CT, & London: Yale University Press, 1998)

GORDON, ROBERT, *A Difficult Modernity: An Introduction to Twentieth-century Italian Literature* (London: Duckworth, 2005)

GREEN, JULIEN, *Le Langage et son double* (Paris: La Différence, 1985)

—— *The Apprentice Writer* (New York & London: Marion Boyars, 1993)

GREENBERG, ROBERT, *Language and Identity in the Balkans* (Oxford: Oxford University Press, 2004)

GRENFELL, MICHAEL, and DAVID JAMES (eds), *Bourdieu and Education: Acts of Practical Theory* (London: Continuum, 2007)

GRINBERG, LEON, and REBECA GRINBERG, *Psychoanalytic Perspectives on Migration and Exile* (New Haven, CT: Yale University Press, 2004)

GROSJEAN, FRANÇOIS, *Life with Two Languages: An Introduction to Bilingualism* (Cambridge, MA: Harvard University Press, 1982)

GRUTMAN, RAINIER, *Des langues qui résonnent: l'hétérolinguisme au XIX siècle québécois* (Saint-Laurent, Quebec: Fides, 1997)

—— 'Les Motivations de l'hétérolinguisme: réalisme, composition, esthétique', in *Eteroglossia e plurilinguismo letterario: atti del XVIII convegno interuniversitario di Bressanone*, ed. by Furio Brugnolo and Vincenzo Orioles (Rome: Il Calamo, 2002), pp. 329–49

GUAGNINI, ELVIO, *Una città d'autore: Trieste attraverso gli scrittori* (Reggio Emilia: Diabasis, 2009)

HA, JIN, *The Writer as Migrant* (Chicago, IL: University of Chicago Press, 2008)

HALLER, HERMANN, *The Other Italy: The Literary Canon in Dialect* (Toronto: University of Toronto Press, 1999)

HERMAN, JUDITH, *Trauma and Recovery* (New York: Harper-Collins, 2002)
HEYMAN, JOSIAH McC., 'Culture Theory and the US-Mexico Border', in *A Companion to Border Studies*, ed. by Thomas M. Wilson and Hastings Donnan (Oxford: Blackwell, 2012), pp. 48–65
HOBSBAWM, ERIC, *Nations and Nationalism since 1780: Programme, Myth, Reality* (Cambridge: Cambridge University Press, 1990)
HOFFMAN, EVA, *Lost in Translation: A Life in a New Language* (London: Vintage, 1998)
HOFFMANN, CHARLOTTE, *An Introduction to Bilingualism* (London & New York: Longman, 1991)
HOKENSON, JAN, 'History and the Self-translator', in *Self-translation: Brokering Originality in Hybrid Culture*, ed. by Anthony Cordingley (London: Continuum, 2013), pp. 39–60
HOKENSON, JAN, and MARCELLA MUNSON, *The Bilingual Text: History and Theory of Literary Self-translation* (Manchester: St. Jerome, 2007)
HOLMSTRÖM, JOSEFIN, '"Born into absence": Trauma and Narration in W. G. Sebald, Anne Michaels and Pat Barker', *Bristol Journal of English Studies*, 2 (2012), 1–18
HONG, ZENG, *The Semiotics of Exile in Literature* (New York: Palgrave Macmillan, 2010)
HOWELLS, CORAL ANN, *The Cambridge Companion to Margaret Atwood* (Cambridge: Cambridge University Press, 2006)
ISER, WOLFGANG, *The Act of Reading: A Theory of Aesthetic Response* (Baltimore, MD: Johns Hopkins University Press, 1978)
ISRAEL, NICO, *Outlandish: Writing between Exile and Diaspora* (Stanford, CA: Stanford University Press, 2000)
JACOBSON, ROMAN, 'On Linguistic Aspects of Translation', in *The Translation Studies Reader*, ed. by Lawrence Venuti (London: Routledge, 2000), pp. 113–18
JOHNSON, LONNIE, *Central Europe: Enemies, Neighbors, Friends* (New York: Oxford University Press, 1996)
JUNG, VERENA, *English-German Self-translation of Academic Texts and its Relevance for Translation Theory and Practice* (Frankfurt am Main: Peter Lang, 2002)
KAPLAN, CAREN, *Questions of Travel: Postmodern Discourses of Displacement* (Durham, NC, & London: Duke University Press, 1996)
KEDOURIE, ELIE, *Nationalism* (London: Blackwell, 1993)
KELLMAN, STEVEN, 'Translingualism and the Literary Imagination', *Criticism*, 33:4 (1991), 527–41
KIŠ, DANILO, *A Tomb for Boris Davidovich* (New York: Penguin, 1980)
KNITTEL, SUSANNE, *The Historical Uncanny: Disability, Ethnicity, and the Politics of Holocaust Memory* (New York: Fordham University Press, 2015)
KOŠUTA, MIRAN, *Scritture parallele: dialoghi di frontiera tra letteratura slovena e italiana* (Trieste: Lint, 1997)
KRAMER, LLOYD, *Threshold of a New World: Intellectuals and the Exile Experience in Paris, 1830–1848* (Ithaca, NY: Cornell University Press, 1988)
LACAN, JACQUES, 'The Mirror Stage as Formative of the Function of the I as Revealed in Psychoanalytic Experience', in *Ecrits: A Selection*, trans. by Alan Sheridan (New York, Norton, 1977), pp. 1–7
—— 'The Unconscious and Repetition', in *The Four Fundamental Concepts of Psychoanalysis*, trans. by Alan Sheridan (New York: Norton, 1981), pp. 17–64
—— *Le Séminaire de Jacques Lacan. Livre X, L'Angoisse* (Paris: Seuil, 2004)
LACAPRA, DOMINICK, *Writing History, Writing Trauma* (Baltimore, MD: Johns Hopkins University Press, 2001)
—— 'Trauma Studies: Its Critics and Vicissitudes', in *History in Transit: Experience, Identity, Critical Theory* (Ithaca, NY: Cornell University Press, 2004), pp. 106–43

LAGOS-POPE, MARÍA-INÉS (ed.), *Exile in Literature* (Lehigh, PA: Bucknell University Press, 1988)
LAPLANCHE, JEAN, and JEAN-BERTRAND PONTALIS, *The Language of Psycho-Analysis*, trans. by Donald Nicholson-Smith (London: Hogarth Press, 1973)
LAVAGETTO, MARIO, *Lavorare con piccoli indizi* (Turin: Bollati Boringhieri, 2003)
LEOUSSI, ATHENA, *Encyclopedia of Nationalism* (New Brunswick, NJ: Transaction Publishers at Rutgers University, 2001)
LEPSCHY, GIULIO, and HELENA SANSON, 'Native Speaker', in *Reflexivity: Critical Themes in the Italian Cultural Tradition: Essays by Members of the Italian Department at University College London*, ed. by Prue Shaw and John Took (Ravenna: Longo Editore, 2000), 119–29
LEPSCHY, GIULIO, 'Mother Tongues in the Middle Ages and Dante', in *Dante's Plurilingualism: Authority, Knowledge, Subjectivity*, ed. by Sara Fortuna, Manuele Gragnolati, and Jürgen Trabant (Oxford: Legenda, 2010), pp. 16–23
LEVI, PRIMO, *La tregua* (Turin: Einaudi, 1963)
——*Il sistema periodico* (Turin: Einaudi, 1975)
LEVY, DANIEL, and NATAN SZNAIDER, 'Memory Unbound: The Holocaust and the Formation of Cosmopolitan Memory', *European Journal of Social Theory*, 5:1 (2002), 87–106
LEVY, SUSAN, and ALESSANDRA LEMMA, *The Perversion of Loss: Psychoanalytic Perspectives on Trauma* (London: Whurr, 2004)
LEYS, RUTH, *Trauma: A Genealogy* (Chicago, IL: University of Chicago Press, 2000)
LUCKHURST, ROGER, *The Trauma Question* (London & New York: Routledge, 2008)
LUTI, GIORGIO, 'Il Novecento', in *Storia letteraria d'Italia* (Padua: Piccin, 1989), pp. 513–78
MACKEY, WILLIAM, 'Determining the Status and Function of Languages in Multinational Societies', in *Status and Function of Languages and Language Variety*, ed. by Ulrich Ammon (Berlin & New York: Walter de Gruyter, 1989), pp. 3–20
MAGRIS, CLAUDIO, 'Equivoci e compiacimenti sull' "antiletterarietà" triestina', *Trieste*, 16:87 (1969), 3–11
——*Microcosmi* (Milan: Garzanti, 1997)
——*Utopia e disincanto: saggi, 1974–1998* (Milan: Garzanti, 1999)
——'Identità ovvero incertezza', *Lettere italiane* (2003), 519–27
MAHLER-SCHÄCHTER, ELIZABETH, 'Svevo e Schnitzler: affinità culturali', in *Italo Svevo scrittore europeo: atti del convegno internazionale, Perugia, 21 marzo 1992*, ed. by N. Cacciaglia and L. Fava Guzzetta (Florence: Olschki, 1994), pp. 547–60
MANACORDA, GIACINTO, *Storia della letteratura italiana contemporanea (1940–1975)* (Rome: Editori Riuniti, 1981)
MANEA, NORMAN, *The Fifth Impossibility: Essays on Exile and Language* (New Haven, CT, & London: Yale University Press, 2012)
MANZONI, ALESSANDRO, *I promessi sposi* (Florence: Salani, 1985)
MARQUES, ISABELLE SIMOES, 'Autour de la question du plurilinguisme littéraire: la textualisation des langues dans les écritures francophones', *Les Cahiers du Grelcef*, 2 (2011), 227–43
MATVEJEVIĆ, PREDRAG, *Mediterranean: A Cultural Landscape* (Los Angeles: University of California Press, 1999)
MAY, STEPHEN, *Language and Minority Rights: Ethnicity, Nationalism and the Politics of Language* (New York: Longman, 2001)
MCCLENNEN, SOPHIA, *The Dialectics of Exile: Nation, Time, Language, and Space in Hispanic Literatures* (West Lafayette, IN: Purdue University Press, 2004)
MCGOWAN, DI MATTHEW, *Ovid in Exile: Power and Poetic Redress in the Tristia and Epistulae ex Ponto* (Leiden: Brill, 2009)

McNally, Richard, *Remembering Trauma* (Cambridge, MA, & London: Belknap Press, 2003)

Milani, Nelida, *La comunità italiana in Istria e a Fiume fra diglossia e bilinguismo* (Trieste: Università popolare; Rovigno: Unione degli Italiani dell'Istria e di Fiume, 1990)

Miller, Jane, 'Writing a Second Language', *Raritan*, 1 (1982), 115–32

Molloy, Sylvia, 'Bilingualism, Writing, and the Feeling of Not Quite Being There', in *Lives in Translation: Bilingual Writers on Identity and Creativity*, ed. by Isabelle de Courtivon (New York: Palgrave Macmillan, 2003), pp. 69–78

Morante, Elsa, *La storia* (Turin: Einaudi, 1974)

Mori, Anna Maria, and Nelida Milani, *Bora* (Milan: Frassinelli, 1998)

Morris, Jan, *Trieste and the Meaning of Nowhere* (London: Faber & Faber, 2001)

Moslund, Sten Pultz, *Migration Literature and Hybridity: The Different Speeds of Transcultural Change* (Basingstoke: Palgrave Macmillan, 2010)

Murphy, Michael, *Poetry in Exile: A Study of the Poetry of W. H. Auden, Joseph Brodsky & George Szirtes* (London: Greenwich Exchange Press, 2004)

Muysken, Pieter, *Bilingual Speech: A Typology of Code-mixing* (Cambridge: Cambridge University Press, 2000)

Nabokov, Vladimir, *Lolita* (New York: Putnam, 1955)

—— *Pnin* (New York: Avon Books, 1969)

—— *Speak, Memory: An Autobiography Revisited* (New York: Putnam, 1989)

Naipaul, Vidiadhar Surajprasad, *Reading and Writing: A Personal Account* (New York: New York Review, 2000)

Nien-Ming Ch'ien, Evelyn, *Weird English* (Cambridge, MA: Harvard University Press, 2004)

Nochlin, Linda, 'Art and the Conditions of Exile: Men/Women, Emigration/Expatration', in *Exile and Creativity: Signposts, Travelers, Outsiders, Backward Glances*, ed. by Susan Rubin Suleiman (Durham, NC: Duke University Press, 1998), pp. 37–58

O'Brien, George, 'The Muse of Exile: Estrangement and Renewal in Modern Irish Literature', in *Exile in Literature*, ed. by María-Inés Lagos-Pope (Lehigh, PA: Bucknell University Press, 1988), pp. 82–101

Okey, Robin, 'Central Europe/Eastern Europe: Behind the Definitions', *Past and Present*, 137 (November 1992), 102–33

Oustinoff, Michaël, *Bilinguisme d'écriture et auto-traduction: Julien Green, Samuel Beckett, Vladimir Nabokov* (Paris: L'Harmattan, 2001)

Pahor, Boris, *Kres v pristanu* (Ljubljana: Mladinska knjiga, 1959)

Pancrazi, Pietro, 'Scrittori triestini', *Corriere della Sera*, 16 June 1930, p. 3

Pavlenko, Aneta, *The Bilingual Mind: And What it Tells Us about Language and Thought* (Cambridge: Cambridge University Press, 2014)

Petacco, Arrigo, *L'esodo: la tragedia negata degli italiani d'Istria, Dalmazia e Venezia Giulia* (Milan: Mondadori, 2000)

Petrucciani, Mario, *Segnali e archetipi della poesia: studi di letteratura contemporanea* (Milan: Mursia, 1974)

Pirandello, Luigi, *Uno, nessuno, centomila* (Milan: Mondadori, 1980)

Pirodda, Giovanni, *L'eclissi dell'autore: tecnica ed esperimenti verghiani* (Cagliari: Editrice democratica sarda, 1976)

Pizzi, Katia, *A City in Search of an Author: The Literary Identity of Trieste* (London: Sheffield Academic Press, 2001)

—— 'Triestine Literature between Slovenia and Italy: A Case of Missed Transculturalism?', *Primerjalna književnost*, 36 (2013), 145–54

Pohl, J., 'Bilinguismes', *Revue Romaine de Linguistique*, 10 (1965), 343–49

POLISH, GEORGE GASYNA, *Hybrid and Otherwise: Exilic Discourse in Joseph Conrad and Witold Gombrowicz* (New York: Continuum, 2011)
POPOVIČ, ANTON, *Dictionary for the Analysis of Literary Translation* (Edmonton: Department of Comparative Literature, University of Alberta, 1976), p. 19
PORTER, ROGER, *Self-same Songs: Autobiographical Performances and Reflections* (Lincoln: University of Nebraska Publisher, 2002)
PRESSBURGER, GIORGIO, *Il sussurro della grande voce* (Milan: Rizzoli, 1990)
PYM, ANTHONY, MIRIAM SHLESINGER, and ZUZANA JETTMAROVA (eds), *Sociocultural Aspects of Translating and Interpreting* (Amsterdam: John Benjamins, 2006)
PYRAH, ROBERT, and JAN FELLERER, 'Redefining "sub-culture": A New Lens for Understanding Hybrid Cultural Identities in East-Central Europe with a Case Study from Early 20th Century L'viv-Lwów-Lemberg', *Nations and Nationalism*, 21:4 (October 2015), 700–20
QUARANTOTTI GAMBINI, PIER ANTONIO, *Il poeta innamorato* (Pordenone: Edizioni Studio Tesi, 1984)
RADULESCU, DOMNICA (ed.), *Realms of Exile: Nomadism, Diasporas, and Eastern European Voices* (Lanham, MD: Lexington Books, 2002)
RANK, OTTO, *The Double: A Psychoanalytic Study* (New York & London: New American Library, 1979)
REBULA, ALOJZ, *Da Nicea a Trieste: saggi, riflessioni, commenti* (Cinisello Balsamo: San Paolo, 2012)
RESTELLI, GIANCARLO (ed.), *Le foibe e l'esodo dei giuliano-dalmati: una storia rimossa* (Milan: Raccolto Edizioni, 2007)
RINDLER SCHJERVE, ROSITA, and EVA VETTER, *European Multilingualism: Current Perspectives and Challenges* (Bristol: Multilingual Matters, 2012)
ROBINSON, RICHARD, *Narratives of the European Border: A History of Nowhere* (Basingstoke: Palgrave, 2007)
ROBSON, KATHRYN, *Writing Wounds: The Inscription of Trauma in Post-1968 French Women's Life-writing* (Amsterdam: Rodopi, 2004)
ROTH, JOSEPH, *The Emperor's Tomb* (London: Hogarth Press, 1984)
SABA, UMBERTO, *Quello che resta da fare ai poeti* (Milan: Henry Beyle, 2012)
SAID, EDWARD, 'Reflections on Exile', in *Reflections on Exile and Other Essays* (Cambridge, MA: Harvard University Press, 2002), pp. 173–86
SALOUL, IHAB, '"Exilic Narrativity": The Invisibility of Home in Palestinian Exile', in *Essays in Migratory Aesthetics: Cultural Practices Between Migration and Art-making*, ed. by Sam Durrant and Catherine M. Lord (Amsterdam & New York: Rodopi, 2007), pp. 111–28
SANTOYO, JULIO-CÉSAR, 'On Mirrors, Dynamics & Self-translations', in *Self-translation: Brokering Originality in Hybrid Culture*, ed. by Anthony Cordingley (London: Continuum, 2013), pp. 27–38
SCHÖPFLIN, GEORGE, *The Dilemmas of Identity* (Tallinn: Tallinn University Press, 2010)
SEIDEL, MICHAEL, *Exile and the Narrative Imagination* (New Haven, CT: Yale University Press, 1986)
SHEPHERDSON, CHARLES, *Lacan and the Limits of Language* (New York: Fordham University Press, 2008)
SICARI, CARMELINA, *Lo specchio e lo stigma* (Ravenna: Longo, 1979)
SILONE, IGNAZIO, *Romanzi e saggi* (Milan: Mondadori, 2008)
SIMBOROWSKI, NICOLETTA, *Secrets and Puzzles: Silence and the Unsaid in Contemporary Italian Writing* (Oxford: European Humanities Research Centre, 2003)
SLATAPER, SCIPIO, *Alle tre amiche* (Milan: Mondadori, 1958)

―― *Il mio Carso* (Milan: Il Saggiatore, 1970)
SLUGA, GLENDA, *The Problem of Trieste and the Italo-Yugoslav Border: Difference, Identity, and Sovereignty in Twentieth-century Europe* (New York: SUNY Press, 2001)
SOROKA, MYKOLA, *Faces of Displacement: The Writings of Volodymyr Vynnychenko* (Montreal & Ithaca, NY: McGill-Queen's University Press, 2012)
STEINER, GEORGE, *Language and Science* (New York: Atheneum, 1967)
―― *After Babel: Aspects of Language and Translation* (Oxford: Oxford University Press, 1992)
STEINITZ, TAMAR, *Translingual Identities: Language and the Self in Stefan Heym and Jakov Lind* (Rochester, NY: Camden House, 2013)
STEVENSON, ROBERT LOUIS, *Master of Ballantrae* (Newcastle upon Tyne: Cambridge Scholars Publishing, 2008)
STUSSI, ALFREDO, *Lingua, dialetto e letteratura* (Turin: Einaudi, 1993)
SUK, JEANNIE, *Postcolonial Paradoxes in French Caribbean Writing: Césaire, Glissant, Condé* (Oxford: Clarendon, 2001)
SULEIMAN, SUSAN RUBIN (ed.), *Exile and Creativity: Signposts, Travelers, Outsiders, Backward Glances*, (Durham, NC: Duke University Press, 1998)
SUN, EMILY, EYAL PERETZ, and ULRICH BAER (eds), *The Claims of Literature: A Shoshana Felman Reader* (New York: Fordham University Press, 2007)
SVEVO, ITALO, *La coscienza di Zeno* (Milan: Mondadori, 1998)
TABORI, PAUL, *The Anatomy of Exile: A Semantic and Historical Study* (London: Harrap, 1972)
THOMSON, IAN, *Primo Levi: A Life* (New York: Metropolitan Books, 2003)
TODOROVA, MARIA, *Imagining the Balkans* (New York: Oxford University Press, 1997)
TOMASEVICH, JOZO, *War and Revolution in Yugoslavia, 1941–1945: Occupation and Collaboration* (Stanford, CA: Stanford University Press, 2001)
TURNER, FREDERICK JACKSON, *The Frontier in American History* (New York: Krieger, 1976)
VAN DER KOLK, BESSEL, and ONNO VAN DER HART, 'The Intrusive Past: The Flexibility of Memory and the Engraving of Trauma', in *Trauma: Explorations in Memory*, ed. by Cathy Caruth (Baltimore, MD: Johns Hopkins University Press, 1995), pp. 158–82
VANVOLSEN, SERGE, 'La lingua e il problema della lingua in Svevo: una polimorfia che non piacque', in *Italo Svevo scrittore europeo: atti del convegno internazionale, Perugia, 18–21 marzo 1992*, ed. by N. Cacciaglia and L. Fava Guzzetta (Florence: Olschki, 1994), pp. 429–45
VENUTI, LAWRENCE, *The Translator's Invisibility: A History of Translation* (London & New York: Routledge, 1995)
VERGA, GIOVANNI, *I Malavoglia* (Milan: Treves, 1881)
―― *Lettere a Luigi Capuana* (Florence: Le Monnier, 1975)
VLADISLAV, JAN, 'Exile, Responsibility, Destiny', in *Literature in Exile: Conference Transcripts and Papers*, ed. by John Glad (Durham, NC, & London: Duke University Press, 1990), pp. 14–27
WEINRICH, URIEL, *Languages in Contact: Findings and Problems* (The Hague: Mouton, 1953)
WEISSMANN, GARY, *Fantasies of Witnessing: Postwar Efforts to Experience the Holocaust* (Ithaca, NY: Cornell University Press, 2004)
WHITE, HAYDEN, 'Historical Discourse and Literary Writing', in *Tropes for the Past: Hayden White and the History/Literature Debate*, ed. by Kuisma Korhonen (Amsterdam: Rodopi, 2006), pp. 25–34
WHITEHEAD, ANNE, *Trauma Fiction* (Edinburgh: Edinburgh University Press, 2004)
WHITEHOUSE, ROGER (ed.), *Literary Expressions of Exile: A Collection of Essays* (Lewiston, NY, & Lampeter: Edwin Mellen Press, 2000)
WOLFF, LARRY, *Inventing Eastern Europe: The Map of Civilization on the Mind of the Enlightenment* (Stanford, CA: Stanford University Press, 1994)

—— *Venice and the Slavs: The Discovery of Dalmatia in the Age of Enlightenment* (Stanford, CA: Stanford University Press, 2001)

WOODS, MICHELLE, *Translating Milan Kundera* (Clevedon: Multilingual Matters, 2006)

YILDIZ, YASEMIN, *Beyond the Mother Tongue: The Postmonolingual Condition* (New York: Fordham University Press, 2011)

YOUNG, ROBERT, *Colonial Desire: Hybridity in Theory, Culture and Race* (London & New York: Routledge, 1995)

ZANINI, PIERO, *Significati del confine: i limiti naturali, storici, mentali* (Milan: Mondadori, 1997)

INDEX

Aciman, André 7
Aeneid 30
Albahari, David 163
Aleksić, Tatjana 163–64
Anderson, Benedict 47
Andrić, Ivo 1, 2, 4, 38, 164
Anokhina, Olga 97, 151
Anselmi, Simona 53
Anzaldùa, Gloria 6, 44
Ara, Angelo 13, 21
Assenza, Silvia 6, 43
Austro-Hungarian Empire 14, 78, 95
autobiographical novel 128, 142–43, 159–61

Bakhtin, Mikhail 46, 50
Baldi, Guido 75
Balkans:
   definition 46–48
   languages 87, 92
Ballinger, Pamela 20, 56, 64, 91
Bassnett, Susan 54, 154
Beaujour, Elizabeth Klosty 53, 141
Bellucci, Maria Claudia 33
belonging 1, 2, 4, 13, 14, 21, 23, 25, 37, 44, 48, 56, 73,
   75, 102, 104, 112, 115, 120, 129, 131, 133, 142, 144
Benjamin, Walter 132
Bergamini, Giorgio 104
Berruto, Gaetano 6, 50, 85
Berto, Gabriella 114
Bertone, Giorgio 6, 42
Besemeres, Mary 146
Bhabha, Homi 6, 45, 65 n. 11
Bienek, Horst 128
bilingual writer 141
bilingualism:
   definition 50–53
   and creativity 151
   and dialect in Tomizza 77–85, 130, 133
   in *Materada* 85–92
   in *La miglior vita* 95–98
Bisanti, Tatiana 51
Blagoni, Robert 142
Bloomfield, Leonard 49, 50
border:
   and frontier 6, 42–44
   definition 42
   fascism 19

   in Istria 21–29
   in *La ragazza di Petrovia* 110, 113, 121–24
   in *L'albero dei sogni* 124–25
   literature 34, 38
   see also borderland
borderland 1, 22, 23, 32–35, 39, 42–45, 47, 49, 64–65
Bosetti, Gilbert 14
Bourdieu, Pierre 93
Brison, Susan 63
Brodsky, Joseph 4, 7, 77, 102, 121
Brooke-Rose, Christine 55
Brubaker, Rogers 48
Brugnolo, Furio 50

Camerino, Aldo 105
Canetti, Elias 5
Cankar, Ivan 31, 38, 71–73
Caruth, Cathy 6, 7, 8, 60, 61, 63, 162
Casagrande, Marco 36
Cavarero, Adriana 8, 160
Cernecca, Domenico 149
Cervigni, Dino 59
Chambers, Iain 5, 46
Chomsky, Noam 49
chorus 73–76, 159, 161
cold war 20, 34
Conrad, Joseph 53, 77
Crainz, Guido 38

Damiani, Alessandro 95
Damiani, Roberto 33, 74
De Leo, Gaetano 119
De Michelis, Cesare 33, 130
Derrida, Jacques 49
dialects:
   Čakavian 3, 5, 52, 76, 79, 82, 95, 97, 133
   Istro-Venetian 3, 5, 52, 71, 76, 79–89, 95
   see also diglossia
displacement 2, 21, 25, 26, 29, 45, 55–57, 59, 60, 62,
   63, 102–04, 108, 114, 116, 120, 121, 124, 140
double:
   and exile 7
   belonging 4, 14, 25–26, 28, 102, 103
   definition 102–14
   heritage 17
   language 53, 80, 92, 133, 141
dreams 3, 30, 31, 63, 133, 151

Edwards, John 50
Elwert, Wilhelm Theodor 51
Englund, Axel and Olsson, Anders 2
estrangement 7, 57, 60, 87, 101, 114–25
exile:
   and language 2–3, 127–33, 141–47
   as trauma 2, 7, 8, 55–65, 154–55
   creativity 127
   counter-exile 58
   definition 7, 55–56, 102
   internal 57–58
   Istrian 19–22
   metaphysical 56, 105, 121, 122

Farah, Nurrudin 150
fascism 16, 19, 64
Fellerer, Jan 6, 45, 48
Fenoglio, Beppe 34–35
Ferguson, Charles 51
Ferreri, Rita 151
Fishman, Joshua 93–94
Foot, John 64
Forlenza, Rosario 64
Freud, Sigmund 7, 37, 60, 103, 112, 114
frontera, see Anzaldùa, Gloria
frontier:
   and border 6, 42–44, 120–21
   definition 42–47
   condition 1–6
   exile from 1–2, 59–60
   in Tomizza 31–34, 70
   writer 22–23, 28–29
   see also border, borderland
Fusillo, Massimo 7, 111

Galli, Lina 17, 21
Gardini, Nicola 108
Gilmore, Leigh 62
Glad, John 6, 58
glagolitic 17–18
Goldsworthy, Vesna 47
Gordon, Robert 33, 34
Green, Julien 83, 153
Greenberg, Robert 87
Grinberg, Leon 60
Grinberg, Rebeca 60
Grutman, Rainier 51
Guagnini, Elvio 34, 70, 75

Herman, Judith 103
Heym, Stefan 128
Hoffman, Eva 7, 77, 102
Hoffmann, Charlotte 51
Holmström, Josefin 62
homeland 1, 2, 4, 11, 12, 16, 21, 24, 27, 55, 58, 63, 70, 71, 102, 106, 109, 125, 131, 140, 158, 164

hybridity:
   definition 44–48
   in *Materada* 93–98
   Istrian 12, 16, 24, 28, 30, 82–83
   linguistic, *see* Bakhtin, Mikhail
   see also borderland, subcultures and Bhabha, Homi

identity 5, 7, 8, 11, 13–16, 21–23, 44–48, 70, 75–76, 91, 93–94, 101–03, 109–21, 124, 128, 133, 141–43, 150, 159, 164
imagined communities, *see* Anderson, Benedict
iper-correttismi, *see* un-literariness
Iser, Wolfgang 63, 107
Istria:
   borderland 46–48
   exile 21–23, 56–58
   history 16–23
   languages 52, 77–92

Jacobson, Roman 132, 141
Jacobson Schutte, Anne 37
Jung, Verena 54

Kaplan, Caren 6, 56, 59
Kedourie, Elie 120
Kiš, Danilo 3
Kramer, Lloyd 2

Lacan, Jacques 8, 60, 61, 103, 117–18, 162
LaCapra, Dominick 6, 8, 62, 162–63
Lagos-Pope, María-Inés 6, 55, 57
language:
   and ethnicity 87
   contaminations 6, 82, 88, 97, 127, 133, 143, 147, 152
   code-switching, code-mixing, hybridization, and interference 6, 71, 85–88, 135
   diglossia 6, 51, 52, 71, 129, 130
   see also dialects
Laplanche, Jean 60
Lavagetto, Mario 106
Lemma, Alessandra 3
Lepschy, Giulio 7, 49
Levi, Primo 34, 35, 36, 38, 77
Levy, Susan 3
linguistic habitus, *see* Bourdieu, Pierre
loss 3, 4, 21, 29, 34, 55, 59, 61, 63, 101, 102, 117, 122, 127, 128, 142, 154, 155
Lunetta, Mario 76, 149

Mackey, William 53
Magris, Claudio 5, 13, 21–23, 31, 64, 147
Mahler-Schächter, Elizabeth 37
Maier, Bruno 105, 148
Manea, Norman 127
Marin, Biagio 13, 21, 147–48

Matvejević, Predrag 18
McClennen, Sophia 127
memory:
  divided 64
  and trauma 61–65
mestiza, see Anzaldùa, Gloria
migration 18, 33, 34, 43, 46, 48, 53, 56, 58, 60, 78
Milani, Nelida 18, 52, 56–57
Milano, Paolo 28, 38, 149
Miller, Jane 83
minority 19, 34, 38, 46, 47, 48, 49, 52, 133, 134, 150
mirror 7, 8, 15, 25, 54, 55, 64, 71, 77, 79, 103, 114, 115, 116, 117, 118, 119, 128
  see also estrangement
Modena, Anna 34
Molloy, Sylvia 130
monolingualism 2, 4, 5, 6, 7, 49, 50, 151, 164
Moretto, Marta 142
multilingualism 3, 4, 5, 6, 8, 34, 42, 49–54, 71, 75, 77, 83, 92, 97, 120, 129–31, 140, 141, 155
  see also plurilingualism
Murphy, Michael 6
Muysken, Pieter 6, 80, 82

Nabokov, Vladimir 8, 53, 77, 128, 143, 144, 145, 146
Naipaul, Vidiadhar Surajprasad 162
nationalism 19, 20, 26, 47, 106, 120, 121
Neirotti, Marco 16, 35
Nochlin, Linda 142

O'Brien, George 56
origin, see homeland
otherness 44, 63, 115–18
Oustinoff, Michaël 54
Ovid 4, 55

Pahor, Boris 152
Pampaloni, Geno 73
Pancrazi, Pietro 12
Petrucciani, Mario 30, 33, 107
Pirandello, Luigi 7, 37, 112, 116, 117
Pizzi, Katia 64
Plurilingualism 3, 6, 7, 8, 32, 34, 35, 39, 50–52, 96, 127, 129, 133–35, 138, 145, 146, 150–55
Pohl, J. 51
Pontalis, Jean-Bertrand 60
Popovič, Anton 53
Pressburger, Giorgio 134, 137, 139, 142
Pyrah, Rogers 6, 45, 48

Quigly, Isabel 22

Radulescu, Domnica 7, 101, 164
Ragusa, Olga 134
Rank, Otto 7, 103
Rebula, Alojz 80

refugee 4, 20, 21, 27, 29, 38, 56, 58, 102, 104, 113, 121, 122, 124
return 29, 59, 60, 102
Robinson, Richard 6, 46
Robson, Kathryn 61
Roth, Joseph 19

Saba, Umberto 11, 12, 14, 147, 148
Said, Edward 6, 7, 61, 101, 103, 105, 113
Saloul, Ihab 104
Scotti Jurić, Rita 131, 136, 137, 154
Seidel, Michael 62
self-translation:
  definition 53–55
  interior 8, 54, 129, 133, 153
  in *L'amicizia* 133–41
  in *La miglior vita* 93–98
  in *Materada* 85–92
  and multilingualism 6, 49, 53
  see also Pressburger, Giorgio
Sgorlon, Carlo 30, 90
Shepherdson, Charles 61
Sicari, Carmelina 119
Siciliano, Enzo 31
Silone, Ignazio 92
Simoes Marques, Isabelle 135
Slataper, Scipio 3, 9, 11–15, 22, 147, 148
Slavs 2, 3, 13, 14, 15, 16, 17, 18, 19, 21, 22, 25, 26, 27, 30, 34, 45, 72, 76, 79, 80, 82, 83, 86, 90, 106, 136, 143
Sommavilla, Guido 104
Spaini, Alberto 147, 148
Spinazzola, Vittorio 32
Steiner, George 61, 77
Steinitz, Tamar 128
storytelling 22, 31, 63, 74, 76, 104, 162
stranger 1, 7, 103, 106, 108, 116, 117, 119, 162
subcultures 6, 42, 48
Suk, Jeannie 103
Svevo, Italo 3, 8, 9, 11, 12, 14, 22, 23, 37, 85, 108, 134, 148, 149

Tabori, Paul 6
Thompson, Ian 2, 36
Tito, Josip 20, 58
Todorova, Maria 47
Tomasevich, Jozo 47
Tomizza, Fulvio:
  biblio-biography 24–32
  works:
    Materada 4, 5, 6, 21, 22, 24, 25, 28, 29, 32, 34, 35, 70–80, 83–87, 89, 90–93, 97, 101, 103, 129, 133, 153, 154, 158–61
    La ragazza di Petrovia 4, 7, 29, 74, 101–04, 109, 119, 120–22, 163
    La quinta stagione 29, 129, 130
    Il bosco di acacie 29

Trilogia istriana 29
L'albero dei sogni 4, 7, 8, 25, 29, 30, 31, 101–07, 114, 115, 118–20, 124, 149, 153, 159, 160, 163
La città di Miriam 31
La miglior vita 4, 6, 17, 31, 70, 71, 75, 76, 77, 85, 93, 95, 96, 97, 101, 103, 129, 133, 154
L'amicizia 4, 8, 127, 133–41, 153
Il male viene dal nord: il romanzo del vescovo Vergerio 32, 37
Ieri un secolo fa 152
Gli sposi di via Rossetti 131
I rapporti colpevoli 25, 32, 33, 151
Franziska 4, 8, 127, 133, 141–47
La casa col mandorlo 160
Il sogno dalmata 24, 27
Alle spalle di Trieste 5, 15, 32, 77
Destino di frontiera 11, 13, 32
Tozzi, Federigo 35, 98
Trieste 3, 4, 7, 8, 11–21, 25–36, 48, 56, 64, 73, 86, 88, 102–10, 114, 117, 121, 128, 133, 134, 143, 147, 150, 152, 159, 160
Triestine literature 8, 9, 12–16, 37, 147, 148
triglossia 52

un-literariness 147–55

Van der Hart, Onno 61
Van der Kolk, Bessel 61
Vanvolsen, Serge 148
Venetians 18, 24, 78, 80
Venuti, Lawrence 131
Verga, Giovanni 35, 73, 75, 77, 91, 92, 98
violence 4, 19, 20, 21, 29, 64
Vittorini, Elio 28, 84, 85, 150
Vladislav, Jan 58
Von Humboldt, Wilhelm 153

White, Hayden 62
Whitehouse, Roger 158
Woods, Michelle 132

Yildiz, Yasemin 3
Young, Robert 6, 45, 46
Yugoslavia 3, 4, 16, 19, 20, 21, 22, 24, 25, 26, 27, 28, 31, 34, 37, 47, 56, 58, 72, 85, 88, 102, 103, 106, 108, 120, 163

Zanini, Piero 6, 43